JCMS Annual Review of the European Union in 2010

Edited by

Nathaniel Copsey
and
Tim Haughton

General Editors: Michelle Cini and Amy Verdun

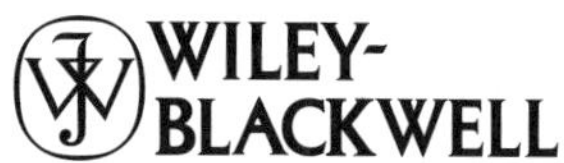

This edition first published 2011

Blackwell Publishing was acquired by John Wiley & Sons in February 2007. Blackwell's publishing program has been merged with Wiley's global Scientific, Technical and Medical business to form Wiley-Blackwell.

Registered Office
John Wiley & Sons Ltd, The Atrium, Southern Gate, Chichester, West Sussex, PO19 8SQ, United Kingdom

Editorial Offices
350 Main Street, Malden, MA 02148-5020, USA
9600 Garsington Road, Oxford, OX4 2DQ, UK
The Atrium, Southern Gate, Chichester, West Sussex, PO19 8SQ, UK

For details of our global editorial offices, for customer services, and for information about how to apply for permission to reuse the copyright material in this book please see our website at www.wiley.com/wiley-blackwell.

ISBN 978-1-4443-3905-5
ISSN 0021-9886 (print) 1468-5965 (online)

Set in 11/12.5 Pt Times by Toppan Best-set Premedia Limited
Printed in Singapore

2010

CONTENTS

JCMS 2011 Volume 49 Annual Review pp. 1–6

Editorial: 2010, Kill or Cure for the Euro?

NATHANIEL COPSEY
Aston University
TIM HAUGHTON
University of Birmingham

Another year, another set of crises. The year 2010 brought the EU fresh difficulties, with renewed pressure on the single currency precipitated by bail-outs first for Greece and then for the Irish Republic. Two dramas were played out over the course of the year: the first was the sovereign debt crisis on the eurozone's periphery that at one point seemed to imperil the single currency's future; the second was a Brussels-based crisis that passed largely unobserved beyond the city's ring road and concerned the details of the implementation of the Lisbon Treaty.

Although one of the roots of the new treaty had been the Laeken Declaration's call to bring Europe closer to its citizens, outside Brussels most Europeans know little and care less about the provisions of Lisbon. Their interests in the common European project (if they have any) lie in what the Union actually does. Notwithstanding this, the changes made by Lisbon should allow the Union to build more effectively 'a Europe of results' (Barroso, 2009). But no sooner had the treaty come into force than some began to muse over additional tinkering to the Treaty provoked in large part by the crisis in the eurozone.

In early 2010, the government of Greece – the country hit most severely by the economic crisis in the eurozone – began to experience serious problems in borrowing money at a reasonable rate of interest. This in turn prompted fears of a default on its sovereign debt by the Greek government. A bail-out to prevent default was mooted but initially resisted by the eurozone's anchor, Germany. Back in the 1990s, the German people had been made an explicit promise that there would be a no bail-out clause in the institutional architecture of the euro as the price for relinquishing their beloved Deutschmark. Chancellor Angela Merkel found herself in something of a quandary, therefore, as public opinion back home turned hostile, testing the bonds of solidarity between Member States to the limit. German wags suggested that Greece should sell a few islands, or perhaps more reasonably, increase the retirement age to the levels prevailing in Germany. By April, the interest rate on two-year Greek government bonds had climbed above 15 per cent, bringing matters to a head. The following month, the Greeks were provided with a bail-out (of sorts) in the form of €110 billion in loans from the EU and the IMF (International Monetary Fund).

Greece was not the only other eurozone country at risk. Indeed, as soon as the Hellenic Republic was forced into a bail-out, other economies on Europe's southern periphery began to appear vulnerable. The Irish Republic, Portugal and Spain were also touted as potential recipients of emergency loans and €720 billion was set aside by the EU and the IMF for this purpose. By the end of 2010, despite the introduction of painful austerity measures, the government of the Irish Republic was also obliged to send for the IMF. At the time of writing in April 2011, the Portuguese government had recently been forced to seek a rescue package following the collapse of its government.

It remains to be seen at what point the crisis in the eurozone will be contained. In a similar vein to the previous year, the EU managed to weather the storm in 2010. The European Financial Stabilization Mechanism and European Financial Stability Facility offered some respite from the inclement economic weather, but 'dark clouds continued to lurk menacingly' (Copsey and Haughton 2010, p. 5). Indeed, as Dermot Hodson writes in his contribution to this year's Annual Review, to paraphrase Churchill, it was 'not so much the beginning of the end for the eurozone's sovereign debt crisis as the end of the beginning'.

Nevertheless, amongst all the doom and gloom surrounding the euro, Estonia completed the final preparations for joining the single currency on 1 January 2011. On the stroke of midnight and with a beaming smile, Estonian Prime Minister Andrus Ansip, alongside his counterparts from Latvia and Lithuania, withdrew euro notes from an ATM in Tallinn, providing a modest vote of confidence in the single currency, perhaps highlighting that even in the midst of a crisis small states realize the benefits of being inside the eurozone.

The rescue package imposed on the Irish and the Greeks was harsh. The loans offered were at a real rate of interest (less than the 15 per cent offered to Greece by the markets, but above that paid by creditworthy Germany or the Netherlands) and the much tighter austerity packages imposed in the short term made their economic situation worse. The medicine doled out to the Greek and Irish patients was bitter. Their conditions were considered so severe that a specialist consultant with long and controversial experience of prescribing kill-or-cure remedies was engaged – in the form of the IMF. This economic chemotherapy brought Greeks out onto the streets to protest in the hundreds of thousands. The Irish were more quiescent. In 2010, the Greek economy contracted by 4.8 per cent; in 2011 it is forecast to contract by 3.6 per cent. The Irish Republic fared slightly better in that its economy shrank by a lesser degree, although its budget deficit rose to over 30 per cent of GDP and the outlook was bleak.

Whilst the global financial turmoil that started in 2007 (see Trichet, 2010) had initially engulfed all the Member States of the Union, 2010 was the year where divergences became apparent. Indeed, the 'all in this together' mentality which was encouraged as all Europe's economies bar Poland had slipped into recession was strained during 2010 as the recovery highlighted divergences. In particular, Germany's economy bounced back from a 4.7 per cent drop in GDP in 2009 with GDP growth of 3.7 per cent in 2010. But it was not just in the richer northern states where resentment grew, fuelling Eurosceptic sentiment. In the then newest member of the eurozone, the expectation that poorer Slovakia, for example, would contribute to a bail-out of richer Greece was unpopular even amongst pro-Europeans. Moreover, the dangers of taking the 'Greek route' became a theme of a number of parliamentary elections during the year – most notably in Slovakia, the Czech Republic and the United Kingdom (Haughton *et al.*, 2011).

Crises often bring reality into sharper relief. The euro crisis highlighted that no rescue deal in the eurozone is possible without Germany, but Germany shrinks from leadership. It is a reluctant hegemon but there are, however, no obvious other leaders in economic matters. President Sarkozy is unpopular at home and leading a country that feels it is losing its way. In May 2010, the United Kingdom elected a coalition government whose European policy is more or less identical to that of the previous Labour administration in substance, but whose appetite for European leadership seems non-existent.

The Lisbon Treaty was envisaged to bring leadership and an ability to rise to the challenges confronting the Union. Although it is still too early to come to a definitive judgement, the scorecard is mixed. Whereas the President of the European Council Herman Van Rompuy seems to have performed quite well, the verdict on Catherine Ashton has been more critical. Although acutely aware of the limitations of his office, Van Rompuy mustered all of his coalition-building experience from running the fractious Belgian state to push European heads of government gently towards agreement on measures to deal with the euro crisis.

In contrast, Ashton had a less happy 2010. Her dual role was challenging enough in itself. She was not helped by constant sniping in the press and the long drawn out process of getting the EEAS (European External Action Service) budget approved by the European Parliament which was keen to assert its new enhanced powers under Lisbon. Nonetheless, the long delay in producing the organogram outlining the organizational structure of the new service and the slow appointment of individuals to key posts failed to inspire confidence amongst many officials in Brussels and sent a signal that the 'European External *Action* Service' was falling short of the necessary dynamism. Nevertheless, 2010 was always going to be a year of institution-building, whereas 2011 was intended to be the year when the EEAS would be up and running and could begin to be measured against its results.

The EU appears to be undergoing one of its periodical bouts of consolidation and catch-up as the necessary refinements to make the eurozone work are implemented. There is too much at stake, both economically and politically, for the euro project to fail – and for that reason it is highly unlikely that the Member States will allow this to happen. What is more likely to occur is that the spillover from the eurozone crisis will lead to increased pressure for the creation of a European economic government within the eurozone. The non-eurozone Member States have good reason to fret about the creation of this club-within-a-club, especially those who spent years struggling to get into the negotiating room in the first place and remain for the most part outside the eurozone.

The year 2010 not only marked the beginning of the term of the second Barroso Commission and the launching of the External Action Service, it also marked the date by which Europe was supposed to become the most competitive knowledge-based economy in the world as envisaged in another agreement struck in the Portuguese capital. Although these Lisbon goals were not achieved, EU leaders responded with a new strategy, Europe 2020, aiming at 'smart, sustainable and inclusive growth' with greater co-ordination of national and European policy. These were fine words, but to make it happen in the age of austerity will require a quality often absent in European politics and never mentioned in the wording of treaties: political will.

***

This is our third issue of the *JCMS* Annual Review as editors. Continuing in the vein of previous Annual Reviews we have commissioned contributions from practitioners and commentators from outside the academic world. Following Commission President Barroso's (2009) clarion call to deliver a 'Europe of results' and ECB (European Central Bank) President Trichet's

(2010, p. 18) trenchant analysis of the financial crisis and the ECB's role as a 'reliable anchor of stability and confidence', we are delighted that this year's State of the Union address comes from the President of the European Parliament Jerzy Buzek, who argues that the Lisbon Treaty is 'best placed to make the EU a power ready to face the challenges of the 21st century [. . . and] increases the quality of European democracy'.

Our second commissioned article comes from one of the most astute observers of the single currency, David Marsh, author of two leading works on the single currency's creation and its future (Marsh, 2009, 2011). Marsh argues that for all the euro's numerous sources of strength, the expectations of what it would achieve for Europe – politically, economically and in terms of further integration – formed an 'improbably long wish-list'. It is, in part, the weight of these unrealistic and over-optimistic expectations that has caused the eurozone to buckle since 2007. Central not just to the survival and future success of the euro, but of the European project as a whole, is Germany. Two decades on from German reunification and with Angela Merkel playing a pivotal role in key developments affecting the Union in 2010, we commissioned perceptive, long-time observer of German politics, William Paterson, to assess Germany's stance towards Europe and European integration. In his contribution he assesses the causes and consequences of the 'reluctant hegemon' being pushed to the front of the European stage.

Loukas Tsoukalis of the University of Athens and the Hellenic Foundation for European and Foreign Policy, who has long bridged the divide between academia and policy-making circles, accepted our invitation to give the *JCMS* Annual Review lecture. Following on from Vivien Schmidt's (2009) call to 're-envision the European Union' and Kalypso Nicolaïdis' (2010) appeal for 'sustainable integration', Tsoukalis argues that Europe runs the risk of becoming a 'victim of complexity in times when mass politics turns into populism and simple messages'. The financial and economic crisis, however, offers an opportunity. Indeed, he maintains, Europe is better qualified than other parts of the world to adopt new ways of thinking thanks to its deeply rooted democratic traditions, deeply ingrained notions of social justice and environmental concern, long history of a mixed economy and a healthy scepticism earned through bitter experience. Nonetheless, European politicians need to work hard to articulate and explain choices to citizens and demonstrate the centrality of a European component to policies which will deliver both security and prosperity.

We would like to thank all contributors to this issue of the *JCMS* Annual Review for their efforts and efficiency in producing such excellent copy on time. One of our long-standing contributors to the Annual Review, Michael Dougan, stood down this year and we extend our thanks to him for his many contributions to this journal. We are delighted to welcome on board as the author of the 'Legal Developments' chapter, the distinguished scholar of European Union law, Fabian Amtenbrink of the Erasmus University in Rotterdam. Last but not least, we would also like to thank the new editors of the *JCMS*, Michelle Cini and Amy Verdun, with whom we have enjoyed a friendly and productive relationship over the past year.

References

Barroso, J. (2009) 'State of the Union: Delivering a "Europe of Results" in a Harsh Economic Climate'. *JCMS*, Vol. 47, s1, pp. 7–16.

Copsey, N. and Haughton, T. (2010) 'Editorial: 2009, a Turning Point for Europe?' *JCMS*, Vol. 48, s1, pp. 1–6.

Haughton, T., Novotná, T. and Deegan-Krause, K. (2011) 'The 2010 Czech and Slovak Parliamentary Elections: Red Cards to the "Winners" '. *West European Politics*, Vol. 34, No. 2, pp. 394–402.

Marsh, D. (2009) *The Euro: The Politics of the New Global Currency* (New Haven, CT: Yale University Press).

Marsh, D. (2011) *The Euro: The Battle for the New Global Currency* (New Haven, CT: Yale University Press).

Nicolaïdis, K. (2010) 'The JCMS Annual Review Lecture – Sustainable Integration: Towards EU 2.0?' *JCMS*, Vol. 48, s1, pp. 21–54.

Schmidt, V. (2009) 'Re-envisioning the European Union: Identity, Democracy, Economy'. *JCMS*, Vol. 47, s1, pp. 17–42.

Trichet, J.-C. (2010) 'State of the Union: The Financial Crisis and the ECB's Response between 2007 and 2009'. *JCMS*, Vol. 48, s1, pp. 7–19.

JCMS 2011 Volume 49 Annual Review pp. 7–18

State of the Union: Three Cheers for the Lisbon Treaty and Two Warnings for Political Parties

JERZY BUZEK
President of the European Parliament

Introduction

It is too early to say whether the Lisbon Treaty will rank as a decisive turning-point in the institutional history of the European Union (EU). Some present it as a quiet revolution, while others see it as simply a natural evolution. Either way, it has streamlined the architecture of the new European political system and offered the chance to improve the efficiency and quality of decision-making within the Union. Jean Monnet's famous dictum that 'nothing is possible without man, nothing is lasting without institutions' is often used to defend the necessity of EU institutions, to stress that the unity among Europeans cannot be reached through good intentions alone, and that progress has to be locked in through norms, procedures and legislation. In this article, after stressing the strength and necessity of the Lisbon Treaty, I would like to look at the first part of Monnet's motto: the importance of man, of political will and of leadership. The continuity of the European project's success rests not only in the solidity of its institutional structure, but also on the vitality of political intentions and of party and civic political organization. To an important degree, the latter is the fuel which makes the European engine work. Political parties at the European level will determine whether, in the future, Europe is a confident and leading force, or a defensive and stagnant one, responding to and ultimately dictated by national interests.

I. The Genesis of the Lisbon Treaty

Many critics look down on the Lisbon Treaty as a kind of 'back-up strategy' or 'plan B' on the part of Brussels bureaucrats to induce European citizens to swallow the less palatable pill of the European Constitution after its rejection by French and Dutch voters. The new Treaty, which followed 'no' votes in the 2005 referendums, is presented as the tamer version of a more ambitious federalist project. The critics of the Lisbon Treaty pointed to the need for repeated Irish referendums as evidence of an intrusive and unbending Europe. However, gradually and patiently, the Treaty managed to convince the public, and it has succeeded where its predecessor had failed. The new Treaty deserves to be seen as an ambitious consensus that tested the limit for support of EU integration, and not simply as a second-best option.

The ratification of the Lisbon Treaty was the result of lengthy discussions, rulings by constitutional courts, opt-outs and debates on the merits and necessity of a new text. It was the end-product of a decade-long process that began with the Laeken European Council of 2001 and was concluded with the Czech ratification and the entry into force of the Treaty on 1 December 2009. The Lisbon Treaty was also the first treaty to be ratified in 27 Member States. No other treaty had to overcome such a challenging threshold. This long gestation period has made it more widely understood, and states feel a much stronger sense of ownership of it. We could say that by the time of its birth, the Lisbon Treaty was already 'mature'. More importantly, its genesis marks a clear point in its legitimacy: its acceptance has been hard-earned and its support was ultimately genuine. That is why the narrative of the coming into being of the Lisbon Treaty is one of democratic legitimacy.

When looking at the narrative of the Treaty, there is another point worth mentioning: it might easily turn out to be the last treaty – save for amendments necessary to strengthen economic governance. From the Single European Act to the Nice Treaty, every change has been accompanied by a major relaunch based on the reform of the preceding treaty. If we consider the rhetoric and nature of the debate that accompanied and followed the ratification of the Lisbon Treaty, it is not unlikely that some Member States now see it as the ultimate legal frontier of European integration.

The Lisbon Treaty as a Tool of Reinforced Parliamentary Oversight

The Treaty has reshaped some of the architecture of the Union by reforming existing institutions and creating new ones. The European Parliament was convinced that the newly acquired importance of these institutions could not go unchecked. Thanks to the principle of parliamentary oversight that permeates the new Treaty, the European Parliament has ensured that EU institutions are firmly anchored to the accountability of the only directly elected component of the European legislature.

The most important example is the institutionalization of the European Council and the creation of the post of permanent President of that new institution. Even if the European Council is the Union's intergovernmental body par excellence, the Lisbon Treaty and practical understandings between the Council and the Parliament can help ensure that the proceedings and the conclusions of the heads of state and government will be properly scrutinized.

The European Parliament can attempt to influence the workings of the European Council in a number of ways: through the adoption of timely resolutions ahead of summits, through the presence and address of the President of the European Parliament at the beginning of each European Council, by holding a meeting of the Conference of Presidents of political group leaders with the President of the European Council immediately after each summit, and by holding a comprehensive discussion with the European Council President during the plenary session that follows the meeting of heads of state and government. President Van Rompuy and I meet once a month in order to discuss co-operation between the European Council and the European Parliament and to follow up on each summit's conclusions. These timely and recurrent consultations ensure that when providing the political impetus for the development of general EU political priorities, the European Council is aware of the possible reaction of the European Parliament and can take it into account.

An example of this was the discussion I had with heads of state and government over the 2011 EU Budget during the European Council in October 2010. In my opening remarks, I stressed how the Parliament was asking for an ambitious budget in line with the expectations posed over the policies of the EU and highlighted the paradox between continuously increasing competences and diminishing funding, crippling the EU's ability to deliver. In doing so, I was seeking to highlight how the annual EU Budget still represents only 1 per cent of the EU-27's collective national income, that the Budget has not risen as a share of the European economy over the last two decades, that the EU does not and cannot run a Budget deficit, that the Budget has in recent years been consistently underspent, and that in most years the Union in fact returns some unspent money to the Member States. Ironically, if the Member State governments had managed their own public finances as well as the Union – by respecting the legally binding Stability and Growth Pact, for example – they might be facing a much less acute fiscal crisis today. A debate ensued concerning the substance of the proposals presented by the

Parliament. The debate is ongoing. This will be a particularly difficult issue as we enter the negotiations over the next Multiannual Financial Framework.

The Lisbon Treaty also provided for a streamlining of the action of the Union in external relations by merging the post of Commissioner for External Affairs with that of High Representative for Common Foreign and Security Policy – and also intertwining with this the traditional functions of the Council Presidency in foreign policy – to create a new enhanced High Representative for Foreign Affairs and Security Policy, assisted by a European External Action Service. This change has given rise to important questions about parliamentary oversight. Whilst respecting the Member States' prerogatives on security and defence policy, the Parliament decided to make use of its power in foreign affairs and external relations so as to ensure that the new service would not become an unaccountable island lost between the Council and the Commission, and between supranational and national levels. The External Action Service was successfully established, but the biggest challenges lie ahead. The bloc's external action should not be the reflection of a lowest common denominator among the 27, but rather a more ambitious and cohesive European foreign policy.

The best example to date of the effects of the Lisbon Treaty on parliamentary scrutiny of other institutions remains the vote of 11 February 2010 on the agreement between the EU and the United States on the transfer of financial data for the purposes of the Terrorist Finance Tracking Programme – the so-called 'SWIFT Agreement'. This allows for the transfer of bulk financial data of European citizens from the EU to the American authorities in the framework of their anti-terrorist investigations. After the entry into force of the Lisbon Treaty, the European Parliament had to give its consent to agreements negotiated by the Council with third countries. The Council believed that the Parliament, despite its serious misgivings about several aspects, would not use its new power to block the agreement for the sake of transatlantic relations. In my eyes, and those of my colleagues, there were serious reasons to reopen the discussions: an asymmetry between the requirements of the American and EU authorities, and a disproportion in the management of private data for security concerns. This was the first time the European Parliament had blocked an international agreement in the field of justice and home affairs: the renegotiated text that resulted some months later was significantly better on many fronts.

Over the last year, we have also made important strides towards greater accountability by the European Commission towards the Parliament, as well as improved inter-institutional dialogue more generally. Many of these changes were not set down in the precise wording of the new Treaty, but are very much in the spirit of it. Most notably, we have signed a new Framework

Agreement between the Parliament and the Commission for the current (2009–14) parliamentary term. The two institutions now co-operate through a truly 'special partnership' and the negotiation has led to a very satisfactory outcome. A key achievement was an acceptance of the principle of equal treatment by the Commission of the Parliament and the Council in legislative and budgetary matters for the first time. I now meet personally with the College of Commissioners every six months or so. Similar dialogues will occur between the Commission and the Parliament's Conference of Presidents (comprised of the political group leaders), under my chairmanship, and the Conference of Committee Chairs. Major improvements were also secured on rules on keeping MEPs informed of progress of international negotiations, on the Parliament's participation in international conferences, and on the Parliament's access to classified and confidential information.

There have been some other important reforms. Before his re-election last autumn, the President of the European Commission, José Manuel Barroso, at my suggestion, presented a personal manifesto to the Parliament, on which he was questioned in detail by each of the political groups. This process is now institutionalized in the new five-year Framework Agreement. Last autumn, we introduced a Question Hour with the Commission President so that Mr Barroso may now answer unscripted questions for an hour from MEPs during the monthly plenary session in Strasbourg. We have also instituted an annual 'State of the Union' debate each September, at which the Commission President presents his overall priorities and thinking for the coming political year.

This more intensive dialogue between the Commission and the Parliament has a twofold advantage. First, the Commission is subject to reinforced parliamentary oversight: the College of Commissioners as a whole and the Commissioners individually are constantly under the scrutiny of MEPs. Every angle of their legislative and other priorities is inspected. This scrutiny applies not only to legislation, but also to the Commissioners personally. If the Parliament doubts the integrity and quality of their performance, it can push the President of the Commission to review his or her choices, with the possibility of a 'vote of no-confidence' always looming over the whole Commission. Second, the legislative process is reinforced in the 'Community method'. The European Parliament puts the European Commission at the centre of the institutional architecture of the EU. The Parliament favours a powerful, efficient and active Commission: a more accountable EU executive leads in turn to a better-performing Union. The European Council might provide for important political impetus, but ultimately it is for the Commission to be at the centre of the Union system by leading the day-to-day process of converting priorities into action.

The 'Parliamentarization' of European Democracy

In any consideration of the Lisbon Treaty by the President of the European Parliament, it would be normal to expect a bias in labelling the new text as the 'Treaty of the European Parliament'. The institution I represent has gained enormously from the Lisbon Treaty. We have come a long way from the 78 MPs of the appointed consultative assembly of the European Coal and Steel Community that first met in September 1952 to the directly elected 736 MEPs of today. The Treaty marked the end of the long march that made the Parliament a co-legislature with the Council in almost all areas of law-making. It has ended the unjustifiable asymmetry between the Council and the Parliament, and this is in itself a welcomed improvement in the quality of European democracy. However, when I refer to the Lisbon Treaty, I prefer to label it as 'The Treaty of Parliaments' in the plural – and not just of the chamber I represent. The Treaty has promoted a genuine parliamentarization of the EU, furthering the involvement of national parliaments in law- and policy-making. National parliaments have to be informed and consulted, they now police the subsidiarity process and can force the Commission to explain its activity, and they are extensively included in matters concerning civil liberty, judicial co-operation, defence and enlargement.

This increased involvement has three advantages. First, it gives real meaning to the controversial concept of 'subsidiarity'. National parliaments are best placed to determine whether a piece of legislation or an action proposed by the Commission is best undertaken at the EU level. The Commission and the Parliament always look at whether subsidiarity and proportionality are respected, but it is fair to admit that national parliaments' interests are more directly at stake when the EU proposes new legislation and their assessment on the necessity and level from which a new law should emanate is necessary and legitimate.

Second, the increased involvement of national parliaments increases their sense of ownership of the European integration process. EU law-making was, up to now, left to national ministers and EU institutions. National parliamentarians could influence the legislative process only indirectly by holding their executives accountable for their actions in the European sphere. Whilst this way of proceeding is and should be still in place, it has the shortcoming of giving national parliaments information that may be partial, subjective or out of date. National parliaments have delegated to their governments the task of negotiating European directives and regulations on their behalf. Yet this exercise can prove unsatisfactory to national parliaments because they sometimes see results that differ substantially from their own goals. The increased direct involvement of national parliaments in EU legislation tackles this problem.

Third, reinforced consultation of national parliaments can increase the efficiency of EU law-making. National parliaments are responsible for turning EU directives into national legislation. The quality, speed and communication of this transposition may determine the success in practice of a directive on the ground. Ultimately, all European legislation boils down to the quality of implementation. Multi-level governance in the Union can only work effectively if all relevant partners are committed and willing to make the process a success. If national parliaments perceive a piece of legislation as a top-down 'imposition', it is unlikely to be a success. The inclusion of national parliaments helps to move away from a sense of 'the Union made me do it' back to an approach that says 'we have made a key contribution to make this legislation a success'.

In recent years, the European Parliament has greatly increased the involvement of national parliaments. We have been holding interparliamentary meetings with great frequency. We have invited MPs to committee meetings on a very regular basis. I have already met personally and collectively the Speakers of national parliaments on a number of occasions, and we also have intensive, more informal consultations through correspondence and phone calls. The partnership between the EP and national legislatures has truly entered a new phase with Lisbon.

The Lisbon Treaty as a Tool of Direct Democracy

Parallel to the steady and continuous growth in the power of the European Parliament, in the last two decades another development has strengthened the democratic foundations of the European Union: the rise of the concept of 'European citizenship'. The idea entered the Maastricht Treaty discretely. Part two of the then EC Treaty stated that: 'Citizenship of the Union shall complement and not replace national citizenship'. Yet as it was to be clarified by a series of judgments by the European Court of Justice (ECJ), complementarity did not render the idea of European citizenship void. On the contrary, through a number of cases, the ECJ gave meaning to the rights that came with European citizenship. Europeans are members of a transnational community which has legal personality, within which they enjoy a number of freedoms that are granted – not curtailed – by virtue of their being a national of a Member State of the Union. More importantly, however, the EU is a community of values based on respect for the rule of law, human rights, minorities, pluralism, the widely shared idea of a balanced social market economy, and the rejection of the death penalty as a form of redress. Citizenship in the EU has a political, as well as legal, connotation.

Whilst recognizing the common traits that lie behind the idea of European citizenship, the treaties that came before the Lisbon Treaty gave scant incentives for the direct participation of European citizens at the EU level. Thanks to Article 11(4) of the Treaty of the European Union, after the entry into force of the Lisbon Treaty a whole new dimension has been added to the idea of active citizenship. Thanks to the agreement reached by the Parliament, Council and Commission, starting on 1 April 2012, 1 million signatures from residents in a quarter of Member States will suffice, under certain conditions, to make the European Commission take action, either causing a negative reply or prompting it to take on board the suggestions stemming from the citizens' initiatives. The European Parliament fought hard to have an ambitious, citizen-friendly and not overtly bureaucratic citizens' initiative.

We have been so keen on lowering the bureaucratic requirement of the European Citizens' Initiative (ECI) because we believe that the concept of 'active citizenship' cannot be isolated from the idea of public participation and civil society. Moreover, a strong and functioning citizens' initiative increases the standing, recognition and prominence of the European Commission. The EC still maintains its right of initiative, but becomes the focal point as the institution responsible for actions and reactions. To put it differently, the ECI is welcomed because it will reinforce the successful Community Method. People's awareness of the centrality of the European Commission will be strengthened.

I am confident that the ECI will bring fresh insights into the necessary initiatives needed to reinvigorate our Union. It will do so by equipping EU institutions with the lateral thinking that may be absent in the often inward-looking Brussels triangle. The grass-roots initiatives proposed by the Commission, even if not adopted, will certainly serve to enhance the awareness in EU institutions of the existing gaps perceived by European citizens. The Parliament will as always be an attentive player in the scrutiny not only of the initiatives, but also of the replies that the European Commission will offer.

I would nevertheless stress a warning on the ECI. Whilst I think that its introduction adds to the democratic quality and overall legitimacy of the EU, I would not say that a piece of legislation introduced as a result of the Initiative will be more legitimate than one autonomously initiated by the Commission. An ECI provides a different source of legitimacy, but it does not surpass the legitimacy of indirect democracy.

II. Political Parties and the Quality of European Democracy

When we look at the quality of European democracy, the Treaty of Lisbon is only one side of the equation. We have not only one, but two elephants in the room. The first elephant is the fact that the European Parliament's increase in power has not been supplemented by an increase in participation in European elections – in fact the opposite is true. Although hugely important, European elections are very often treated as or perceived by the public as second-order elections. European legislators should not shy away from recognizing the lack of knowledge and even interest which still surrounds European elections.

The second elephant in the room is that although democracy needs political parties – and as the Treaty succinctly explains: 'Political parties at European level contribute to forming European political awareness and to expressing the will of citizens of the Union' – pan-European political parties are still in their infancy. This happens paradoxically against the backdrop of very deeply rooted and effective political groups within the European Parliament. The pre-eminence of the political cleavage over the national cleavage in the voting of the European Parliament has reached almost the status of an academic consensus. However, the cohesiveness of political parties is hardly visible when we look at European elections within Member States.

As a politician, I know that the inability of political parties to create a European public space and the continuing abstention in European elections are problems that trouble many of my colleagues. At stake are not only their prominence, but also the nature, the outlook and the legitimacy of the European Parliament and European democracy.

The answers need to come largely from MEPs as national parties and Member States will not take up this challenge. The discussion is ongoing and prolific, and two camps have started to emerge (Menon and Peet, 2010): on the one side, there is a strand of politician who wants to progress through an ambitious reform of European electoral practices. In the first half of 2011, the European Parliament considered the Giannakou Report on the regulations governing political parties at European level and the rules regarding their funding. More importantly, it also considered the Duff Report on the revision of the law concerning the election of MEPs. In this respect, it is interesting to mention the suggestions of the former Secretary General of the European Parliament, Sir Julian Priestley, who sees the relative inactivity of European political parties to be the 'missing link' in the creation of a genuine European polity (Priestley, 2010). The other camp sees the European Parliament as already having exceeded its competences and regrets the lack of scrutiny of national parliaments over the work of EU institutions (MacShane, 2011).

Both camps see the status quo – of increasing disengagement on the part of electorates from the EU – as unsustainable. Both sides have different diagnoses and thus propose different cures. One side sees EU legitimacy increasing only through a self-imposed scaling down of its action so as to focus on a definite number of areas in which the citizens could more easily identify themselves with the Union. 'Do less better', say the partisans of this camp. The claim is often that the Union should care only about core historic functions, such as the single market. By sticking to a few main issues, the EU would become more understandable and less political. In an era of supposedly increasing mistrust toward politicians, it is argued, this should serve to enhance the legitimacy of the EU project.

This third way between self-styled 'Eurosceptics' and 'Europhiles' might be appealing, yet I consider it flawed. First, no matter how minimalist the definition of the 'single market' might be, an area of free exchange would never have been efficiently realized if it was not supported by strong central institutions to enforce it and a number of policies to sustain it. For example, a coherent single market would not exist without a coherent external trade policy or competition policy, or indeed consumer protection policy. To supplement this, I should stress that the internal market is far from complete. It should suffice to look at the service sector within the EU to realize that we are still far away from a perfect internal market. In my view, a complete single market requires further strengthening with free movement granted to all workers and citizens in the Union and a single currency for as many countries as meet the convergence criteria.

Second, I am sceptical of this third way as it does not view the Union as an essentially political project, but rather as a purely technocratic one. The single market is an extraordinary tool for increasing prosperity, competitiveness and even peace among Europeans, but it is, in itself, without a political goal. Having come from a repressive and authoritarian system, the European Union was for me much more than a space of prosperity and security: it was a community of values which upheld human rights, the rule of law, civil liberty and a free and independent press. Depicting the EU as a mere 'union of markets' is both inaccurate and dangerous. If economic opportunism is what keeps us together, our achievements will be volatile and ephemeral. In any case, we live in a multipolar world of rising powers, and we are faced with challenges that go beyond the capabilities of the nation-state. This is true not just for the smaller Member States, but also for the bigger and mightier. Whether we look at trade, development, crisis management or diplomatic representation in international forums, we need a high degree of European unity. To safeguard our common interests and advance our common values, we need to act together, more than ever before.

This thinking makes it clear why I believe that the process of European integration is far from finished. Yet whilst we need further deepening, we cannot let it take place in a political vacuum. The choices the EU is facing are delicate and can be divisive, but citizens should be fully engaged in crucial debates that concern their future and that of the generations to come. Political parties have to root the future of the European project firmly in the genuine aspirations of their electorate, not in a permissive consensus of national politicians. If this process of anchoring the European project to a European electorate which is both responsive and responsible for the action of European political parties does not take place, we are likely to witness an ever growing corrosion of the support for the EU as a whole. The European Parliament must be at the centre of this political renewal. Anti-European populism, both from the far left and far right, is alive and kicking. It would be naïve to think that people will keep their faith in Europe if political parties do not actively defend our previous gains and debate the way forward in an open, inclusive and far-reaching discussion. In a few weeks, governments pressured by public opinions might be tempted to undo achievements it has taken decades to build. The current discussion over the reform of Schengen might be taken as a case in point.

Conclusions

I might be accused of being biased towards the Lisbon Treaty. My Presidency in the European Parliament has coincided with its entry into force. I have campaigned vigorously for its adoption in the last reluctant Member States, including my own. I genuinely believe that the new Treaty is best placed to make the EU a power ready to face the challenges of the 21st century, whether we look at economics or foreign policy. Here I have tried to explain why the Lisbon Treaty increases the quality of European democracy and should not be used as a scapegoat for criticisms of the Union. My impression is that if we are really looking for a culprit, we should look elsewhere. The main problem is that, although we need further European integration, this cannot be provided without a strengthening of political parties at the European level. A genuine party system at the EU level would lead to greater legitimacy, greater accountability and better communication between the EU and its citizens, breaking the vicious circle of abstentionism and Euroscepticism.

In the last three years, seismic changes have taken place in the world order with the financial crisis, the democratic upheavals in Northern Africa and the Middle East, and the push in the world economy's centre of gravity away from the west. Facing these challenges, either we will have a united European stance, or we will not have a relevant stance at all. Yet the definition of our common position needs to be the reflection of popular will. This will happen only if the political parties that represent and shape a European polity become a reality.

As we learned after the fall of the Iron Curtain, history had not ended. Indeed, today it seems that the march of human history has actually quickened its pace. If Europe does not want to be left behind, it needs to proceed with political deepening. Our experience from Laeken to Lisbon shows that the process of institutional deepening has largely been completed, but that the political deepening has still fully to occur.

References

MacShane, D. (2011) *Europe's Parliament: Reform or Perish?* (London: Centre for European Reform).

Menon, A. and Peet, J. (2010) *Beyond the European Parliament: Rethinking the EU's Democratic Legitimacy* (London: Centre for European Reform).

Priestley, J. (2010) 'European Political Parties: The Missing Link'. Policy Paper (Paris: Notre Europe).

JCMS 2011 Volume 49 Annual Review pp. 19–44

The JCMS Annual Review Lecture
The Shattering of Illusions – And What Next?*

LOUKAS TSOUKALIS
University of Athens/ELIAMEP

I. Ten Years of Fast Learning . . . the Hard Way

The European Union (EU) entered the new century on a wave of euro-enthusiasm. Many people were convinced that integration was running fast again, and the process would be unstoppable. Some went further, predicting that the 21st century would be the century of Europe, and many more were ready to believe them.[1] It was too good a prospect to dismiss lightly. For the fainthearted, and those with a more sceptical, or just narrowly utilitarian, approach to European integration, it was of course all rather threatening. They felt they were being swept aside. They were in a minority, not strong enough to resist the wave of euro-enthusiasm, but always alert to take advantage of any future change in the direction of the wind. And the opportunity eventually did come their way.

* This article is dedicated to the memory of Tommaso Padoa-Schioppa, a leading European thinker and practitioner, who played a major role in the European construction and the creation of the euro in particular, and Susan Strange, a pioneer in the study of international political economy, who analysed the workings of casino capitalism and its internal explosive dynamics at an early stage. They both stood up against the intellectual orthodoxy of their time – what the French call '*la pensée unique*'. I should like to thank the editors of the Annual Review, Nathaniel Copsey and Tim Haughton, for their very useful comments; Nikos Koutsiaras for many constructive exchanges of ideas; Eleni Panagiotarea for research assistance; and numerous colleagues from whom I have learned so much in joint projects and discussions across Europe and beyond.

[1] Leonard (2005) and Rifkin (2004) are good examples.

The EU was meant to proceed on yet another combination of deepening and widening, even more ambitious this time than in the past. The creation of the single currency was, undoubtedly, the most important act of integration since the very beginning. It was daring in its economic significance and broader implications; it was based on the use of economic means for political ends, thus continuing an old tradition going back to the Schuman plan of 1950; and it was heavy with symbolism. This had been decided back in the early 1990s as part of a package deal that linked money to the redrawing of the map of Europe and German reunification, after the collapse of the Soviet empire. The more directly political part of the package was to follow some years later with the attempt to turn the founding European treaties into a constitution. What the advocates of political union had failed to deliver with the Maastricht, Amsterdam and Nice revisions of the treaties, they were determined to achieve this time round. Treaty revision as a never-ending process?

The conditions seemed to be more propitious this time round. The other big project of the first decade of the new century was further enlargement of the EU: much more ambitious than ever before in terms of numbers of candidates and the size of the *acquis*, as well as in terms of the economic distance between candidates and those already in, not to mention the differences in political culture and collective memory between old and new members. The southern enlargement of the 1980s had surely been difficult, but ultimately successful. The challenge of incorporating the newly liberated countries of central and eastern Europe, plus the two island states in the Mediterranean, looked even bigger by comparison.

Crash Landing of the European Constitution

More than a decade later, we are surely much wiser – chastened by reality, one might say. The Constitutional Treaty – with the word 'compromise' written all over it, including the name – hit the rocks in the French and Dutch referendums of 2005 before it reached the lands of the usual suspects. As a result, some of the symbols that had caused offence to the non-believers were thrown overboard, while the text became more complex and even more unreadable before it was finally signed as the Treaty of Lisbon. From the noble aspiration to engage the European demos in the writing of Europe's first post-national constitution, we were back again to marathon committee meetings with crafty lawyers and diplomats in search of the long-winded compromise that still (unavoidably?) characterizes the European process. The revamped treaty did not enjoy a smooth passage either, thanks to the Irish who were the only ones to be consulted in a referendum – and since they did not vote the right way the first time, they were asked to do so again! After years of agony, the Treaty of Lisbon finally entered into force in December 2009.[2]

From beginning to end, the latest attempt at treaty revision had lasted eight years. The process proved traumatic for all concerned – not to be repeated again for a long time, politicians and diplomats involved in the process vowed. Apparently, they had not counted on the strong will of the German chancellor, operating under the sword of Damocles of her constitutional court in Karlsruhe. Only a few months later in 2010, the EU was to embark on yet another revision of the new treaty, though we were assured that this would be a small operation without much political fuss. It remains to be seen.

During those eight years, we all discovered that European citizens were no longer ready to give their leaders a carte blanche on the future of European integration. A yawning gap had opened between elected politicians and their electors on things European: parliamentary ratifications of the Lisbon Treaty (and its predecessor) were mostly comfortable, voted by large majorities, while referendum results revealed much unhappiness and also large amounts of ignorance on behalf of citizens. The elitist conspiracy of European integration, full of good intentions and with pretty remarkable results, had probably reached its limits. European political leaders were apparently good at getting their officials to negotiate complex compromise documents, but most proved singularly incapable of explaining the end products to their fellow citizens.

Europe runs the risk of becoming a victim of complexity in times when mass politics turns into populism and simple messages. There is surely a problem of communication, but this is not the only explanation. Has Europe finally hit against the hard rock of national and local identities – the European and the global being things that only small cosmopolitan elites can understand and identify with?

Political discourses remained predominantly national, and there was precious little effort, even less success, in incorporating a European narrative in them. It was also a time of growing inequalities and uncertainty in our societies, often perceived as being directly linked to the opening of frontiers and global financial markets. European integration became increasingly identified with globalization, and there was growing resistance, especially in the more dysfunctional national systems that could not adjust to a changing environment. There were losers in the process, real, potential or even

[2] There is a vast literature on the workings of the European Convention, the failed referendums and the travails of the intergovernmental conference that finally led to the Treaty of Lisbon. See Norman (2005); Taggart (2006); Moravcsik (2006); and Piris (2010), among others.

imaginary.[3] Most national politicians (and others) were too late in realizing the problem, not to mention trying to deal with it.

Others spoke about the legitimacy deficit[4] of the EU and its institutions, which is not the same as the democratic deficit that had been much talked about in the literature earlier. Eurobarometer surveys have been pointing to weaker popular support for integration, while the 2009 elections of the European Parliament (EP) registered a record low rate of participation, mixed with heavy doses of apathy during the campaign. As the powers of the EP kept growing from one treaty revision to the next, popular interest in it was apparently on the way down: an inverse relationship that most analysts had not predicted.

Ambitions had thus to be scaled down significantly – and this was painful. The constitutional ambition had produced a political crisis which threatened to paralyse the EU. But the collective sigh of relief that accompanied the setting into force of the Lisbon Treaty was soon followed by another shock when people heard the names of those appointed to fill the posts of President of the European Council and High Representative. Those two posts were after all the major novelty of the Treaty and many expectations had been invested in them. Was the shock (and the disappointment that went with it) justified because the names clearly lacked political glamour, or did it rather stem from false expectations about what Mr (and Ms) Europe might have been allowed to do or say on behalf of members always alert to keeping the strings tight?

No national politician apparently wants a European (high or less high) representative to be able to stop the traffic in Beijing and other capitals – and there would be absolutely no point in doing so, the seasoned observer of the European scene might add. Back to reality, so read the message. But for euro-enthusiasts it was like a crash landing. It will take some time before we can pronounce on the effects of the new Treaty and what the new appointees, together with national political leaders, will be willing (or able) to make of it.[5] And we may well end up with very different conclusions about Mr Herman Van Rompuy, the President of the European Council, and Baroness Ashton, the High Representative, respectively. Personal qualities will play a role here, as will the nature of the job, together with what Harold Macmillan[6] famously

[3] I talked about losers inside countries and how this was beginning to affect European integration back in 2003 (Tsoukalis, 2005 [2003]). For a recent, in-depth analysis, see Fligstein (2008). The creation of the European Globalization Adjustment Fund in 2006 was one modest attempt to deal with the problem (Tsoukalis, 2006). It proved to be completely ineffectual: the kind of symbolic gesture that European leaders often resort to, and later ends up like an empty shell.

[4] See, for example, various articles on the subject in Cramme (2009). See also Neyer (2010); Piret (2008); and Scharpf's (1999) classical work on input- and output-oriented legitimacy.

[5] For an early, albeit very provisional, attempt, see CEPS, Egmont and EPC (2010), and Dinan (this volume).

[6] Harold Macmillan was prime minister of the United Kingdom in 1957–64.

referred to as 'events, my dear boy, events'. After all, European treaties, like national constitutions, only set the parameters for decisions and policies; they do not determine the contents.

Enlargement and Saint Panteleimon

There was no crisis as such with the big bang enlargement that brought ten new members in May 2004, and two more in January 2007. From 15 to 27: no small deal. The new members were much poorer than existing ones, most of them with relatively short experience of democratic institutions, while some were also novices in the exercise of statehood. Many observers argue that enlargement has been the most successful foreign policy of the Union, extending *Pax Europeae* to some of the less privileged and unstable parts of the European continent. This may indeed be true: the best application of European soft power, or Europeanization at its best and most efficient.[7]

Alas, few things come free in today's world. Successive enlargements have had a negative effect on the internal cohesion of the EU – and the latest ones arguably even more so. Numbers also make a big difference. Councils of 12 or 15 still looked like a group. With 27, European councils of different denominations resemble a (mini-UN) conference. This is bound to affect the workings of those institutions. It also tends to encourage bigger countries to circumvent official channels of negotiation deemed to be too slow and tedious and with little correspondence to the distribution of power in the real world. The nature of the game has changed. This is a common secret in Brussels among the old hands, although not often expressed in public for the sake of political correctness.[8]

We have discovered in the process that some countries may not have been ready to join, and that the process of Europeanization, especially after accession, has narrow limits. Yet we should have known that from previous experience. With the economic crisis that followed, we later painfully discovered that economic convergence between the core and the periphery of the Union was not so much of an automatic process either. The crisis hit particularly badly the new members of the eastern periphery of the EU, especially the Baltic countries, as well as Romania and Bulgaria (Poland being a notable exception). They were soon followed by southern Europe, plus Ireland. Many

[7] The literature on Europeanization is rich and with a relatively long history. See, among others, Featherstone and Radaelli (2003).

[8] Various authors have tried to assess the effects of enlargement on EU decision-making and the functioning of the EU as a whole. Wallace (2007) and Zielonka (2007) remain among the best. As with many econometric studies, there is always the risk that the researcher measures things that can be measured and leaves out those that really count.

years of economic convergence were at least partly rolled back in a short space of time.

I am certainly not arguing here that the latest rounds of enlargement should not have taken place, although they could have been better prepared. The argument is rather that enlargement comes with a price: the nature and the internal operation of the EU have changed significantly and enlargement has been an important factor in this change. Those who have always preferred a loose, more intergovernmental EU may be happy with this development; if anything, they had always seen it as one of the advantages associated with enlargement.[9]

Now, there is precious little appetite to take more members in. Most of the official candidates are to be found in southeastern Europe. On the one hand, there is Turkey – a big country and a rising power in the region, big but also very different (Grigoriadis, 2008; Oniş, 2007; Oktem, 2011). On the other, there are the small countries of the Western Balkans – namely the successor states of Yugoslavia, plus Albania (Rupnik, 2009): with few exceptions, those countries still have some distance to travel before they become functional political and economic entities. The appetite (and capacity) to integrate them in the EU is not there. Croatia will most probably sneak in. What about the others? Only a few people still consider the EU as a modern incarnation of Saint Panteleimon, the all-merciful healer of all kinds of disease. The miracle of Europeanization has been cut down to size through experience.

There is, however, the other side of the argument, equally valid, which says that the EU door should be kept open to all European countries that fulfil the basic criteria for entry. Closing the door would be like denying a key part of the European project. Squeezed between those two sets of arguments, the Union is tempted to resort to the old habit of procrastination. Hopefully, it may also try to think out of the box, linking further enlargement to the reshaping of the European project while also inventing new intermediate stages between membership and non-membership, and not only of the virtual kind.

EMU as a Postmodern Construction

Before the internal political crisis ended, associated with the adoption of the new (no longer constitutional) treaty, a new crisis had begun. The biggest financial crisis of the developed world soon turned into a European crisis.

[9] Vivien Schmidt (2009) wrote about the different discourses on Europe, and expectations associated with them, among member countries (and political families, one might add). Most of the new members belong to the group of pragmatists (usually translated in institutional and policy terms as minimalists), led by the United Kingdom.

Many people then discovered what a currency without a state really meant (Padoa-Schioppa, 2004). EMU (economic and monetary union) was indeed a highly ambitious and risky project. Economists have always been divided on the balance between pros and cons; the decision to proceed had been after all highly political. Several people have wondered all along whether Europe was ready for such a big jump, while others relied instead on the well-worn strategy of successive disequilibria leading to ever higher levels of integration. The construction designed at Maastricht reflected economic orthodoxy and the internal balance of power at the time of creation. True, it was itself unbalanced, but that was all that was politically feasible at the time.

Before the crisis, I used to compare EMU to a postmodern construction (Tsoukalis, 2005 [2003]) that defies the laws of gravity (and economics?). It did so successfully for more than ten years, and there were those who were lulled into believing that the good times would last forever. Alas, the laws of gravity finally began to take their revenge – and they did so with great force. The year 2010 became the year of the crisis of the eurozone.

II. The Bursting of the Bubble and the Euro

The crisis began back in 2007 in an obscure segment of the American financial industry, the so-called 'sub-prime loans market'. European political leaders first thought it was of no concern to them; little did they know. It soon spread to what was the most globalized (and unregulated) sector of the world economy. To be precise, it became a crisis that affected the whole of the western financial system, and in their typically arrogant fashion, Americans and Europeans branded it as 'global'. It did not stop there either. The financial crisis quickly spilled over to the real economy, leading to negative rates of growth in Europe and North America that had not been experienced since the Great Depression. In some countries of the eastern periphery of Europe, the decline was in double-digit figures in a single year (Connolly and Copsey, 2011). And that was not the end of the story. As many national governments opened their purse in order to save banks and jobs in the real economy, markets were seized by panic when they saw sovereign debt rising fast. The previous run on banks was thus succeeded by a run on states.[10]

There were three main underlying factors in the big crisis that hit the eurozone in 2010. The first had to do with the rapid rise of sovereign debt in several member countries, largely although not exclusively, the result of states running big deficits to mitigate the effects of a crisis born out of a financial

[10] For a good analysis of the crisis and its broader economic, social and political effects from different perspectives, see Hemerijck *et al.* (2009). See also the special issue of *JCMS* (Hodson and Quaglia, 2009).

system that had previously run amok. The second was related to growing current account imbalances inside the eurozone, typically between the north and the south. And the third was about the perception, widely held in Wall Street and the City of London (although much less so in most European countries), that Europe had neither the instruments nor the political will to deal with the problem.

And then markets began to bet massively against the euro, leading those politically naïve and more easily excitable to think that the demise of the euro (and also the EU?) might not be very far off. They had never understood the political investment made in the euro, and there was of course more than an element of *Schadenfreude* among those who had never welcomed the creation of the European single currency, not to mention the closer political union that would probably have to follow.

Greece served as the catalyst for the crisis of the euro because it had the worst combination of three different deficits – namely a large budget deficit being added to an already huge debt, an unsustainable current account imbalance, and a deficit of credibility since Greek politicians had been repeatedly economical with the truth and flexible with the use of statistics (see also Featherstone, 2011). Greece was a big problem on its own; it was also perceived as a precursor of things to come and a test case of how other European countries and the EU would deal with the twin problem of sovereign debt and imbalances.

The perception proved right this time: the big rescue operation soon mounted by the EU, with the assistance of the IMF (International Monetary Fund), was indeed the precursor of a Europe-wide crisis mechanism and broader changes in the governance structures of the euro, while the programme of stabilization imposed on Greece by its lenders served as a test of political, economic and social endurance in the adjustment to a world after the bubble. Ireland soon followed, and Portugal too. One thing, however, is sure: we are nowhere near the end of a crisis causing different kinds of collateral damage. After all, the political and social consequences of financial crises usually follow with a time lag. In Europe, they do not respect national borders, and this is complicating matters further.

The crisis is the result of colossal failures in markets and institutions; it also marks a big failure for the economics profession. The efficient market hypothesis, resting on the behaviour of rational actors armed with perfect information, which had provided the intellectual basis for financial deregulation, was shown to bear little resemblance to real life financial markets in which greed and moral hazard met in an explosive mix, with the old herd instinct being added for extra effect. Financial power often translates into political power: there were too many instances of politicians being hijacked by financial lobbies. And the academic profession was shown to be particularly prone to mainstream thinking – for some, attachment to mainstream thinking was also apparently related to pecuniary interest.[11]

Of course, the bursting of the bubble was not specifically related to Europe. It acquired though a strong European dimension because of the existence of the euro and the weakness of its governance structures. Market integration had raced far ahead of policy integration; with the crisis, there was an urgent need to catch up. Financial regulation was found to be hopelessly weak. The Stability and Growth Pact was inadequate from its very conception; it was weakened in the process and poorly implemented. Surveillance by European institutions was also found to be very poor, and there was no crisis mechanism at all when it was sorely needed: some people had feared that the existence of a crisis mechanism would add to moral hazard.

Sure, there was systemic failure, but there was also gross irresponsibility by those elected or appointed to guard the gates. Much of the Greek political class (and those who elected them) had been adding for years to an already very large public debt: clientelism was coupled with gross mismanagement, and the results were appalling. Sure, the party had been great fun as long as it lasted. But were Greek politicians more irresponsible than their Irish colleagues who allowed a small group of bankers to bankrupt the Irish economy? What about British politicians, including those of New Labour, who had led for years the crusade of financial liberalization and deregulation? As for German politicians (and regulators), were they blameless and hence morally justified in chastising the others? After all, German banks had been allowed to play a big role blowing into the bubble for years by translating German savings into loans to other countries. Most of those loans went to consumption and construction bubbles, while the competitiveness gap between the north and the south in Europe kept on increasing.

When the bubble finally did burst, several politicians in different countries, egged on by tabloids and eager to ride the wave of rising populism at home, engaged in the game of finger pointing and the exchange of insults and national stereotypes. They should have known better, given the fragile nature of the European construction. It was like throwing stones in a glasshouse.

[11] Padoa-Schioppa (2007) wrote that European financial supervision was neither super, nor did it have any vision. In *What Kind of Europe?* (Tsoukalis, 2005 [2003]), I wrote about the inherent instability of financial markets, the risk of systemic crisis in a deregulated environment, and raised the question about who will pay the costs when the crisis does eventually break out: the finance industry, consumers or taxpayers? Others, of course, expressed similar views: an old-fashioned minority allegedly unable to understand, among other things, what a huge difference sophisticated computer models made in the functioning of financial markets. Now we all do, although having drawn very different conclusions from the ones propagated by the economic orthodoxy at the time. In a remarkable piece of self-criticism, the independent evaluation office of the IMF (IEO, 2011) wrote about groupthink, intellectual capture and incomplete analytical approaches behind policies that had led to the crisis.

With exceptions, the European political class will not come out of the crisis with high marks. This is meant as an understatement: in fact, much of the political class in some countries risks being wiped out.

III. New Economic Governance: Will It Work?

Crisis is the mother of change, and crises in the past have often provided the catalyst for further integration in Europe. The functionalist strategy seems to be back again and in full swing: we need to strengthen the 'E' in order to secure the 'M' of EMU. In other words, we need more effective institutions and rules of economic governance to safeguard the single currency. And this has been indeed happening in successive stages since European leaders admitted in the early months of 2010 that there was a collective problem that required collective action. It has been happening slowly and reluctantly, as is customary in EU affairs. In this particular case, the mental adjustment required was indeed huge and extremely painful at a time when the appetite for further integration is clearly lacking.

Having reached the edge of the precipice, European leaders have taken decisions that would have been completely unthinkable only a short time ago, thus so far disproving the Cassandras who had been betting on disintegration. We will end up with stronger and more effective governance structures, including new rules and institutions for the regulation of financial markets, closer and more binding co-ordination of national economic policies with a much broader agenda, backed up with the threat of (more or less) automatic sanctions and more effective surveillance procedures, greater emphasis on structural reform aiming at restoring the competitiveness of national economies that have been lagging behind, as well as a mechanism for crisis management on a permanent basis with large sums of money, strong conditionality and close IMF involvement in order to convince markets that European leaders mean business.[12] In the meantime, individual members, starting with Greece, followed by Ireland and Portugal, have been going through the purgatory of large-scale budgetary consolidation, accompanied by structural reforms, as a condition for the provision of financial assistance by the other members of the eurozone.

Will it work? The optimists point to the high stakes and remind us that when it comes to the crunch European leaders finally take the necessary decisions in order to save the integration project – the euro being

[12] There is a rapidly growing literature on the new European economic governance. For a good summary description, albeit unavoidably rather sterilized in political terms, see ECB (2011). For a cogently argued and critical paper on the subject, see also De Grauwe (2011).

undoubtedly a key part of it. The new governance structures will have to work, they add, and remaining gaps will be filled as we go along. The pessimists, however, point to the enormity of the challenge ahead and the big questions that still remain unanswered. Of course, the one trillion euro question is whether the crisis will stop there. Extending beyond those three countries of modest size, it would stress test the endurance of the new crisis mechanism. No doubt, we live in interesting times: for the Chinese, this is meant as a curse, not a wish – this is presumably also true for Europeans today. We have clearly reached a new integration frontier, and we are not at all sure what lies ahead. EMU looks like a make-or-break issue for Europe.

Co-ordination of policies is much easier said than implemented, and the political basis on which it rests remains shaky. We are all very much aware of the implementation gap in an EU so often forced to resort to long communiqués as a poor substitute for action. For example, the so-called 'European semester', which aims at a simultaneous assessment of national budgetary and structural measures, has a noble intention behind it. But how will national parliaments react, especially those of the bigger countries (we are surely all equal, but some are still more equal than others!), when they begin to receive more or less binding instructions from Brussels? Even more so, what will heads of state or government of the eurozone make of the collective ownership they have taken of the new Euro-plus Pact, which is meant to extend co-ordination to policy areas beyond those coming under the more constraining rules of the Treaty? The experience with the old Lisbon Agenda is hardly promising. Is it again the triumph of hope over experience?

Provisions for closer co-ordination of national economic policies do not automatically resolve the problem of who actually sets the priorities for the eurozone (and the EU as a whole), and how. To put it differently: how will the burden of adjustment be distributed between surplus and deficit countries, with direct implications for the general macroeconomic stance for the eurozone and the EU as a whole? In the long debate and negotiations on European monetary union that go back more than 40 years, the French have been persistently trying to ensure some symmetry between the two: judging from results, mostly in vain (Tsoukalis, 1997). This is an old problem acknowledged by Keynes during the Bretton Woods negotiations. At the time, the Americans represented the surplus countries, although not for very long.

Should fiscal consolidation in southern Europe (and elsewhere) be accompanied by measures to bolster domestic demand in surplus countries? And is there room for EU instruments, including a more flexible use of Structural

Funds, to promote investment and growth?[13] Germany plays the role of China in the eurozone with a large surplus in its current account. Much of this surplus is the counterpart of deficits in the south. Admittedly, the intra-European debate on the delicate matter of distributing the burden of adjustment has been more diplomatic and polite than the international one pitting the United States against China: for obvious reasons, we can guess. Yet, it has also been a political *bras de fer*, in which the view of the strongest, backed by markets, has so far prevailed.

Austerity may be indeed the right message after many years of excessive borrowing in Europe and the rest of the developed world. But austerity can go too far with the risk of Europe plunging into another recession. And what if prolonged budgetary austerity proves too much for the economies and societies of the European periphery? Structural reform is also fine, indeed urgent in some countries, but can, or should, all countries imitate the German model and try to keep wages down as a way of winning the competitiveness race? We usually discover the threshold of social tolerance once we have crossed it. Greece seems dangerously close to it.[14] The convergence machine of European integration is now going into reverse gear, with the less prosperous periphery being left behind. It is a threatening prospect and a dramatic reversal of earlier trends, if it were to continue for long.

The crisis began a few years ago with runs on banks and it has been followed by runs on states. Large bank exposure and rising sovereign debt have been operating like communicating vessels across national borders. In other words, there is a close interdependence between the banking and the sovereign crises in Europe.[15] They need to be tackled jointly in the transition to a post-bubble world. However, this raises in turn the awkward question of how to distribute the burden of adjustment between taxpayers and private lenders (or bondholders). Markets anticipate so-called 'haircuts' of sovereign debt of one or more of the most vulnerable countries in the foreseeable future; and this has added to the panic. It does not help that this issue has been

[13] The President of the European Commission, José Manuel Barroso, has proposed the issuing of Eurobonds for the financing of large investment projects in partnership between governments and the private sector. On the so-called 'project bonds', see Haug *et al.* (2011). There have also been proposals for the frontloading of money spent through EU Structural Funds as a way of boosting investment in the crisis-stricken countries (Marzinotto, 2011).

[14] The cases of Latvia or Lithuania, which have gone through an internal devaluation while experiencing a fall of 15–18 per cent of GDP in one year, have sometimes been presented as examples to follow. God protect us from the virtuous – and some economists too!

[15] See also Buiter *et al.* (2011); Darvas *et al.* (2011); Kopf (2011). Several people, including prominent politicians and analysts, have put forward proposals for the issuing of Eurobonds, partially replacing national sovereign bonds, as a way of restoring stability and confidence in financial markets (Juncker and Tremonti, 2010; Steinmeier and Steinbrück, 2010; Gros and Mayer, 2010). Such a move would constitute a first, big step towards fiscal union, considered by a good number of economists as an essential component of EMU. However, some of the key political players are not ready for it – at least not as yet.

formally raised in association with the establishment of a permanent crisis mechanism (European Stability Mechanism – ESM) in 2013. Trying to buy time while everybody knows that some of the most difficult decisions lie ahead does not help to calm the nerves. Is sovereign default an option, or even an inevitability, and with what consequences? Democracies and financial markets do not operate on the same clock. The lack of synchronization becomes highly destabilizing in a world where markets set the pace.

Honest stress tests for European banks will probably have to be followed in more than a few cases by recapitalization and restructuring. But who will then provide the invisible hand to guide them since there is no political authority in Europe to match a highly integrated banking sector? Recapitalization and restructuring of banks may have to precede any attempt to deal with the highly sensitive political question of how to distribute the burden of adjustment to a world after the bubble between taxpayers and private creditors. And this in turn overlaps with another difficult problem of distribution – namely the one between countries. In other words, who should pay for the toxic assets of European banks, being the product of excessive lending to both private and public sectors? Should it be taxpayers in Ireland, Greece, Germany or France? And how much should creditors or shareholders of those banks share the burden? Distributional issues are difficult to handle, even more so when they cross borders. This remains very much true of the EU, despite long years of integration. Such issues are now at the very top of the European political agenda.

Let us try another way of looking at the problem. Do German politicians, for example, find it politically easier to pay for the rescue of Greece or Ireland, painful though it may be domestically, than face squarely the problem of their own *Landesbanken*? This would be a fascinating question to address for political economists. The place that banks and the financial industry in general will (be allowed to) occupy in the brave new world after the crisis has not yet been settled. True, the enthusiasm for bold reforms seems to have dissipated rather rapidly. Is the next financial crisis an accident waiting to happen?

IV. The Broader Picture

The crisis has been international as well as European in its range, although the effects have varied significantly from one country to the other. There is now more economic divergence inside Europe because of the crisis, and the odds are that the divergence will continue, if not worsen, in the foreseeable future. Germany and the countries around it have entered a phase of economic recovery, robust as it seems, while those in the south and the west of Europe (also Britain?) face the prospect of very slow growth, if not stagnation: fiscal retrenchment surely does not help.

In times of diverging economic performance, agreement on a common European approach, not to mention a comprehensive European solution, to the crisis is understandably difficult to reach. There are competing strategies between countries, mainly between creditors and debtors, but there are also competing strategies within countries. The intra-European negotiation is still predominantly intergovernmental, but there is also growing public debate on alternative strategies and policy choices that are no longer confined within national boundaries – and this is a very good sign for Europe.

Political leaders have to cope with growing dissatisfaction in their societies, which in places goes one step further and turns into anger and social unrest. Populism is on the rise and so are anti-establishment parties. They offer simple solutions for complex, yet real, problems, they love scapegoats, and they carry a strong nationalist message with often anti-European and generally xenophobic undertones. They have a strong presence in France, Austria and the Netherlands. Different versions can be found in Belgium and Italy. They are on the rise in several countries in Europe, even in what used to be social democratic Scandinavia, long perceived as being immune to that kind of problem. And some are pretty ugly. If populism were to obtain a political foothold in Germany, it could have wider consequences given the increasingly central role that Germany plays in the European system. Countries in central and eastern Europe are more familiar with populism: they have already experienced different versions of it in the transition to democracy and capitalism.[16] They may therefore have lessons to teach their fellow members of the European family, those with longer experience in parliamentary democracy but hardly any experience with cuts in living standards and social expenditure until very recently.

There is a host of factors behind the populist phenomenon, of different scale and combinations across European countries: large immigration, widening income disparities, growing uncertainty in times of rapid change, dissatisfaction with the 'Golden Straitjacket'[17] imposed on societies when Left and Right converged that may now get worse if the burden of adjustment after the crisis is perceived to be unfairly distributed. Unhappiness turns into social unrest in those countries where the problems are more acute, the culture of social protest is stronger and the institutions weaker. Financial markets

[16] For an interesting article on populism and different conceptions of nationalism in Europe, see Auer (2010). See also Deegan-Krause and Haughton (2009).
[17] A term introduced by Thomas Friedman (1999).

remain as imperfect as they have always been (and in panic), while national governments are increasingly constrained by their public opinion in seeking solutions which require a strong global and regional component for problems that have long ceased to be confined within national boundaries. It is like trying to navigate between Scylla and Charybdis. We know from Greek mythology that this required enormous skill and courage – qualities that are in short supply among political leaders in today's Europe.

National governments, of course, remain the key players, and public discourse is predominantly national. European public space is small, although growing and largely because of the crisis. True, those who try to intermediate between national discourses often lose themselves in translation. The EP was meant to gradually make the connection: some MEPs have succeeded in that respect, but most do not have much of an audience anywhere, while transnational political parties are still weak players. As for the Commission, steering a European course has become increasingly difficult in recent years, especially since political leaders in the big countries showed little interest in or respect for it. The European Commission might try instead to be more assertive. The one institution that comes much stronger out of the crisis is surely the ECB (European Central Bank). Even diehards of national sovereignty recognize the crucial role it has played in managing the crisis – and we were surely lucky to have Mr Trichet[18] at the helm when the going got really rough. The ECB is a federal institution par excellence. It also follows the venerable tradition of depoliticized policies at the European level: independent central banking at its best. Rightly or wrongly, it is not an example that can be widely imitated or transplanted.

One is tempted to argue that the European political system is turning more intergovernmental, with the European Council being the place where the buck stops. This is certainly true of negotiations leading to the provision of financial assistance to the heavily indebted countries of the eurozone and the European Financial Stability Facility (EFSF), which will be replaced by the European Stability Mechanism (ESM) in 2013. But can a purely intergovernmental system deliver the goods? This is one question that Ms Merkel and Mr Sarkozy have been trying to evade. European economic governance requires collective ownership and institutions that can provide continuity, surveillance and implementation control. Intergovernmental arrangements cannot do that. It is interesting that by calling for more automatic sanctions in the context of a reformed Stability and Growth Pact, member governments will have to accept, albeit reluctantly, a bigger role for the European Commission. This is

[18] See last year's JCMS Annual Review (Trichet, 2010).

precisely what the 'reverse majority voting' rule for the application of sanctions should lead to – not what some member governments originally had in mind.

The crisis has placed Germany at centre stage as the country with the biggest and strongest economy in Europe, the indispensable country in any European comprehensive solution to the crisis, and hence the one that can also dictate the terms (see Paterson, this volume). Many years back, it was monetary policy and exchange rates that had led to the first concrete manifestation of a two-tier Europe, with West Germany leading the first tier. It was in the mid-1970s, when the 'snake' was gradually reduced to a Deutschmark zone (Tsoukalis, 1977). Almost 40 years later with the euro, Germany is again leading the pack.

With the advent of the crisis in the eurozone, leadership was indeed thrust upon Germany. When this happened, its political leaders showed little enthusiasm for taking it on, or any signs of knowing what to do with it. As Germany gradually began to exercise leadership, also setting its own terms and conditions, many of its partners became manifestly unhappy. We were told that Germany had become a normal European country in which EU matters were now seen through the lenses of narrowly defined, short-term national interest. After all, others were behaving so, why not the Germans? Admittedly, many Germans were in a state of shock: the crisis of the euro had confirmed their worst fears about sharing a currency with countries that did not share their approach to public finance and many other things – and their view of European integration, understandably perhaps, turned grey. Some began to think of the EU, and especially its weaker members, as an albatross hanging from their neck that they would much prefer to get rid of, others felt that Germany may be ready to go global on its own, while tabloids stoked the fires of populism.[19] Europe surely cannot afford a Eurosceptical Germany, but nor can it accept a hegemonic one. There should be enough space in between the two for a unified Germany playing a leading role in transforming European integration once again into a positive-sum game.

Franco–German initiatives continue to be a frequent feature of European decision-making: increasingly to disguise German strength and French weakness, the cynical observer might add. The relationship is indeed becoming

[19] There has been intense debate inside Germany about ways of dealing with the crisis, as well as about the pros and cons of bail-outs (a dirty word in German). As would have been expected in any country, the arguments ranged all the way from the sophisticated to the vulgar, from the European to the narrow nationalist. Many spoke of punishment, fewer of forgiveness. For an informative discussion about new Germany and Europe, see Guérot and Leonard (2011); and Paterson (this volume). For representative, yet different, views on ways to handle the sovereign debt crisis, see Belke (2010) and Bofinger (2010). See also the position paper signed by over 180 German economists against further rescue packages (Lucke, 2011).

more unequal, at least in economic terms, although it continues to leave a strong imprint on EU decisions and policies, with the rest often voicing their frustration. The main problem does not always lie with the content of Franco–German initiatives as such. Sometimes, it is the arrogance and sheer lack of diplomatic tact accompanying those initiatives that the other members have found most insulting. The recent 'Pact for Competitiveness', subsequently renamed the 'Euro-plus Pact' as a kind of verbal massage for the national sensitivities of lesser mortals, is a typical example – and not the only one.

Several people in Britain and Poland in particular have voiced their concern as the management of the euro begins to dominate European debate and policy-making because it risks marginalizing the countries outside the eurozone.[20] They raise the spectre of another kind of two-speed Europe, between the 'ins' and the 'outs' of the eurozone, which has been in fact on the cards since Maastricht. Monetary union remains the most important act of integration. It necessitates policy action and co-ordination on behalf of those who share the common good of a single currency that simply does not compare with what is required for the management of the single market. Those outside the eurozone have indeed legitimate views and interests which should be taken into account, but they cannot have an equal say in the decision-making related to the management of the euro. It is both logical and unavoidable.

In the years before the crisis, the EU had become increasingly identified with economic liberalization, hence running the risk of being delegitimized in the eyes of those who found themselves on the losing side of economic change. Parties of the centre-left became very much aware of this problem. Now, the perception is changing, although the political balance sheet may turn more negative. In the north, the spectre of a European 'transfer union' is haunting people: the bail-out of the bankrupt economies of their weaker partners requires ever increasing amounts of financial assistance and guarantees provided by Germany, Austria, the Netherlands and Finland among others; and their citizens (and taxpayers) are manifestly unhappy. On the receiving end of those transfers, which are in effect interest-bearing loans as long as they are being serviced, there are people who go through a long and painful process of budgetary consolidation and who increasingly perceive the EU as the policeman of austerity. The combination could be political suicide for Europe.

[20] The Prime Minister of Poland, Mr Tusk, expressed his concern in public. *The Economist* (2011) had a leading article in which it argued in strong terms against the emergence of a two-speed Europe as a result of measures to strengthen the governance of the euro; it was not, however, clear at all what it proposed instead.

V. What Kind of Europe?

Some years back, I argued that the key question in European integration had long ceased to be '*How much Europe*?' and should be replaced by '*What kind of Europe*?' Different conceptions about the kind of Europe, and the kind of society in which we want to live, were hidden behind the question of more or less integration. There were trade-offs and choices to be made that the still predominantly intergovernmental political system of the EU failed to highlight (Tsoukalis, 2005 [2003]). I believe that this argument holds even more true today.

The biggest financial and economic crisis of the western world since the Great Depression may be the end of an era marked by economic liberalization during which financial markets acted as the spearhead of globalization, an era of rapidly growing consumption paid largely through rising debt and with deleterious effects on the global environment. The financial crisis and global warming are in effect the products of the two biggest market failures of the last two decades or so. Unregulated financial markets caused huge damage to the real economy. Similarly, markets in goods and services have failed to internalize the negative effects on the environment.

If this is indeed the end of an era, we are not yet sure what will succeed it.[21] We are still fumbling in the dark, trying to cope with the damage created by the bursting of a big bubble. The political vacuum created by the collapse of neo-liberal ideology has not been filled as yet; if anything, it tends to be filled by populism. And this has major implications for national as well as European politics and policy-making. It would be dangerously naïve to think that the European dimension of the crisis can be dealt with independently from the rest.

Many people pretend, and have good reasons for it, that the crisis was an unfortunate accident of the kind that can happen all the time ('stuff happens', as Donald Rumsfeld would have said). We should therefore deal with the damage as well as we can and go back to life as usual, they say. After all, there are vested interests to defend, as well as intellectual idleness and well-worn habits to contend with. Against mainstream opinion, there are those, still in a minority, who argue for a radical change in our way of thinking and the way we manage our national and European affairs. This change will have to include the redrawing of boundaries between the state and the market, the taming of the financial beast (an end to casino capitalism,[22] if you prefer), the

[21] In last year's Annual Review Lecture, Nicolaïdis (2010) talks of a 'Tocquevillian moment', in which a doomed era is ending without being replaced by the benefits of a new one.

[22] Back in 1986, Susan Strange began her last book with the sentence '[T]he Western financial system is rapidly coming to resemble nothing as much as a vast casino' (Strange, 1986, p. 1). She then proceeded to

adoption of a new approach to economic development that no longer upsets the planetary balance, and greater emphasis on equity and the quality of life instead of a one-dimensional focus on quantitative growth.[23]

Surely, our economies need to become more dynamic – the economic prospects do not look good and the demographic trends are even worse. Yet economic dynamism needs to be combined with a more qualitative and socially inclusive approach to economic development, thus creating the conditions for a new social contract that would cater more for the interests of the economically weaker, as well as the interests of younger generations who are now expected to foot our bill. European welfare systems surely need to be reformed, but in order to better preserve their essential features in changing conditions. After all, it is not the European social model in its different national incarnations that has brought Europe close to bankruptcy, but rather a particular variety of capitalism that had been advertised for years as the only way forward.

Europe is better qualified than other parts of the world to adopt such new ways of thinking and eventually even providing a model for others to follow. It has democratic traditions with strong roots, deeply ingrained notions of social justice and environmental concern, a long history of a mixed economy, and a healthy scepticism (of the large majority so far) of so many '-isms', including crude forms of nationalism, a scepticism earned through bitter experience. Elsewhere, I have tried to translate the more widely accepted etymological explanation of the word 'Europe', meaning 'broad eyes' in Greek, into a rallying cry for Europe the broad-minded (Tsoukalis, 2011).

For a long time, European integration had been like a car moving uphill: the French usually provided the driver, the Commission the map, the Germans paid for the petrol and the British oiled the brakes. In more recent years, it looked like a car without a driver, the map was replaced by a GPS, going on and off, the Poles insisted on taking an insurance policy with God, nobody wanted to pay for the petrol (and some clearly cheated), while those inside had an argument about how many more could fit into the car.

The European political scene has become more pluralistic, with a wide range of opinions and interests. The interplay of national interests has always determined the course of European integration, the famous Community

---

explain that the new system was both unstable and uncontrolled. It took most people many years to realize this fundamental truth about the new financial system. Today, critiques of the old order do not always stem from the same analytical or ideological basis, nor do they end up with the same, or even similar, policy conclusions. See, for example, two excellent works by Hutton (2010), with the emphasis on inequality, and Kaletsky (2010), who criticizes excessive faith in the efficiency of markets.

[23] See the report submitted to the president of the French Republic by a group of eminent, yet unorthodox, economists, including Joseph Stiglitz, Amartya Sen and Jean-Paul Fitoussi (Stiglitz *et al.*, 2009).

method notwithstanding. Yet as integration deepened and widened, national interest became more relative as a concept, and more directly shaped by partisan preferences. Other interests have begun to raise their pretty or ugly heads. There is no single European narrative,[24] as constructivists would have said. If it ever existed, it has surely suffered several deaths as a result of successive rounds of widening and deepening. And that is not necessarily a bad thing, just another sign of the European political system becoming more pluralistic and hence more mature.

Europe needs political oxygen to breathe. Otherwise, it may suffocate, or die from boredom.[25] True, interminable council meetings conducted through interpreters in search of the long-winded compromise is not the stuff that is likely to attract the old-style politician full of adrenalin. The nature of European politics is indeed different, but no less real. It often looks dull and introverted; there is something stale in the European world of Brussels. But we also know from experience that a few personalities can make a big difference, and we desperately need them today. Politics is about choices, and choices need to be clearly articulated and explained to citizens. In our European countries today, political choices must have a strong European component. Our security and prosperity depend on it.

There is a role for individual countries and for European institutions to play in giving concrete form and shape to the new era. The division of labour between the nation-state and the EU needs to be protected both from the missionary zeal of bureaucrats and judges keen on bulldozing all kinds of national particularities and idiosyncrasies in the name of the four fundamental freedoms of the treaties, but also from the illusions propagated by 'sovereigntists' in a highly interdependent, congested and pretty small, yet highly diverse, continent. There should be enough room for differentiation in order to cater for internal divergence, as well as flexibility for those who may want to stay (temporarily?) out of common policies. And more emphasis should be placed on policy innovation and measures that work in a complementary fashion with those at national and local level.

In some policy areas, however, Europe will require more, not less, co-ordination and integration. Financial markets are a prominent example because interdependence in the marketplace has already gone very far. Interdependence needs joint management, and this has to be explained to people: there is an educational role for politicians as well. The same applies to the environment, the governance of the euro and also parts of the internal market. Can we seriously argue, for example, that in a single market with free

[24] On Europe's narrative diversity, see Pélabay *et al.* (2010).

[25] Politicization in the EU remains, of course, a controversial subject. Hix (2008) has strongly argued in favour, and I have also done so (Tsoukalis, 2005 [2003], 2007). Moravcsik (2006) thinks otherwise.

movement of goods and capital there is no need for co-ordination in the area of taxation, including corporate taxes? Unless, of course, we imply that taxes do not matter, or that free-riding should be elevated into a high principle of the integration project. There is no need for harmonized taxes, only for minimum rates that would put a floor underneath what now looks like a race to the bottom.[26]

Solidarity should remain an integral part of the overall European bargain, but it needs to be explained and defended against all kinds of populists and narrow nationalists. It also needs to be connected to common projects and common goods, in which most if not all see tangible benefits for themselves; and it has to be subject to conditions and rules.[27] No free lunch, in other words. This surely applies to the governance of the euro, and it should increasingly apply to immigration and free internal borders. Solidarity does not enjoy ample space in our increasingly atomized societies – and this is only more true across borders. We shall need to rediscover the meaning of society and the value of public goods in the years to come, thus partly reversing a trend that has lasted for too long and has gone too far.[28]

In his valedictory message, Tony Judt (2010, p. 225), one of the best minds of our time, wrote: ‘Social democracy does not represent an ideal future; it does not even represent the ideal past. But among the options available to us today, it is better than anything else to hand’. This may indeed be true, but judging from the state of social democracy in Europe today, the staleness of the message and the defensive, almost apologetic, stance of its official representatives, we will have to go further. Social democracy needs to reinvent itself; and it will surely have to acquire again a strong European and global dimension.

The Neighbours and the World Further Afield

No word has been mentioned so far about Europe’s global role, or European soft power, with the exception of enlargement as a form of foreign policy that eventually transforms itself into internal policy. The cynical explanation would be that there is little to say given experience. Alas, the gap between expectations and official promises on the one hand, delivery on the other, remains wide. Trying to forge unity out of 27 independent-minded foreign

[26] This is an argument put forward by Mario Monti in his report to the President of the European Commission (Monti, 2010), as part of a new European bargain for the relaunching of the internal market programme.
[27] Jacques Delors has repeatedly and convincingly argued the case for solidarity as a key part of the European bargain.
[28] In Margaret Thatcher’s famous words: ‘[T]here is no such thing as society, there are only individual men and women, and there are families’ (*Women’s Own Magazine*, 31 October 1987).

chancelleries is, admittedly, no simple matter. You cannot undo history and geography in one stroke. Yet there has been a shattering of illusions in that area too in recent years. Europeans have often tended to confuse rhetoric with soft power, while on the big issues of war and peace Europeans have been too complacent, too weak or divided, to be able to influence events outside their borders. The world is indeed becoming multipolar, but Europe does not necessarily represent one of those poles (see also Howorth, 2011; Vasconcelos, 2010; Tsoukalis *et al.*, 2009; Smith, 2009).

Foreign policy normally starts with the neighbours, and Europe's Mediterranean neighbourhood, for example, has a long history of grand initiatives that have tended to fall flat on their face. Here again, ambition has not been matched by the policy instruments available. There have been contradictory goals and plenty of hypocrisy as well. The Europeans have for long followed the Americans in pretending to believe there is a real peace process on the Israeli–Palestinian conflict, while Israel was creating new 'facts on the ground' almost every day. The Europeans were not able, or they did not dare, to take a stronger and united stance. They have also pretended for long they had 'shared values' with all kinds of autocracies in the Arab world. Brussels was trying to export democracy and human rights through trade and aid, while individual member countries were supporting the local dictators: the soft power of the EU as a fig leaf? The new Arab revolt has forcefully removed it, while sweeping away any illusions entertained about the benevolent role and influence of Europeans in this highly unstable part of their neighbourhood. They are now trying to pick up the pieces and find ways of getting back on the scene (Vasconcelos, 2011).

In the next few years, the key challenge for Europeans will be to identify and collectively defend common interests and values in a rapidly changing world where size still matters a great deal. A divided, ageing and shrinking Europe would unavoidably court with strategic irrelevance and decline, and the signs are already there. 'Speak European' and 'Help Change the World in Your Own Image', so should read the message (Tsoukalis, 2011). In other words, speak with one voice (preferably also having something to say), back your words with action (this being surely more difficult), and use your own experience in promoting co-operation and collective management at the global level. It would be in Europe's interest to do so; a world of power politics and martial arts offers a very grim prospect for Europeans. And this is a mission that could mobilize many people on the old continent of Europe, especially the younger generations: another manifestation of Europe the broad-minded.

Will it happen? Honestly, the chances are not good. Decline may be indeed an irreversible trend in Europe; and if so, it may not necessarily happen with much grace or even internal peace. The stakes are high. We risk losing some of the things we used to take for granted after many years of integration in Europe. A new political message for our societies requires a strong, yet realistic, European component. Will there be political forces that dare to articulate such a message and try to get it across with confidence and determination against the forces of inertia here and the rising populist tide there? Hopefully, we shall not have to wait for too long.

References

Auer, S. (2010) 'New Europe'. *JCMS*, Vol. 48, No. 5, pp. 1163–84.

Belke, A. (2010) 'Driven by the Markets: ECB Sovereign Bond Purchases and the Securities Markets Programme'. *Intereconomics*, Vol. 45, No. 6, pp. 357–63.

Bofinger, P. (2010) 'Germany has a Vital Interest in Ensuring Irish Solvency', *Spiegel online*. Available at: «http://www.spiegel.de/international/europe/0,1518,729819,00.html».

Buiter, W. *et al.* (2011) 'The Debt of Nations'. *Citigroup Global Markets*, 7 January.

CEPS, Egmont and EPC (2010) *The Treaty of Lisbon: A Second Look at the Institutional Innovations*. Available at: «http://www.egmontinstitute.be/SD/Joint_Study_complet.pdf».

Connolly, R. and Copsey, N. (2011) 'The Great Slump of 2008–09 and Ukraine's Integration with the European Union'. *Journal of Communist Studies and Transition Politics*, Vol. 27, forthcoming.

Cramme, O. (ed.) (2009) *Rescuing the European Project: EU Legitimacy, Governance and Security* (London: Policy Network).

Darvas, Z. *et al.* (2011) 'A Comprehensive Approach to the Euro-Area Debt Crisis', *Bruegel Policy Brief*, 02/2011, February. Available at: «http://www.bruegel.org/publications/publication-listing/topic/41-the-euro-area-debt-crisis/».

De Grauwe, P. (2011) 'Governance of a Fragile Eurozone', CEPS Working Document, May (Brussels: Centre for European Policy Studies).

Deegan-Krause, K. and Haughton, T. (2009) 'Towards a More Useful Conceptualization of Populism: Types and Degrees of Populist Appeals in the Case of Slovakia'. *Politics & Policy*, Vol. 37, No. 4, pp. 821–41.

The Economist (2011) 'Can Angela Merkel Hold Europe Together?' *The Economist*, 12 March.

European Central Bank (ECB) (2011) 'The Reform of Economic Governance in the Euro Area: Essential Elements'. *ECB Monthly Bulletin*, March, pp. 99–119.

Featherstone, K. (2011) 'The JCMS Annual Lecture: The Greek Sovereign Debt Crisis and EMU'. *JCMS*, Vol. 49, No. 2, pp. 193–217.

Featherstone, K. and Radaelli, C.M. (eds) (2003) *The Politics of Europeanization* (Oxford: Oxford University Press).

Fligstein, N. (2008) *Euro-Clash: The EU, European Identity and the Future of Europe* (Oxford: Oxford University Press).

Friedman, T. (1999) *The Lexus and the Olive Tree* (London: HarperCollins).
Grigoriadis, I.N. (2008) *Trials of Europeanization: Turkish Political Culture and the European Union* (Basingstoke: Palgrave Macmillan).
Gros, D. and Mayer, T. (2010) 'Towards a Euro(pean) Monetary Fund'. CEPS Policy Brief 202, May (Brussels: Centre for European Policy Studies).
Guérot, U. and Leonard, M. (2011) 'The New German Question: How Europe Can Get the Germany It Needs'. ECFR Policy Brief, May (Madrid: European Council on Foreign Relations).
Haug, J. *et al.* (2011) *Europe for Growth: For a Radical Change in Financing the EU* (CEPS/Notre Europe).
Hemerijck, A. *et al.* (eds) (2009) *Aftershocks: Economic Crisis and Institutional Choice* (Amsterdam: Amsterdam University Press).
Hix, S. (2008) *What's Wrong with the European Union and How to Fix It* (Cambridge: Polity).
Hodson, D. and Quaglia, L. (2009) Special Issue. *JCMS*, Vol. 47, No. 5, pp. 939–1128.
Howorth, J. (2011) 'Why the EU Needs a Grand Strategy'. In Tsoukalis, L. and Emmanouilidis, J.A. (eds) *The Delphic Oracle on Europe: Is There a Future for the European Union?* (Oxford: Oxford University Press).
Hutton, W. (2010) *Them and Us: Politics Greed and Inequality – Why We Need a Fair Society* (New York: Little, Brown).
Independent Evaluation Office of the International Monetary Fund (IEO) (2011) 'IMF Performance in the Run-Up to the Financial and Economic Crisis: IMF Surveillance in 2004–07', IEO Evaluation Report, February (Washington, DC: IEO).
Judt, T. (2010) *Ill Fares the Land* (London: Allen Lane).
Juncker, J.C. and Tremonti, G. (2010) 'E-bonds Would End the Crisis'. *Financial Times*, 5 December.
Kaletsky, A. (2010) *Capitalism 4.0: The Birth of a New Economy in the Aftermath of Crisis* (London: Bloomsbury).
Kopf, C. (2011) 'Restoring Financial Stability in the Euro Area'. CEPS Policy Brief 237, March (Brussels: Centre for European Policy Studies).
Leonard, M. (2005) *Why Europe Will Run the 21st Century* (London: Fourth Estate).
Lucke, B. (2011) *Stellungnahme zur EU-Schuldenkrise*. Plenum der ökonomen. Available at: «http://www.wiso.uni-hamburg.de/lucke/?p=581».
Marzinotto, B. (2011) 'A European Fund for Economic Revival in Crisis Countries'. Bruegel Policy Contribution, February (Brussels: Bruegel).
Monti, M. (2010) *A New Strategy for the Single Market: Report to the President of the European Commission*. Available at: «http://ec.europa.eu/bepa/pdf/monti_report_final_10_05_2010_en.pdf».
Moravcsik, A. (2006) 'What Can We Learn from the Collapse of the European Constitutional Project?' *Politische Vierteljahresschrift*, Vol. 47, No. 2, pp. 219–241.
Neyer, J. (2010) 'Justice, not Democracy: Legitimacy in the European Union'. *JCMS*, Vol. 48, No. 4, pp. 903–21.

Nicolaïdis, K. (2010) 'The JCMS Annual Review Lecture – Sustainable Integration: Towards EU 2.0?' *JCMS*, Vol. 48, s1, pp. 21–54.

Norman, P. (2005) *The Accidental Constitution: The Story of the European Convention* (Brussels: EuroComment).

Oktem, K. (2011) *Angry Nation: Turkey since 1989* (London: Zed Books).

Oniş, Z. (2007) 'Conservative Globalists versus Defensive Nationalists: Political Parties and Paradoxes of Europeanization in Turkey'. *Journal of Southern Europe and the Balkans*, Vol. 9, No. 3, pp. 247–61.

Padoa-Schioppa, T. (2004) *The Euro and Its Central Bank: Getting United after the Union* (Cambridge, MA: MIT Press).

Padoa-Schioppa, T. (2007) 'Europe Needs a Single Financial Rulebook'. *Financial Times*, 11 December.

Pélabay, J. *et al.* (2010) 'Echoes and Polyphony: In Praise of Europe's Narrative Diversity'. In Lacroix, J. and Nicolaïdis, K. (eds) *European Stories: Intellectual Debates on Europe in National Contexts* (Oxford: Oxford University Press).

Piret, E. (2008) 'Competing Models of EU Legitimacy: The Test of Popular Expectations'. *JCMS*, Vol. 46, No. 3, pp. 619–40.

Piris, J.C. (2010) *The Lisbon Treaty: A Legal and Political Analysis* (Cambridge: Cambridge University Press).

Rifkin, J. (2004) *The European Dream* (Cambridge: Polity).

Rupnik, J. (2009) 'The Challenges of EU Enlargement in the Balkans'. *ISS Opinion*. Available at: «http://www.iss.europa.eu/uploads/media/EU_enlargement_in_the_Balkans.pdf».

Scharpf, F. (1999) *Governing Europe: Effective and Democratic?* (Oxford: Oxford University Press).

Schmidt, V. (2009) 'Re-envisioning the European Union: Identity, Democracy, Economy'. *JCMS* Vol. 47, s1, pp. 17–42.

Smith, M. (2009) 'A Liberal Grand Strategy in a Realist World? Power, Purpose and the EU's Changing Global Role'. *Journal of European Public Policy*, Vol. 18, No. 2, pp. 144–163.

Steinmeier, F.W. and Steinbrück, P. (2010) 'Germany Must Lead Fightback'. *Financial Times*, 14 December.

Stiglitz, J.E. *et al.* (2009) *Report by the Commission on the Measurement of Economic Performance and Social Progress*. Available at: «http://www.stiglitz-sen-fitoussi.fr/document/rapport_anglais.pdf».

Strange, S. (1986) *Casino Capitalism* (Oxford: Basil Blackwell).

Taggart, P. (2006) 'Keynote Article: Questions of Europe – The Domestic Politics of the 2005 French and Dutch Referendums and Their Challenge of the Study of European Integration'. *JCMS*, Vol. 44, s1, pp. 7–25.

Trichet, J.C. (2010) 'State of the Union: The Financial Crisis and the ECB's Response between 2007 and 2009'. *JCMS*, Vol. 48, s1, pp. 7–19.

Tsoukalis, L. (1977) *The Politics and Economics of European Monetary Integration* (London: Allen & Unwin).

Tsoukalis, L. (1997) *The New European Economy Revisited* (Oxford: Oxford University Press).

Tsoukalis, L. (2005 [2003]) *What Kind of Europe?* (Oxford: Oxford University Press).

Tsoukalis, L. (2006) 'The *JCMS* Lecture: Managing Diversity and Change in the European Union'. *JCMS*, Vol. 44, No. 1, pp. 1–15.

Tsoukalis, L. (2007) 'Une Europe plus politique'. *Raison Publique*, No. 7, pp. 131–9.

Tsoukalis, L. (2011) 'The Delphic Oracle on Europe'. In Tsoukalis, L. and Emmanouilidis, J.A. (eds) *The Delphic Oracle on Europe: Is There a Future for the European Union?* (Oxford: Oxford University Press).

Tsoukalis, L. *et al.* (2009) *An EU 'Fit for Purpose' in the Global Age* (London: Policy Network).

Vasconcelos, A. (ed.) (2010) 'A Strategy for EU Foreign Policy'. *ISS Report*, No. 7, June.

Vasconcelos, A. (ed.) (2011) 'The Arab Democratic Wave: How the EU Can Seize the Moment'. *ISS Report*, No. 9, March.

Wallace, H. (2007) *Adapting to Enlargement of the European Union: Institutional Practice since May 2004* (Brussels: TEPSA).

Zielonka, J. (2007) 'Plurilateral Governance in the Enlarged European Union'. *JCMS*, Vol. 45, No. 1, pp. 187–209.

JCMS 2011 Volume 49 Annual Review pp. 45–55

Faltering Ambitions and Unrequited Hopes: The Battle for the Euro Intensifies*

DAVID MARSH
Official Monetary and Financial Institutions Forum (OMFIF)

It was not supposed to turn out like this. At the core of the euro, the supranational currency at the heart of EMU (economic and monetary union), is a tale of faltering ambitions and unrequited hopes. Launched in 1999 as one of the Old Continent's brightest success stories, the European single currency became a saga of Wagnerian intensity, full of interweaving sub-plots, where the grandest designs were subverted, the most beguiling intentions contorted, the most elaborate political calculations turned to dust. Monetary union threw a veil of comfort and well-being over the fortunes of the continent. In 2009–10, the veil was ripped away.

With a unified monetary and interest rate policy that by 2011 encompassed 17 countries, EMU and its key institution – the Frankfurt-based European Central Bank (ECB) – were conceived as breaking down barriers between people, companies and markets: a force for unity and prosperity following the fall of the Berlin Wall, the reunification of Germany and the ending of the communist–capitalist divide. Some of the euro's achievements are incontestable. In 2011 the eurozone made up one-fifth of the global economy with a population of 330 million – in economic size, roughly equivalent to the United States. The ECB had built up respect and acumen in the councils of monetary power around the world. The euro is the second most important international currency after the dollar, of major significance in financial market transactions and in the holdings of central banks, pension funds,

* This article is an edited extract from the new edition of my book, *The Euro: The Battle for the New Global Currency*, published in July 2011 by Yale University Press.

insurance companies and government agencies around the world. In cash terms, there were 15 to 20 per cent more euros in worldwide circulation than dollars in 2011.[1]

Yet, a dozen years after its birth, EMU had become Europe's melancholy union. The factors behind its travails included some with their roots outside Europe: the build-up of massive footloose investment capital by fast-growing developing nations like China; straitened conditions for international borrowing and lending after the American home loans crash in 2007 and the downfall of American investment bank Lehman Brothers in 2008; and then, in 2009, the worst world recession since the 1930s. But the central reasons for the dashing of European dreams have been relentlessly homemade. They lay in EMU's inherent encouragement, through the 'one-size-fits-all' interest rate policy, of vulnerable Member States to live beyond their means, and in the extraordinary failure of Europe's governments and financial authorities to heed the warning signs and take corrective action until it was far too late.

A project that was often (rightly) said to be mainly political rather than economic in inspiration was ill-served by Europe's 21st-century leaders, who displayed enormous incompetence in operating and safeguarding it. The basic causes of the problems, however, went back to the previous generation of politicians who agreed the treaty for monetary union at a summit meeting in Maastricht in the Netherlands in 1991 that hailed the dawning of a new Europe. The dawn broke, but the day darkened. As Ruud Lubbers, the Dutch prime minister who orchestrated Maastricht, put it: 'I thought that the euro would be so successful that it would lead to political union and that it would be attractive for other states to join. This was a mistake'.[2]

Another former government leader, Helmut Schmidt, who presided over West Germany as chancellor between 1974 and 1982 and ranks as one of the spiritual fathers of the euro, points to governments' mistake at Maastricht of aspiring to a wide membership of disparate states.

> They invented the Euro and invited everybody to become a member of the Euro area. And this was done without changing the rules or clarifying the rules beforehand. This was when the great mistakes were made. What we are suffering now is the consequence of that failure.[3]

Angela Merkel, the daughter of an East German pastor who became Germany's first female chancellor nearly a quarter of a century after

[1] According to ECB and United States Treasury figures, euro notes and coins in circulation overtook those in dollars in October 2006 (*Financial Times*, 27 December 2006). In March 2011, euro currency in circulation totaled €820 billion (US$1,100 billion), against $940 billion in dollars.

[2] Lubbers' comments to author, Amsterdam, 24 March 2011.

[3] Schmidt interview with author, Hamburg, 25 November 2010.

Schmidt left office, was at the forefront of the battle to salvage the euro in what she herself termed an 'existential' struggle – a fight for survival.[4] As Europe's largest economy and most important creditor nation, Germany led the list of countries that profit if the euro performs well, but had most to lose if it fared badly. Merkel said the 'wondrous' pre-2009 contraction in borrowing rates for different countries gave the impression that financial and economic conditions in Europe were harmonized. 'As a result of the crisis, the differences are much more visible – and of course they were there all along.'[5]

The euro's advantages were meant to be self-fulfilling; success would feed on itself. Yet as a result of the shortcomings revealed in 2009–10, European countries had to embark, within a period of just two years, on a massive programme of financial overhaul for which they were almost completely unprepared and which dwarfed, in real terms, the sums of money mobilized to repair Europe after the end of the World Wars I and II.[6] The single currency bloc was revealed as a zone of semi-permanent economic divergence, corrosive political polarization and built-in financial imbalances, beset by 'a perpetual penumbra of hope and pain'.[7] Both for the better- and worse-off members of the eurozone, the financing of these disequilibria created burdens that were increasingly irksome for creditors and debtors alike – and could, in some instances, become intolerable. For the broad mass of the European electorate, the notion of 'Europe' became a byword for unpopular and painful economic restructuring. In allocating funds to prevent payments and debt disparities from destroying the euro, EMU governments decided to commit colossal sums of taxpayers' money they could afford to heal internal disparities they could not conceal to shore up an edifice many believed could not stand – at least, not in its current form.

The success of the euro is its diversity, its devotees say; therein, too, as the events of 2009–10 have shown, lies its weakness. The sheer incongruousness of the euro's membership, together with the manifest shortcomings in Member States' economic flexibility required for a single currency area to

[4] Merkel speech, Permagon Museum, Berin, 9 November 2010.

[5] Merkel speech, Federation of German Banks Congress, Berlin, 31 March 2011.

[6] The rescue facility for euro states assembled by the EU and the IMF in May 2010 amounted to US$1,000 billion. The most commonly accepted figure for German reparations fixed in 1921 is 132 billion marks, or around US$400 billion in 2010 dollars. Marshall Plan aid to Europe after World War II was US$13 billion, or US$118 billion in 2010 dollars.

[7] To use the memorable phrase of David Lascelles, co-founder of the Centre for the Study of Financial Innovation.

prosper, was exposed as its Achilles heel.[8] EMU's members include three of the world's top seven economies – Germany, France and Italy[9] – as well as the Netherlands, Belgium and Luxembourg, the three other founders of the original six-nation European Economic Community that started in 1958 and in the 1990s became the much-enlarged European Union (EU). Of the other 11 euro adherents, Ireland, Cyprus and Malta were formerly under British dominion. Slovenia, Slovakia and Estonia (the latter as part of the Soviet Union) were communist states up to the end of the cold war. Austria and Finland were neutral. Greece, Portugal and Spain (in 2010 the world's 12th largest economy) were dictatorships up to the 1970s.[10]

Confirming its long-held ambivalence over European integration, Britain decided – resolutely, maybe permanently – to stay outside EMU. Two of the other top ten economies in the European Union – Sweden and Poland – remained, too, on the sidelines, although for different reasons. Formerly communist Poland, which benefited from preserving its own currency outside EMU and was the sole EU member to expand its economy in recession-hit 2009, was one of the central and eastern Europe states that were candidates to join in the second decade of the 21st century. But the pressures on EMU's existing membership increased the Poles' scepticism about joining; other wavering EU members such as Denmark, the Czech Republic and Hungary showed similar reactions. The repercussions of the euro's misfortunes were global, since they had a sobering impact on plans for setting up monetary unions in Asia, Latin America, the Middle East and Africa, where in various forms the euro supplied a template for monetary integration.[11] One of the more curious repercussions of the euro malaise was that countries as far down the development scale as Uganda said that the mishandling of EMU had taught them valuable lessons for their own economic policies.[12]

[8] There is a vast literature on the need for flexibility of product, capital and labour markets to allow appropriate economic adjustment mechanisms to make a single currency area function satisfactorily, starting with that of Robert Mundell (1961). The theory lays down a further condition in the existence of fiscal redistribution to allow tax income to flow from regions of high economic activity to weaker areas hit by falling output and rising unemployment (see also Eichengreen, 2002).

[9] IMF database, 2011. In 2010 the world's top economies ranked by nominal GDP measured in dollars were: the United States, China, Japan, Germany, France, the United Kingdom, Italy, Brazil, Canada, Russia, India, Spain, Australia, Mexico and Korea.

[10] Britain, Denmark and Ireland joined the European Community in 1973; Greece in 1981; Spain and Portugal in 1986. Austria, Finland and Sweden joined the EU in 1995; Cyprus, the Czech Republic, Estonia, Hungary, Latvia, Lithuania, Malta, Poland, Slovakia and Slovenia in 2004; Bulgaria and Romania in 2007. Slovenia joined the EMU in 2007; Malta and Cyprus in 2008; Slovakia in 2009; Estonia in 2011.

[11] Asia is pressing ahead with monetary integration, but this will fall a long way short of monetary union.

[12] For example, Emmanuel Tumusiime-Mutebile, Governor of the Bank of Uganda, wrote, with reference to the case of Greece in EMU: 'The issue of a member state lying with statistics is a real threat to the sustainability of a monetary union' (*OMFIF Bulletin*, March 2011).

The club which many countries in Europe and beyond once regarded as a model was truly tarnished. To correct the malignant effects of years of economic recklessness, Europe, backed up by the International Monetary Fund (IMF), imposed austerity and belt-tightening on the problem-ridden peripheral states led by Greece, Ireland and Portugal, in exchange for emergency financing to help them pay their massive debts. These countries, three of the smaller economies in the euro, ran into serious problems in 2009–11 as a result of a large increase in debts built up as the result of low interest rates and faulty supervision after monetary union started, with the Greek imbroglio considerably worsened by government manipulation of key statistics that camouflaged the true extent of economic deterioration. As part of crisis measures, the creditor nations – with Germany in the vanguard – were asked to join in the sacrifices by taking a soft line over repayment of the problem states' existing debts, as well as guaranteeing new ones.

European banks, severely weakened in many cases by the collapse of the pre-2007 global credit boom, were drawn into the fray through their involvement as owners of hundreds of billions of dollars of government bond issues of the hard-hit peripheral states. European governments were reluctant to see the banks suffer outright losses through restructuring of the deficit nations' debts. The result was that responsibility for bailing out the errant euro members has been inexorably shifting away from the banking sector to taxpayers in the better-off countries. The chief characteristic of this new European interdependence – neither expected nor, for the most part, properly explained by political or monetary leaders – was not freely exchanged solidarity, but growing resentment and recrimination. In a spiral of mutual discontent in some ways reminiscent of the atmosphere engendered by demands for reparations from defeated Germany after World War I, both creditors and debtors look likely to revolt: the former, against the prospect that they would not be repaid, and the latter, against the onerous conditions attached to loans made in the spirit of an economic union that had become increasingly disturbed.

Whatever the setbacks it faced and the strains it may continue to suffer, the euro is most unlikely to collapse and disappear. In the intricate work on assembling a common European money, too great was the expenditure of political and economic capital, too arduous were the efforts of many governments from many nations over many years, for the product of their labours simply to wither and die. Nonetheless, the system clearly faced the danger of fragmentation, with either strong or weak countries separating from the system and reintroducing – despite all the costs and upheaval – some form of national currency management more suited to their economic requirements.

One development helping the bloc to hold together was that preserving the euro had become a strategic priority for China, the world's no. 2 economy, no.1 reserve currency owner and main creditor nation, holding one-third of world foreign exchange reserves in 2011. The People's Bank of China, the Chinese central bank, and the State Administration of Foreign Exchange (SAFE), the country's premier sovereign wealth fund, emerged as strong buyers of the euro in a bid to diversify their reserves away from the dollar. To a more moderate extent, Japan – the second-biggest official holder of foreign exchange reserves after China, and the world's no. 3 economy after the United States and China – had been following the same policy. China does not want to be exposed to a chronically weak European currency when its own exports are being hit by rising inflation at home and by the threat of protectionism in some of its main markets, led by the United States. Nor did either China or Japan wish the Americans to benefit indefinitely from the unchallenged monopoly power of the dollar. The single currency had thus been caught up in a global battle over the future of the world economy between the two pivotal economies of the United States and China.

However, in their involvement in these skirmishes, European policy makers were reduced to the role of bystanders rather than central players. The European objective was to become an essential part of a new tri-currency system in which America, Europe and China would parley over power; the monetary future of the globe would be in the hands of a triumvirate of central banks, the Federal Reserve in Washington, the ECB in Frankfurt and the People's Bank in Beijing. In fact, for all the ECB's undoubted accomplishments, grave flaws in political governance of the euro placed the Europeans in positions of weakness rather than strength. In the eyes of its supporters as well as its detractors, the euro was signally downgraded. The single currency that emerged from the economic wreckage left by the European sovereign debt upheavals was significantly different from that planned by its protagonists. The construct seemed to be divided rather than united by diversity, fragmented into opposing blocs of creditor and debtor states, and condemned to years of costly and complex financial underpinning through the monetary equivalent of medical life-support machinery. A two-speed Europe became reality, made up of a northern group of relatively integrated, homogeneous and cohesive creditor states around Germany and the Netherlands, and a more diverse collection of hard-hit debtors on the periphery – Italy, Spain, Portugal, Greece and Ireland. France, which was politically and economically close to Germany yet prone to long-lasting tensions with the Germans over running monetary union, was sandwiched uneasily between the two groups.

As many sceptics had earlier predicted, events in Europe between 2009 and 2011 produced a textbook display of the drawbacks of establishing a 'one-size-fits-all' monetary policy without thoroughgoing political interlinkages and especially fiscal solidarity offering automatic redistribution of tax income among stronger and weaker countries. The fiscal rules of the so-called 'Stability and Growth Pact' established in 1997 as a means of maintaining EMU members' macroeconomic and budgetary probity proved woefully inadequate. The 'no-bail-out clause' at the heart of EMU's statutes agreed in Maastricht, laying down that Member States had no liability for each other's debts, was insufficient to prevent financial contagion under which individual states' payments difficulties upset other members' fiscal health.

At the heart of the euro's gradual transition to a long-running state of misery was a gargantuan misunderstanding of the laws of economics. The architects of monetary union believed that individual euro countries' disparities in their balance of payments performances – caused by diverse economic growth and inflation rates – would have a negligible impact on the resilience of the eurozone a whole. According to this notion, individual countries' current account deficits – especially *vis-à-vis* other member countries – would be largely self-financing (Commission, 1990).[13] This turned out to be pure fiction, but, since it appeared to be true in the early years of EMU, the thesis attracted a great deal of support from within and beyond the eurozone – and ended up promoting a self-perpetuating process in which spendthrift governments, companies and consumers were rewarded rather than penalized by the financial markets.

Because within a single currency area devaluations are no longer possible, states on the southern and western fringes, such as Ireland, Portugal, Spain and Greece with higher inflation than the core group around Germany, effectively had exchange rates that were far too high, pricing their goods and services out of business in international trade. The Europe-wide fall in interest rates to German levels that accompanied the start of the single currency was used in the more inflation-prone peripheral countries not to build up productive capacity and prepare economies for the challenges of technological change and foreign competition, but to fuel wasteful consumption and speculative purchases of financial assets and real estate whose values subsequently plummeted. Since interest rates in the first eight years of the euro were plainly too low in peripheral states, these countries experienced credit booms leading to above-average growth rates and also higher inflation and thus a loss of competitiveness – sparking off increasing current account balance of payments deficits that had to be financed by foreign borrowing. Countries such as Germany had the opposite experience: lower growth rates and inflation,

[13] For a prophetic treatment of the likelihood of credit risks opening up in monetary union, see Te Velde and Taylor (2001).

resulting in higher competitiveness and large current account surpluses that were subsequently channelled back as loans to the deficit states, effectively pouring oil on a slow-burning monetary fire.

In August 2007 – the month when the transatlantic credit crisis erupted internationally with the bursting of the bubble in the American sub-prime mortgage sector– the ECB published a 12-page article devoted to global imbalances in current account surpluses and deficits (for more detail on the ECB's response, see Trichet, 2010). It failed to mention the imbalances within the eurozone, on the grounds that the current account position of the EMU countries had been 'broadly balanced'. In an unwitting prophecy of the unrest sparked by Greece just two years later, the ECB wrote in August 2007: 'It is hard to define which countries are systemically important: some past financial crises have been triggered by relatively small economies'. However, the ECB failed completely to spot how the seeds of turbulence were being sown within the eurozone. Unregistered by the ECB's statistical coverage, euro members in 2006 recorded some of the world's largest balance of payments disequilibria. Greece, Portugal and Spain, respectively, ran up deficits of 11 per cent, 10 per cent and 9 per cent of GDP, while Germany and the Netherlands earned surpluses of 6.5 per cent and 9 per cent. In all cases, these imbalances were even larger than that displayed by the United States, with a current account deficit of 6 per cent of GDP that year.[14]

As the illusion of safety persisted, inflows of international capital – fuelled by belief in economic convergence and solid growth prospects – allowed governments across the eurozone to borrow more or less at the same low interest rates as the government of the European country with the most stable post-war economic track record: Germany. The ECB was only too happy to accept the apparently benevolent interpretation of international bond investors, accepting government paper from banks as part of its refinancing operations at virtually the same price throughout Europe, in line with the fiction that the eurozone really had become one single political and economic bloc in which individual governments could borrow on near-identical terms, regardless of their economic circumstances. As well as buttressing the notion that monetary union had come of age, the equivalence of borrowing eased the ECB's task of establishing harmonizing economic conditions throughout the eurozone. Financial markets compounded the sense of well-being by setting aside traditional analytical tools (or even common sense) governing the pricing of financial risk, and valuing government debt as though Greece and other less well-off states really did have the same creditworthiness as

[14] OECD and IMF data. Revised figures show that the eurozone as a whole recorded a surplus of 0.4 per cent of GDP in 2006.

Germany. This resulted in a self-perpetuating process in which the sharp reduction in interest rate 'spreads' between better-class and less good borrowers persuaded the politicians that monetary union was succeeding far more resoundingly than many had expected.

Once the complacency was punctured in the more trying times that followed the ending of the enormous expansion of sub-prime American mortgage lending and the subsequent recession, the apparently benevolent European cycle suddenly became vicious, turning out to be as short-lived and as illusory as the asset bubbles on which it was built. As Herman Van Rompuy, the former Belgian prime minister who in 2010 became President of the EU's governmental body, the European Council, put it in June 2010 with more than a hint of rueful pathos: 'The Euro became a strong currency with very small interest rate spreads [on government bonds]. It was like some kind of sleeping pill, some kind of drug. We weren't aware of the underlying conditions'.[15]

Warnings that monetary union would lead to unsustainable surges in borrowing were in fact made by authoritative figures such as Hans Tietmeyer, president of the Bundesbank during preparations for EMU in 1993–99. Tietmeyer spoke frequently in the pre-euro years of the risk that EMU states that generated higher inflation than Germany would suffer losses in competitiveness that could no longer (as in the past) be offset by devaluation but could be withstood only by lowering the internal prices of internationally traded goods and services and, in the last resort, through higher unemployment.[16] Gerhard Schröder, Helmut Kohl's successor as German chancellor, who presided over the advent of the single currency in 1999, commented in 1998 that EMU would increase Germany's industrial domination of Europe because its competitors would be unable to devalue their currencies.[17] Another prescient admonition came from Norman Lamont, Britain's chancellor of the Exchequer in 1992, who will always be remembered as presiding over the debacle of the United Kingdom's departure from the exchange rate mechanism (somewhat unfairly, since he was not responsible for taking Britain into the ERM, the forerunner of monetary union). An avowed opponent of the single currency project, Lamont wrote in 1999:

> Members [of the euro] with weak public finances benefit from lower interest rates on their borrowing. Convergence of bond yields across the Euro-zone members show that the markets expect that countries like Italy and Belgium would be bailed out if they ran into difficulties. Because their own currencies no longer exist, it removes pressure from the markets on

[15] Interview with the *Financial Times*, June 2010.
[16] Tietmeyer, Interview with the *Financial Times*, June 2010.
[17] Schröder, Conversation with the author, Hanover, March 1988.

> individual governments to take unpopular decisions and stabilise their public finances. Market discipline has been replaced by the peer group pressure of European finance ministers, few of whom are in a position to lecture their colleagues on sound public finances. (Lamont, 1999, p. 453)

Such statements represent strikingly accurate predictions of what actually happened. Many similar warnings were given by academic economists in many countries, but during the period of 'Europhoria' these were more or less ignored. In the early years of the single currency, experienced monetary technocrats such as ECB president Jean-Claude Trichet, the Frenchman who took over running the central bank in 2003, certainly witnessed warning signs, such as rising current account deficits and lowered competitiveness in the peripheral countries of Europe. But they did not speak much – or at all – about these signals in public. Trichet was wary about telling the rest of the world about the eurozone's weak spots, which is why he tended to concentrate on positive statements, and downplayed the negative news or left it out of his speeches altogether.[18]

As Europe awoke from the narcotic spell identified by Van Rompuy, the bitter truth was that very few of the strategic motivations for the formation of the single currency had been fulfilled. The progenitors of the Maastricht Treaty – led by France and Italy, as well as smaller countries such as Belgium and the Netherlands, but including, too, most of Germany's leading politicians – foresaw a variety of benefits. The four main reasons for the euro were to promote European growth and prosperity by eliminating exchange risks and boosting trade; to complete Franco–German post-World War II political rapprochement by establishing a path towards political union; to create a rival and complementary force to the dollar as a pivotal world money; and to constrain the perceived dominance of newly reunited Germany by constructing a more closely knit European community. The supporters of the euro wrote an improbably long wish-list: it would ban strife; promote social progress; control the Germans; increase growth, trade, wealth, investment and employment; quell inflation; counter the pre-eminence of the dollar; and buoy Europe's standing in the world. Never before had a new currency been so replete with anticipation, so desirous of achievement in so many fields; it was almost inevitable that, under the weight of these expectations, it would buckle.

To take just one example, in the crucial field of Franco–German friendship and co-operation, there had been a significant weakening of the relationship under Chancellor Angela Merkel and President Nicolas Sarkozy – a

[18] In 1994, speculator and philanthropist George Soros named this psychological displacement phenomenon 'the emotional amplifier'.

development heavily linked to the economic difficulties of the eurozone and Germany's political unwillingness to take more energetic action to relieve the debtor states. Perhaps in greatest contradiction to the earlier hopes, Germany was stronger than ever in European politics and economics, having used the new euro framework much more successfully than other EMU members to revitalize its economy and position itself for new challenges with and outside Europe. Fixed European exchange rates provide disproportionate support for Germany's export-orientated economy by making its industrial sales extremely competitive both within and outside Europe, increasing Germany's export surplus to record levels, and deflecting its attention from the necessary task of stimulating domestic demand – an outcome that would help both itself and its neighbours.

Germany's resurgence in Europe appeared to mark a return to its previous years of economic and industrial supremacy – an uneasy history punctuated by deep-seated political malaise and World Wars I and II. Not the least of the many uncomfortable ironies of the euro story was that an exercise in supranational economic management that was supposed to mark a comprehensive break with the past seemed in some ways to have brought it back to life. In the chronicles of national endeavour, forces of history and economics frequently trump stratagems and ambitions of political leaders. In summer 2011, as the euro crisis gains in intensity, it looks as if this pattern is once again being repeated.

References

Commission of the European Communities (1990) 'One market, one money', *European Economy*, October.

Eichengreen, B. (2002) 'Lessons of the Euro for the Rest of the World', Vienna, 4 December. Available at: «http://ies.berkeley.edu/pubs/workingpapers/PEIF-2-Lessons_of_the_Euro.pdf».

Lamont, N. (1999) *In Office* (London: Little, Brown & Co).

Mundell, R. (1961) 'A Theory of Optimum Currency Areas'. *American Economic Review*, Vol. 51, pp. 657–65.

Te Velde, D. and Taylor, C. (2001) 'Balance of Payments Prospects in EMU'. Discussion Paper 178 (London: National Institute of Economic and Social Research).

Trichet, J.-C. (2010) 'State of the Union: The Financial Crisis and the ECB's Reponse, 2007–09'. *JCMS*, Vol. 48, s1, pp. 7–19.

JCMS 2011 Volume 49 Annual Review pp. 57–75

The Reluctant Hegemon? Germany Moves Centre Stage in the European Union*

WILLIAM E. PATERSON
Aston University

Introduction

Among the large Member States of the European Union (EU), the Federal Republic of Germany has been distinctive in its commitment to integration and enlargement and has always played a key role in European integration. The traumatic experience of the short century from 1870 to 1945, when Germany had twice attempted to assert its power unilaterally, meant, however, that the Federal Republic was a 'reflexive multilateralist' who made a practice of 'leading from behind'. There was a self- and external perception of Germany pursuing a European vocation (Paterson, 2010). It therefore avoided a discourse of national interest: the European interest was seen as the national interest. Its preferred mode of presenting European initiatives was in tandem with France. All of these elements have come under pressure in recent years, but the eurozone crisis has proved to be a tipping point for classic German Europeanism while simultaneously Germany has been pushed somewhat reluctantly centre stage to become Europe's reluctant hegemon. In this article we will examine how this tipping point was arrived at, how the German government has performed in this new role and the implications for Germany and the wider EU.

* I would like to thank my long-time collaborator Simon Bulmer who continues to be a source of ideas and inspiration and with whom I am currently working on a book project on Germany and the European Union.

I. The Federal Republic as the Posterboy of European Integration

The Federal Republic that was created in 1949 was much less than a conventional state. It remained under an occupation statute until 1955, and its major city was physically separate from the rest of the territory as well as being under a completely different type of occupation regime. In terms of security, it was totally dependent on the protection of the Western allies, especially the United States. The Federal Republic was therefore very deficient in 'actorness' and European integration offered it an opportunity to expand its role as an actor; by pooling formal sovereignty, the Federal Republic was gaining in actual sovereignty.

The key gains were in the area of economic sovereignty, where participation in European integration allowed the lifting of discriminatory provisions like the International Authority of the Ruhr. A central element in the post-war settlement was West Germany's reinvention as an export-oriented economy after the autarchy of the Third Reich. Such a policy required access to the markets of other European states and, as has been written elsewhere, 'without European integration as a political arena of co-operation, West German economic performance would have been perceived as a threat' (Bulmer and Paterson, 1987, p. 7).

In the arena of co-operation, the Federal Republic stood out from the beginning in the European Coal and Steel Community as a practitioner of 'reflexive' rather than 'instrumental' multilateralism. This policy, sometimes called 'the Rhineland vision', was initially identified with Konrad Adenauer, the first chancellor, but by the mid-1960s there was a very wide consensus on European integration encompassing all the parliamentary parties and the major interest groups. European integration had come to be seen as essential to the economic success that underpinned the growing attachment of the citizens to the Federal Republic, and the Europeanised identity adopted by the Federal Republic was one that addressed the collective insecurities associated with the German past while holding out an acceptable future with a robust affiliational dimension, even if – as seemed increasingly likely – Germany was to remain permanently divided.

Participation in supranational institutions allowed West Germany to modify its subject status, to resume access to export markets and to strengthen its impaired and weak state identity. Its precondition was acceptance of French leadership. The disastrous experience of unilateral attempts to exert German power in the first half of the 20th century would have ruled against attempting to exercise an individual German leadership on prudential grounds, but it is also important to recognize the understandable lack of self-confidence about the establishment of a stable form of democratic government able to sustain peaceful and productive relations with its neighbours after the experience of Imperial Germany and the Third Reich in the founding years of the Federal Republic. As Charlie Jeffery has observed: '[T]he emerging institutions of European Integration were in these circumstances a displacement of responsibility (we are happy to have others govern us) and partly an insurance policy (we are not so sure we trust ourselves to govern)'.[1]

United Germany

The 'Fall of the Wall' was widely seen as presaging a more powerful Germany. William Wallace (1991, pp. 169–70) has argued that the effect would be to reinstate Germany as 'the natural hegemon of any European political system'. The policy pursued by Helmut Kohl, however, was to press for deeper integration on the basis of a reinvigorated Franco–German core – a choice that he had already made before German Unity and which relied on continued close co-operation with Francois Mitterrand and Jacques Delors. He often remarked that he bowed three times to the tricolour before undertaking a new initiative. His deepest instincts grounded in historical memory were to avoid the manifest and singular exercise of German power since this would force others to counterbalance Germany and seek to contain it in other ways. German Unity opened up the space for further integration as other Member States were keen to bind in Germany.

German power resources were to be invested in deeper integration accompanied by an uploading of German preferences which would help shape the regional milieu (Bulmer *et al.*, 2000). In the immediate post-Wall years, German Europeanism reached an apogee in terms both of a more European Germany, the traditional aim of German European policy and increasingly in a second sense reflecting Germany's new self-confidence: a German Europe where German preferences were uploaded to a European level. The most obvious example of these trends was the replacement of the Deutschmark and the Bundesbank by the euro and the ECB (European Central Bank). The Deutschmark was an iconic symbol of West German identity and economic prowess, and the Bundesbank a defining institution in the Federal Republic. Their replacement, therefore, was keenly felt, but a great deal of hope was placed in the Frankfurt location of the ECB and the fact that its governance was based on the Bundesbank. Creating a more European Germany and a more German Europe could both be plausibly presented as part of the federalist project. In calming external anxieties and overcoming considerable internal resistance, Kohl employed a European vision where to be against

[1] Based on Charlie Jeffery, project draft for Madison Trust, unpublished manuscript, 2005.

deeper European integration was to endorse nationalism and nationalism was presented as a threat to peace (Paterson, 1999).

Kohl's strategy was widely seen as successful and there was a widespread expectation that this would continue, and Anderson and Goodman's (1993, p. 60) view would have been widely shared.

> Over the course of forty years, West Germany's reliance on a web of international institutions to achieve its foreign policy goals, born of an instrumental choice among painfully few alternatives, became so complete as to cause these institutions to be embedded in the very definition of state interests and strategies. In effect, this is what we mean when we describe Germany's institutional commitments in the post 1980's period as reflexive, they have become ingrained, even assumed.

II. The Shrinking of Germany's European Vocation

Having reached a zenith under Helmut Kohl, Germany's 'European vocation' has experienced a gradual decline in the years up to the eurozone crisis. This decline has been uneven and has been shaped by a range of internal and external factors. A key factor has been the transformation of the EU through successive rounds of enlargement. Germany has been alone among large Member States in advocating both deepening and widening. The expectation of both Helmut Kohl (and Jacques Delors) was that by deepening first the changes made at Maastricht would be hard-wired into the EU and would be proof against the potential centrifugal effects of widening. In the new enlarged EU, Germany now occupies a central geographical position rather than being, like the former West Germany, on the eastern rim of western Europe, albeit with its then capital, Bonn, in close proximity to Brussels.

Whilst the effects of an altered geographical position are hard to measure, the impact on Germany's material interests of enlargement is much more palpable. Enlargement has threatened to make the costs of core EU policies like the CAP (common agricultural policy) unaffordable leading to a more defensive posture on the part of France and Germany as in the Schröder/Chirac deal on agriculture in 2002. It has resulted in the addition of a large number of smaller and poorer Member States who have been very effective in the Council of Ministers (Thomson, 2010). Traditionally, Germany has relied on side payments to persuade smaller and poorer partners, but the growth of demands from poorer states and Germany's own 'resource crunch' has resulted in Germany defending its financial interests more directly in alliance with other net payers. It has also weakened its traditional role as advocate of the smaller Member States and reinforced a trend towards concentration on the European Council rather than the Council of Ministers. In short, enlargement has sharpened the appreciation of Germany's distinctive interests.

It has often been said that Germany needed France to disguise its strength and France needed Germany to disguise its weakness and the Franco–German alliance was for long the axial relationship in the EU. Whilst there were periods of tension when agreement was difficult, agreement once secured between France and Germany usually carried the day with the other members. Classically seen as the motor of European integration, it has more recently sometimes operated as a defensive alliance as in the flouting of the Stability and Growth Pact by France and Germany in 2001/02. It is, however, enlargement and the significant increase in Member States that has most visibly contributed to a loss of traction by the Franco–German alliance. The sheer increase in the number of preferences to be aggregated makes it unlikely that a dual alliance can deliver agreement in the way it once did. The Franco–German alliance remained important, but the German government could no longer afford to be a 'one club' golf player in an enlarged EU which had moved from the equivalent of a pitch-and-putt course to a full-scale golf course with attendant rough and bunkers.

Resource Crunch

While fiscal difficulties preceded German unity, the incorporation of Eastern Germany (effectively an industrial scrapyard), with the necessity for continuing fiscal transfers, exerted a continual pressure on German public finances. An unfavourable demographic profile (low birth rate and an ageing population) and generous and expanding social welfare payments added to the fiscal misery and a perception that Germany was facing a 'Gathering Crisis' in public finances (Miskimmon *et al.*, 2009). This perception was heightened by the onset of the global crisis and a new balanced budget rule (Article 115 of the Basic Law) was therefore scheduled to take effect from 2011. These developments indicated an end to the era of generous German side payments and cheque book diplomacy. Henceforth Germany would be 'leaner and meaner' (Harnisch and Schieder, 2006).

Change in Discourse

While contrary to some expectations German Unity had strengthened rather than weakened Chancellor Kohl's Europeanist discourse, the effect of generational change in the German leadership after his chancellorship was to weaken it. The view that Europeanism had entered the genetic code of German policy-makers (Goetz, 1996) no longer looked compelling. The succeeding generation with no direct experience of the war or its immediate aftermath and leading a fully sovereign state were no longer so reluctant to talk about German national interests. On becoming chancellor in 1998, Gerhard Schröder expressed this very clearly:

> My generation and those following are Europeans because we want to be not because we have to be. That makes us freer in dealing with others. [. . .] I am convinced that our European partners want to have a self confident German partner which is more calculable than a German partner with an inferiority complex. Germany standing up for its national interests will be just as natural as France or Britain standing up for theirs.[2]

The transition, however, was not to be quite as complete as the initial declaration suggested. Foreign Minister Joschka Fischer remained committed to the Rhineland vision and in his Humboldt lecture in 2000 he launched what became the Constitutional Convention. Chancellor Schröder was prepared to play the national interest card hard on technical and economic issues, but his critical attitude to the Iraq War left him relatively isolated and he became heavily dependent on the Franco–German relationship. Over time, however, the direction of travel was all one way and the occasions on which members of the German political class used the once so ubiquitous Europeanist rhetoric became ever scarcer.

Public and Elite Opinion

Peter Katzenstein's (1997) description of Germany exhibiting a 'Europeanised identity' applied with special force to the political class from the late 1960s. Mass public opinion was pro-European, but less enthusiastically and more conditionally than elite opinion. The principal reservation was on Germany's paymaster role, but Germany's overwhelming prosperity ensured that this never became salient.

Mass support for European integration was further challenged by the decision to drop the popular Deutschmark – the very symbol of post-war German economic prowess. More long-term unification brought in the population of Eastern Germany where pro-Europeanism had no historic roots and whose citizens never made the automatic association of EU membership and prosperity which prevailed for so long in the old Federal Republic. There was short-lived enthusiasm for the EU at the time of German Unity, but disappointment set in when the popular 'D-Mark' was abolished and membership failed to deliver their aspirations on economic and social security (Weidenfeld, 2010).

[2] 'Germany: Annual Country Review', *Financial Times*, 10 November 1998, p. 6.

Elite opinion, however, at least formally remained pro-European:

> [E]lite and mass opinion continue to diverge but the prevailing elite consensus and the relatively low salience of European issues has allowed continued elite autonomy. The question is for how long? (Paterson, 2005, p. 282)

III. The Merkel Chancellorship

Round One

When Angela Merkel became chancellor in 2005 the priorities of the coalition were widely expected to be in the area of economics. The bruising experience of the 2005 election campaign and the rough reception accorded to her plans for more wide-reaching economic reform, however, led the chancellor to soft pedal on economic reform in the Grand Coalition and to allow the heavy lifting to be done by Peer Steinbrück, the SPD's very competent finance minister. The absence of a financial crisis or deep disagreements over economic reform for most of the period of the Grand Coalition allowed Chancellor Merkel rather unexpectedly to develop a major profile in external policy. In transatlantic relations simply not being Gerhard Schröder was enough to guarantee a positive impact, but Schröder was regarded in a more mixed way in the EU.

A number of factors allowed Angela Merkel to play a major and constructive role in the EU. In a new coalition government the foreign minister who heads a huge permanent service normally dominates in the early years, more especially since the foreign minister often heads the junior coalition partner. Each chancellor has to rebuild the foreign policy section in the chancellor's office. Foreign Minister Steinmeier, who had been in the chancellor's office, was constrained in his early years in office by the controversy surrounding the discovery of quite how widespread the CIA rendition programme had been. Chancellor Merkel had also been able to recruit Christoph Heusgen, Javier Solana's Chief of Staff, to head the foreign policy section in the chancellor's office. Heusgen's Brussels experience was a huge advantage in a governmental term that contained a large number of summits, including Germany's double Presidency of the EU and the G8.

At a European level, the leadership constellation in the major European states played in her favour. The big beasts of the jungle were about to retire like Tony Blair, or like Jacques Chirac clearly in the last months of office.[3]

[3] He retired in 2007.

The retirement of these two figures took some of the heat out of the fissures that had opened up in the Iraq War and left a space for a new European leader to appear.

Chancellor Merkel quickly built up considerable capital at the European level. Her no nonsense, pragmatic approach combined with a mastery of the brief quickly commanded respect. The loss in the referendums in France and the Netherlands on the European Constitutional Treaty in May 2005 relieved the pressure on the United Kingdom government. A less pressured British government felt confident enough to conclude a deal on the budget which included a cut in the United Kingdom rebate – a sacred cow of British European policy – and removed Britain from a purely defensive position. Angela Merkel played a notably constructive role in the budgetary negotiations, including making a German contribution.

Her already strong position was greatly strengthened by the German Presidency of the European Council in the first half of 2007 where Chancellor Merkel selected and shaped the two defining issues of the German Presidency: the Constitutional Treaty and climate change. The traditional approach had been to place Germany at the centre of constitutive bargains, usually in tandem with France, and wait until the issue was ready for a decision. Chancellor Merkel took a maximalist position in favour of the Constitutional Treaty from the outset. This was a bold move given the two-year pause for reflection that had been imposed following the referendum defeats of 2005 in France and the Netherlands, the fact that the French elections were to occur late in the Presidency cycle and the stipulation of the Federal Constitutional Court that it would not rule on the constitutionality of the Treaty until it had been ratified in every Member State.

The style of the intergovernmental negotiations was unusually disciplined and focused on the discussion of 'focal points'. The inevitable compromises that came at the end of the negotiations were less than might have been expected. The success of this 'salvage operation' can be explained by Angela Merkel's negotiating skill, her foresight (by helping the United Kingdom in the budgetary settlement in 2005, it was available as a useful ally in the final negotiations), the efficiency of the German-designed negotiating machinery and the interest of the participants by this time in securing a result. Perhaps the most remarkable feature was the lack of resentment at German leadership. Indeed, with the exception of the Polish government which was eventually wholly isolated, the overwhelming attitude was one of respect and gratitude. Angela Merkel was a former minister of the environment and she was also able to secure agreement on German preferences for ambitious emission targets on climate change.

Round Two

The formation of the second Merkel government in late 2009 coincided with the final stages of the ratification of the Lisbon Treaty, widely seen as a triumph for the German government and Chancellor Merkel personally with little attention being paid to the fact that the immediate past foreign minister had launched the whole process. As chancellor of a coalition with a small partner that was much closer ideologically and with few remaining domestic rivals Chancellor Merkel might have been expected to employ the European political capital she had so successfully accrued during her first government. Externally, too, there were no serious rivals. President Sarkozy was losing support domestically and internationally, a weak Brown-led government in the United Kingdom was about to cede power to an inexperienced coalition whose leader had no interest in exercising power at a European level, and Berlusconi was now seen as a figure of fun. Merkel had proved to be a leader of exceptional surefootedness in the exercise of power at a European level and was the pre-eminent European leader whose support was eagerly sought by other European leaders. Germany was now centre stage without having provoked the fears (especially marked in the United Kingdom) that had been created by Chancellor Kohl's ambitious integrationist project.

The subsequent development has been extremely paradoxical. As the dominant economy and key creditor nation, Germany moved even further centre stage with the onset of the eurozone crisis,[4] but Chancellor Merkel's former surefootedness and resolution in European policy has been replaced by missteps and an over-cautious approach. German economic strength has ensured her continuing pre-eminence, but she is a diminished figure. Three sets of explanations have been offered for this development: one centres on the chancellor, the second on the changing domestic context, and the final set is based on the intractability of the eurozone crisis which would test any statesman.

The explanations that centre on the chancellor have to acknowledge her success in the previous government. The first surprising element is the contrast between what appears to be a steady and purposeful pursuit of power in the period leading up to the ratification of the Lisbon Treaty and the apparent absence of a follow-on strategy. Chancellor Merkel did not appear to have strong preferences about the two post-Lisbon leadership positions, concentrating instead on the prospect of Axel Weber as the next head of the ECB (this came to naught when Axel Weber withdrew from contention in February 2011) and the appointment of Uwe Corsepius, her European policy adviser, as

[4] See Marsh's contribution to this volume.

Council Secretary General from June 2011. Surprisingly given the efforts it had taken to salvage the Treaty, no other elements of a post-Lisbon strategy were visible.

Chancellor Merkel had been able to play the key role in European developments without articulating a 'European vision'. She had talked of 'refounding' the European vision shortly after her accession to power (Merkel, 2006), but no content has been given to that vision. This lack of vision was accompanied, understandably enough given her East German origins, by an absence of empathy and emotional warmth for the Europeanist project in the manner of Kohl. This lack of vision had been shared by Helmut Schmidt and was not necessarily an insuperable obstacle to playing an influential role at a European level. Nor is it a precondition of success – as we can see from the example of the United Kingdom, which at times has possessed a strong European vision – unless it commands support at a European level. It is, however, an important component in mobilizing domestic support if the issue is subject to significant contestation at a domestic level. In her first term of government the issues on which she had been so successful had not raised significant domestic opposition and she was able to continue to profit from the elite autonomy that had allowed German governments to place themselves at the centre of EU constitutive agreements. This era was now coming to an end.

The wider explanations for the weakness of Chancellor Merkel's European policy in her second term reflect both the inherent difficulties of the issue and the more contested domestic terrain of German EU policy. The narrowing of the domestic space had been developing as we have seen (see above) in the post-Kohl years. The arbitrary and lawless nature of the Third Reich ensured that the Federal Republic has given especial importance to its character as a *Rechtstaat* (a state based on the rule of law). Within that context the Federal Constitutional Court assumed an especial importance and there has been a muted friction of jurisdictions with the ECJ (European Court of Justice) since the so-called 'Solange Decision' of the Federal Constitutional Court in 1974. In deciding on challenges to the constitutionality of the Lisbon Treaty in 2009, the Federal Constitutional Court ruled that it was not in conflict with the Basic Law (Mueller-Graff, 2009). Four aspects of the ruling, however, circumscribed the future autonomy of the Federal Government in European policy. The Federal Constitutional Court is a highly influential body and its tone in sections of the judgment legitimized a more Eurosceptic discourse in elements of the political elite. It insisted on new parliamentary procedures in relation to the area of the flexibility clause, bridging clauses or any future proposals entailing the transfer of sovereignty which in effect prescribed a more activist role for the *Bundestag* than it had set itself. It also ruled that the state should retain sovereignty in the following areas: criminal law, police, military operations, fiscal policy, social policy, education, culture, media and relations with religious groups. Finally, the judgment which had attracted a huge amount of attention greatly encouraged the developing habit of appealing to the Federal Constitutional Court on EU policy matters – a development which was bound to engender heightened caution in the area on the part of any federal government.

Formally, the German political elite continued to subscribe to a Europeanist code but the commitment had become less intense and the content less prescriptive; a gradual process of hollowing out had occurred. The federalist element of this code had been subject to a progressive dilution which had begun in the last years of Chancellor Kohl when he dropped the phrase 'United States of Europe' and the succeeding changes have been explored above. Party programmes scarcely mentioned the EU – a marked contrast with the 1980s when the Christian Democratic Union's electoral campaign manager referred to the need to take account of the 25 per cent of CDU party members who were in his words 'eurofreaks' (Bulmer and Paterson, 1987, p. 153). The European theme was less present in the 2009 election than in any election in the preceding six decades. Any remaining residue of federalism was further weakened by the Federal Constitutional Court judgment of June 2009. A sense of a European vocation remained, as was demonstrated in the enormous and ultimately successful efforts to salvage the Lisbon Treaty, but the federalist content had been greatly diluted, and beneath the surface of the formal elite Europeanist code there had been a drop in the intensity of the commitment.

While the elite code had to a degree atrophied, mass support for the EU weakened significantly. German mass opinion had not supported the creation of the eurozone, the opening of accession negotiations with Germany's neighbours or with Turkey, and displayed a continuing concern with Germany's paymaster role. These reservations were accompanied by a generalized pro-EU sentiment which now for the first time registered a significant fall. In an Allensbach Survey reported by Thomas Petersen, the percentage of those polled who had little or no trust in the EU grew from 51 to 63 per cent in the year to early 2010 (Petersen, 2011). These figures at the very least indicated that feelings of solidarity towards the EU were likely to be in short supply.

In the earlier section we drew attention to the impact of enlargement, the weakening of the traction of the Franco–German relationship and the resource crunch. These long-term waves were now accompanied by a chancellor without a European vision, a hollowing out of elite opinion and increasingly hostile public opinion. It was clear that German European policy which had seemed to live in a perpetual virtuous circle in fair weather was in a weak position to withstand the perfect storm that was about to break over the eurozone.

The Tsunami Breaks

The creation of an EMU (Economic and Monetary Union) in the Maastricht negotiations was widely regarded as the high point of the post-Wall Europeanist project. The name is something of a misnomer since, while it is a monetary union, it is not an economic union and the original intention to buttress it with a political union did not succeed. The absence of fiscal powers in EMU provoked anxiety, especially in Germany, about the dangers of Member States running up large deficits. A Stability and Growth Pact designed to impede deficits came into force at the insistence of the then German finance minister Theo Waigel in 1997. The introduction of the euro in 2002 coincided with recessionary pressures and the ongoing costs of German unification. A number of states – notably France and Germany – overshot the deficit limits set out in the Stability and Growth Pact and subsequently blocked action by the Commission. As Beverly Crawford (2007, pp. 139–40) expressed it: 'Germany had weakened the very regime it had created. It would now be difficult to ask other eurozone members with chronic deficits to curb their spending, and what the Commission called "fiscal irresponsibility" in one country could very possibly damage others'.

The immediate impact was limited, however, since the European economies picked up very quickly. The euro strengthened and the eurozone area was perceived as a zone of stability and prosperity. Unfortunately this perception was only partial and, as Simon Tilford (2010, p. 3), has pointed out: '[T]he structural differences between a low inflation, slow growing core and higher inflation periphery were supposed to narrow following the introduction of the single currency. In reality these differences grew'. Low interest rates and the availability of cheap credit led to neglect of the need by the peripheral economies to make their economies more competitive and the reform initiative had been weakened by the negative example set by France and Germany in defying the Stability and Growth Pact in 2002–03. Low wage rates and huge efficiency gains by German firms resulted in a quadrupling of Germany's trade surplus in the eurozone in the decade after the introduction of the Stability and Growth Pact.

The onset of the financial recession and the resultant tightening of credit lines left the peripheral economies, especially Greece, dangerously exposed. Given past side payments and the huge benefits accruing to Germany through the eurozone, an early bail-out – or at least an indication that Germany would help Greece to maintain access to credit markets – might have been expected.

In February 2009 Peer Steinbrück, then German finance minister, calmed the sovereign debt markets by indicating that help would be available from other members for those economies in difficulty. Chancellor Merkel's response was to insist that Greece needed to tackle the problem with a drastic austerity programme. This insistence was widely held to be a misstep:

> By refusing to back Greece however, Merkel created uncertainty and scared off investors. She also made sure not only that Greece would fail but also that Germany would pay. More importantly, she helped nurture a wider crisis of confidence in both sovereign debt markets and in the euro itself. She may have had strong domestic reasons for taking this step but it was a mistake. (Jones, 2010, p. 33)

The domestic reasons included a fear of a hostile Constitutional Court ruling (Busse, 2010), a very hostile press campaign led by *Bild Zeitung* and a perceptible cooling of German public opinion. It was unfortunate in this context that some Greek welfare provisions, like the retirement age, lent themselves to the popular perception that hard-working Germans were being asked to pay for lazy Greeks. At the Brussels summit of 25 March 2010, Merkel held to a hard line. Before any loan facility could be agreed Greece must have exhausted its capacity to borrow and other eurozone members would have to accept far harsher sanctions for budgetary indiscipline – conditions which privileged addressing German domestic opinion over a solution to the developing eurozone crisis. She was also keen to involve the IMF (International Monetary Fund) and EU non-members of the eurozone rather than restrict the solution to members of the eurozone who were seen as being more statist.

This position eroded very quickly as the seriousness of the Greek position became apparent and at the eurozone summit on 9 May 2010 agreement was reached on the establishment of a European Financial Stability Facility which, together with the IMF, underwrites a safety net of €750 billion in the period up to June 2013. This came at a very difficult time for Chancellor Merkel. The EFSF did not entail handing over any money immediately, but the German guarantee of 27.13 per cent was significantly larger than those of other Member States and the Greek 'bail-out' issue contributed to the defeat of the CDU/Free Democratic Party (FDP)-led coalition in the North Rhine Westphalian state election and the loss of the coalition's majority in the upper house of parliament, the *Bundesrat*. Chancellor Merkel was thrown on to the back foot by the intensity of the backlash against the proposals on Greece and failed to develop a narrative as to why support was strongly in Germany's own interest. It was only very late in the campaign that she focused on how much Germany benefited from the eurozone and she never alluded to the losses that German banks would incur in the event of a Greek sovereign default. Some relief was provided by the ruling of the Federal Constitutional Court on 21 May which raised no objections to the rescue plan, but although the chancellor survived the parliamentary vote on the eurozone stabilization package on 21 May, the major opposition party, the Social Democratic Party (SPD), abstained – the first time a major German party had departed from the pro-European consensus since the 1960s.

At the eurozone summit in March 2010 Herman Van Rompuy was charged with leading a task force to produce suggestions on dealing with the eurozone crisis for the October European Council summit.[5] In the run-up to the Council Meeting and immediately before the task force reported, Chancellor Merkel met with President Sarkozy in Deauville where agreement was reached on the creation of a permanent crisis resolution mechanism when EFSF lapsed in 2013 and the rules on automatic sanctions for deficit states envisaged by the task force were heavily diluted. Chancellor Merkel wanted a Treaty change to embed the new European Stability Mechanism, but that would have triggered referendum procedures and was very unwelcome to all other governments. Instead, at the 16–17 December European Council, it was agreed to add an amending clause to Article 136 TFEU to enter into force after ratification by Member States on 1 January 2013.

Unfortunately for Chancellor Merkel, both the internal and external environment worsened. Ireland, weighed down by a bank crisis, eventually agreed to an €85 billion bail-out on 25 November but the bond yields for Portugal and Spain remained worryingly high, and fears of contagion to large economies like Spain and even Italy were an ever-present reality. The Luxembourg prime minister Jean Claude Juncker suggested the idea of Eurobonds to relieve the pressure on the weaker economies – a plan that was summarily rejected by the German government to the intense irritation of its proposer who labelled the summary rejection as 'un-European' (*Spiegel*, 2010). It was, however, endorsed by the Social Democratic Party. In a widely cited article, Frank Walter Steinmeier and Peer Steinbrück called on the federal government to support the limited introduction of Europe-wide bonds, a debt restructuring for Greece and Ireland, and greater powers for European institutions to establish tighter controls over fiscal and economic stability. They also made the crucial point that the ECB was in danger of being turned into Europe's 'bad bank' as it laboured to support the liquidity of the banks in the struggling economies who were failing to cope with the harsh terms imposed on them (Steinmeier and Steinbrück, 2010).

[5] See also Hodson's contribution to this volume.

Internally there were to be seven state elections in 2011 where the question of bail-outs could, as North Rhine Westphalia had indicated, have the capacity to inflict damage on the chancellor's party. Surveys indicated a growing public opposition to the euro (Mueller, 2010). In that situation it is perhaps hardly surprising that Chancellor Merkel privileged domestic concerns. She can, however, be criticized for so rarely attempting to point out what Germany gained from the eurozone, though as a last resort she pointed out what Germany would lose if the eurozone collapsed (cited in Peel, 2011). The large exposure of German banks to these economies which would be lost in the case of sovereign default, a strong argument in favour of bail-out, largely remained a 'dirty little secret'. The combined result was a severe denting of Germany's European reputation without any gains at the domestic level.

Conclusions

The year 2010 was an '*annus horribilis*' for German European policy. Chancellor Merkel's European record in her first incumbency, where she managed to salvage the Lisbon Treaty while taking all the other Member States with her, attracted almost universal approval. In her European diplomacy in relation to the Lisbon Treaty she had displayed considerable resolution and German preferences played a central role. There was a winning combination of a manifest strategy and great tactical skill. The contrast with her record on dealing with the eurozone crisis could hardly be starker. Of course, the salvaging of the Lisbon Treaty played to her considerable analytical skills. Dealing with the eurozone crisis touched on elemental material interests and neither Chancellor Merkel nor her senior officials had a lot of previous experience in dealing with the fast moving financial markets and inexperience showed on a number of issues, such as her attempt to ban short selling.

It was possible to come to a 'grand bargain' at the European Council meeting on 24–25 March 2011. This settlement was reached by a quite different route from past agreements. A manifest and narrow reading of German interests and reliance on German structural economic power had led to bruised feelings on the part of Luxembourg Prime Minister Juncker on the Eurobonds issue, Commission President Barroso on a number of occasions and the leaders of the non-eurozone countries (apart from the United Kingdom) on the decision to operate for eurozone members only under Article 136 TFEU. The Franco–German relationship had operated, but only spasmodically and German preferences prevailed in a much more dominant way than in the past. Economic governance, long a *bête noire* of successive German governments as a threat to 'sound money', was retained as a term, but was largely drained of content.

The Erosion of Domestic Support for European Integration

There is a large element of risk in coming to conclusions in the middle of an ongoing crisis and there is no sign of an end to the eurozone crisis, far less any certainty about the eventual end point. However, it does seem possible to come to some preliminary conclusions about the character and role of a new German European policy. This article has two central arguments. The first argument has tracked significant changes in the politics of domestic support for European integration. Mass public support already on a downward curve since German Unification has weakened very visibly during the eurozone crisis. The Europeanist code shared by the political elite has been subject to a process of hollowing out. This does not mean that the elite have become anti-European, but the reflexive multilateralism of traditional German European policy no longer seems possible. The balanced budget rule embodied in Article 115 of the Basic Law significantly reduces the space for German generosity which has been replaced by urging fellow members to emulate German austerity.

The Reluctant Hegemon?

A defining feature of post-war German European policy has been what is sometimes called a 'leadership avoidance reflex' (Paterson, 1993). It was argued that an exposed leadership position would be unacceptable to other members given the history of the past century. Where Germany did exercise leadership it was in tandem with France with the latter normally accorded symbolic priority. Thomas Pedersen characterized this form of leadership as 'co-operative hegemony'. At the core of this concept is the perception that Germany is the potential hegemon and that France was offered 'a share in its evolving regional hegemony and the opportunities for regional hegemonic rule, which such a continental leadership offers both countries' (Pedersen, 1998, p. 198). Co-operative hegemony relied for its acceptance by other Member States on side payments – an option which is now largely closed. The preconditions for co-operative hegemony have also been undermined by the increasingly asymmetric character of the relationship as German structural economic power continues to grow. It has also become less necessary to Germany as the objections by other states to German leadership fade. It was already a feature of the Lisbon Treaty salvage that other Member States actively sought German leadership. The relationship remains vital to France where they view being seen as being close to Germany as a power resource. In that sense the relationship between France and Germany is beginning to resemble the Anglo–American 'special relationship' rather than co-operative hegemony.

The tipping point, however, in Germany's transition to 'reluctant hegemon' came with the onset of the eurozone crisis. Germany had been the hegemon in the exchange rate mechanism, where the Bundesbank dictated which states should leave the system in the 1992–93 crisis and the price to be paid by those that remained (Hix, 2005, p. 324). EMU was designed to alter this situation and French preferences such as the establishment of an ECB Governing Council and a political role for Ecofin in the management of the external exchange rate policy were reflected in the construction. The eurozone crisis catapulted Germany into a hegemonic role. This was not a role sought by Germany. As we have seen, there was no strategy to build a more central role for Germany on the political opportunity structures created by the Lisbon Treaty. As the dominant economy and key creditor state Germany could, however, scarcely avoid a hegemon role. Ultimately, the other members of the eurozone rely on Germany. The ESM, for instance, in case of difficulty envisages being able to call on designated funds from Member States. Whether this would be possible in the case of Italy or Spain remains an open question and helps explain why the other Member States are so keen to press a leadership position on Germany.

German reluctance to take on the inevitable hegemon role in the eurozone has three explanations. Chancellor Merkel's characteristic policy style formed in the coalition environment of German politics is not to lead from the front but to wait until the balance of political forces is ripe for decision. Second, as we have noted, European policy has become more contested at the domestic level and institutions like the Federal Constitutional Court are in a position to constrain the government's European policy. Third, hegemony brings with it costs and obligations. Hitherto, if forced to be a hegemon Germany's preference was to be a 'benign hegemon' (Morisse-Schilbach, 2011). The costs of such a role would now be high in material terms. It would also impose institutional burdens.

> Acting multilaterally needs a willingness to find the better argument and fight for it, to spend more time to convince people, to have more patience and stamina. It is in other words the more costly choice. (Morisse-Schilbach, 2011, p. 39)

The autonomy of the German political elite in the past was a huge advantage in dealing with these institutional burdens, but the change in the terms of the domestic political support base has greatly narrowed these opportunities and the benign aspect may well suffer, though ultimately the need to arrive at agreement and the benefits Germany derives from the eurozone will act as a counter pressure.

The eurozone crisis looks set to remain the central preoccupation of the EU in the coming years and Germany will be the reluctant hegemon in that area. This hegemony is, however, quite unlike that exercised by the United States in post-war Europe which covered all policy areas. Germany, by contrast, will continue, as the Libyan episode indicated, to punch below its weight in foreign and security policy where the United Kingdom and France retain dual leadership.

References

Anderson, G. and Goodman, J.B. (1993) 'Mars or Minerva? A United Germany in a Post Cold War Europe'. In Keohane, R.O., Nye, S.J. and Hoffmann, S. (eds) *After the Cold War: International Institutions and State Strategies in Europe, 1989–1991* (Cambridge, MA: Harvard University Press).

Bulmer, S. and Paterson, W.E. (1987) *The Federal Republic of Germany and the European Community* (London: Allen & Unwin).

Bulmer, S., Jeffery, C. and Paterson, W.E. (2000) *Germany's European Diplomacy: Shaping the Regional Milieu* (Manchester: Manchester University Press).

Busse, N. (2010) 'Unter Aufsicht. Nicht nur im Fall Griechenland: Die Deutsche Europapolitik wartet auf Karlsruhe'. *Frankfuter Allgemeine Zeitung*, 29 April.

Crawford, B. (2007) *Power and German Foreign Policy* (Basingstoke: Palgrave Macmillan).

Goetz, K. (1996) 'Integration Policy in a Europeanised State'. *Journal of European Public Policy*, Vol. 3, No. 1, pp. 23–44.

Harnisch, S. and Schieder, S. (2006) 'Germany's New European Policy: Weaker, Leaner and Meaner'. In Maull, H. (ed.) *Germany's Uncertain Power: Foreign Policy in the Berlin Republic* (Basingstoke: Palgrave Macmillan).

Hix, S. (2005) *The Political System of the European Union* (Basingstoke: Palgrave Macmillan).

Jones, E. (2010) 'Merkel's Folly'. *Survival*, Vol. 52, No. 3, pp. 21–38.

Katzenstein, P. (ed.) (1997) *Tamed Power: Germany in Europe* (Ithaca, NY: Cornell University Press).

Merkel, A. (2006) 'Regierungserklaerung von Bundeskanzlerin Dr Angela Merkel zur Europapolitik'. *Bulletin der Bundesregierung*, No. 44-1, 11 May.

Miskimmon, A., Paterson, W.E. and Sloam, J. (eds) (2009) *The Gathering Crisis: Germany under the Grand Coalition* (Basingstoke: Palgrave Macmillan).

Morisse-Schilbach, M. (2011) 'Ach Deutschland: Greece, the Eurocrisis and the Costs and Benefits of Being a Benign Hegemon'. *Internationale Politik und Gesellschaft*, No. 1, pp. 28–41.

Mueller. P. (2010) 'Opposition to the Euro Grows in Germany', *Spiegel online*, 27 December. Available at: «http://www.spiegel.de/international/germany/0,1518, 8736680,00.html».

Mueller-Graff, P.-C. (2009) 'Das Karlsruher Lissabon-Urteil: Bedingungen, Grenzen, Orakel und integrative Optionen'. *Integration*, Vol. 32, No. 4, pp. 277–308.

Paterson, W.E. (1993) 'Muss Europa Angst vor Deutschland haben?' In Hrbek, R. (ed.) *Der Vertrag von Maastricht in der wissenschaftlichen Kontroverse* (Baden Baden: Nomos).

Paterson, W.E. (1999) 'Helmut Kohl, the "Vision Thing" and Escaping the Semi-sovereignty Trap'. *German Politics*, Vol. 7, No. 1, pp. 17–36.

Paterson, W.E. (2005) 'European Policy Making: Between Associated Sovereignty and Semi Sovereignty'. In Green S.O. and Paterson, W.E. (eds) *Governance in Contemporary Germany* (Cambridge: Cambridge University Press).

Paterson, W.E. (2010) 'Does Germany Still Have a European Vocation?' *German Politics*, Vol. 19, No. 1, pp. 41–52.

Pedersen, T. (1998) *Germany, France and the Integration of Europe* (London: Pinter).

Peel, Q. (2011) 'Europe's Reluctant Superpower'. *Financial Times*, 12 April.

Petersen, T. (2011) 'Gemeinsames Interesse an Europa in Gefahr', *FAZ Net*, 25 January. Available at: «http://www.faz.net/s/Rub99C3EECA60D84CO8AD6B3 E60C4EA807F/Doc-EAE005».

Spiegel (2010) 'Eurocrisis Leaves Germany Increasingly Isolated', *Spiegel online*, 13 December. Available at: «http://www.spiegel.de/international/Germany/0,1518, 734285,00.html».

Steinmeier, F.-W. and Steinbrück, P. (2010) 'Germany Must Lead Fightback'. *Financial Times*, 14 December.

Thomson, R. (2010) 'The Relative Power of Member States in the Council: Large and Small, Old and New'. In Naurin, D. and Wallace, H. (eds) *Unveiling the Council of the European Union: Games Governments Play in Brussels* (Basingstoke: Palgrave Macmillan).

Tilford, S. (2010) 'How to Save the Euro'. Essay (London: Centre for European Reform).

Wallace, W. (1991) 'Germany at the Centre of Europe'. In Kolinsky, E. (ed.) *The Federal Republic of Germany: The End of an Era* (Oxford: Berg).

Weidenfeld, W. (2010) 'Nationalstaat versus Europaeische Integration'. In Glaab, M., Weidenfeld, W. and Weigl, M. (eds) *Deutsche Kontraste: 1990–2010* (Frankfurt/ New York: Campus Verlag).

JCMS 2011 Volume 49 Annual Review pp. 77–89

Spain's EU Presidency: Ambitions beyond Capacity?*

PAUL M. HEYWOOD
University of Nottingham

Introduction

Spain's assumption of the rotating six-month Presidency of the Council of the European Union (EU) on 1 January 2010 took place in decidedly unpropitious circumstances. Not only were EU Member States still struggling to adjust to the impact of the financial crisis which had dominated headlines since 2007, but the Spanish Presidency was charged with implementing the organizational restructuring agreed in the Lisbon Treaty that had finally been ratified in December 2009 following a long and controversial process.[1] Moreover, although Spain had three times previously held the Presidency, this latest period in the driving seat was greeted with a lukewarm, if not downright unenthusiastic, reception across Europe. In particular, given the imperative need to address the continued shock waves that had been unleashed by the so-called 'credit crunch', Spain lacked credibility as a driver of change: its own economy had been particularly exposed to the impact of the financial crisis, with unemployment heading towards 20 per cent (double the EU average), a hugely damaging housing bubble collapse and a toxic two-tier labour market characterized by protected jobs alongside an extensive black economy (see Hodson, 2010). Such structural difficulties damaged Spain's aspirations to be taken seriously as a major international player with global interests, and its desire to become a consolidated member of the G20 sat

* I am very grateful to Dr Tom Purcell for essential research assistance.

[1] See Dinan (2010) and Dinan in this volume.

Figure 1: The Hacked Version of Spain's Official EU Presidency Website

Source: Google images.

uncomfortably with its status as number one recipient of European aid (Elcano Royal Institute, 2009). Thus it was all the more embarrassing for the Spanish government when hackers managed to replace a picture of the premier, José Luis Rodríguez Zapatero, with one of the fictional character Mr Bean on its official EU website (see Figure 1), helping to heap scorn on the idea of Spain advising Europe on economic recovery.

Nonetheless, the Spanish government was undeterred in its ambitions for the Presidency and set out four priority areas, under the global heading of 'Innovating Europe': full implementation of the Lisbon Treaty; the co-ordination of economic policies to promote growth and recovery through the 'Europe 2020' programme; strengthening the EU's foreign policy; and fostering the rights and freedoms of Europe's citizens. Under the trio arrangement first introduced in 2007–08, which entailed close co-operation across three successive Presidencies, Spain's priorities were designed to align with those of Belgium and Hungary, the next two holders of the Presidency.[2] Indeed, meetings between the three countries had been taking place since 2008 when a common logo was adopted, and the overall priorities had been

[2] On the Belgium Presidency, see Drieskens in this volume.

agreed in December 2009. There was therefore an understandable overlap between Spain's own priorities and those of the trio, which were officially launched at the end of January 2010.

In practice, Spain's programme for the EU Presidency read like an election manifesto – and, like many election manifestos, it looked over-ambitious in terms of what could actually be achieved, as well as sadly lacking in detail as to how promises would be put into practice. Even allowing for the proposals being designed to encompass the trio of Presidencies, 18 months was a very short time to achieve the kind of aspirations set out in this document. Carlos Buhigas Schubert, a member of the Spanish Team Europe of the European Commission, acknowledged that 'the agenda looks too ambitious and, as a result, rather unfocused'.[3] Indeed, it would almost be easier to outline what the Spanish Presidency of the EU did not have on its agenda than what it did. There was maybe an element of smoke and mirrors to Spain's approach, substituting what it lacked in capacity for an exaggerated EU programme in which it was difficult to discern the core policy priorities. Even from a logistical point of view, the Spanish Presidency suffered from a lack of resources: it had a team of just 40 people behind it, fewer than half the number deployed by Sweden in 2009, and an austere budget of €55 million, a third of the amount France had spent in 2008 (Molina, 2010).

The prominent emphasis given to overseeing the 'full and fast enforcement of the Treaty of Lisbon' was seen by the *Financial Times* as potentially misguided,[4] entailing an attempt to fine tune institutional arrangements at the expense of dealing with the real problems that were affecting European citizens and leading to the growing disillusionment with the EU. First, there had been a collapse in GDP growth (–4 per cent across the EU-27 in 2009), which had led to a substantial rise in unemployment in parts of the EU (not least, in Spain itself) and growing uncertainty over the capacity of the euro to contain problems in countries such as Greece and Latvia. Second, there was the continued threat of international terrorism, and question marks over the EU's role in dealing with major security challenges. Third, there was evidence of growing scepticism and disillusionment amongst citizens in Europe, reflected in a decline in electoral participation and the rise of populist, extremist and anti-European parties. The 2009 European Parliament elections, for instance, had seen turnout fall for the seventh time in a row to reach a new low of just 43 per cent across the EU-27. In some of the newer Member States, turnout was exceptionally low: 19.6 per cent in Slovakia, 21.0 per cent in Lithuania and 24.5 per cent in Poland. Moreover, global poverty and its

[3] *EurActiv*, 8 December 2009.
[4] *Financial Times*, 3 January 2010.

concomitant impact on immigration, along with the continued economic development of the BRIC (Brazil, Russia, India and China) countries, represented intractable challenges that called into question the very role and function of the EU.

Given this context, it is easy to see how a concern with implementing the organizational reforms outlined in the Lisbon Treaty could be seen as tantamount to rearranging the deck chairs on the Titanic. Even when attention turned to broader issues, it was equally easy to be dismissive. In a biting observation aimed at both Spain and the EU itself, *The Economist* magazine remarked that a bunch of mid-sized powers with lots of ideas about how the world should be run, notably over climate change and financial regulation, should ponder Spain's lesson: if you want your advice to be heeded, you need something credible to say.[5] However, any proper assessment of Spain's fourth period in the Presidency of the EU Council must be based on what was actually accomplished, rather than what was said. The rest of this article therefore focuses on what was achieved across the four principal objectives outlined in the Spanish programme.

I. Evaluating the 2010 Presidency

As Arteaga (2002, p. 1) has noted: '[T]he assessment of any presidency of the Council of the European Union is always a complicated and subjective task because it is contingent upon the accounting criteria used. There can be a range of national or European interests, activities or results and technical or political outcomes'. The accuracy of this assertion is evident in various recent assessments: whereas many international commentators were initially sceptical and subsequently even scathing of the Spanish Presidency, domestic analysis tended to offer more sympathetic accounts. This is shown, for example, in the impact of the EU's new institutional structure following the Lisbon Treaty, the EU 2020 economic agenda spearheaded by Spain, foreign affairs and European social rights; in examining these, the article will assess the specific challenges facing the Spanish Presidency and how it responded to them, but also how these relate to the wider challenges that will continue to face the EU as a whole.

The Limits of the New Institutional Architecture

The 2010 Presidency represented a new departure for the EU in terms of its organizational structure. The Lisbon Treaty introduced new decision-making

[5] *The Economist*, 9 January 2010.

mechanisms, including a full-time President of the European Council and a *de facto* foreign minister (the High Representative for Foreign Affairs and Security Policy), which arguably represented the most important set of innovations in EU institutional workings since 1993 (see Barber, 2010). As a result, the rotating Presidency trio inevitably had less political leeway than previous Presidencies and probably also less media visibility, even as they faced a greater need to ensure co-ordination of the system. Such a situation inevitably generated considerable uncertainty, and may help explain why the new Spanish Presidency should have placed such emphasis on rapid implementation of the Lisbon Treaty provisions.

The new EU institutional structure comprised four titular Presidents: the rotating Presidency, held for a six-month term; the 'permanent' President of the European Council, Herman Van Rompuy (elected for a once-renewable two-and-a-half-year term), the President of the European Commission, José Manuel Barroso (elected for a second five-year term in September 2009) and the President of the European Parliament, Jerzy Buzek (elected for a two-and-a-half-year term in July 2009). In addition, there were two people who could be seen as the EU foreign minister: the High Representative for Foreign Affairs, Baroness Ashton, and the foreign minister of the country holding the rotating Presidency – in this case, Miguel Angel Moratinos. The distinction in role between the rotating and the permanent Presidency was summarized by Francisco Villar, Spain's ambassador to Paris, at the formal launch of the 'Presidency Trio' programme in January 2010: 'Our role is to provide impetus to each dedicated Council, not necessarily to stabilise it, as is the case of the permanent presidency. [. . .] The answer must be given in practice, not in the text'.[6]

According to Molina (2010, pp. 3–4):

> Spain's term as President established a good precedent for co-habitation between the permanent and rotating Presidencies. The distinction between the General Affairs Council and the Foreign Affairs Council went smoothly, the link with the European Council for preparing the order of the day and the conclusions went well, and the distribution of tasks among the working groups that corresponded to Spain or the High Representative did not suffer any major lack of co-ordination.

Such apparent accord, however, is open to dispute. Commentators have suggested that tussles for the lead role with post-Lisbon offices, including that of Van Rompuy in early 2010, damaged the Spanish EU Presidency and stand as testimony to continuing teething problems in the European institutional

[6] *EurActiv*, 26 January 2010.

structure.[7] At the time, Zapatero announced that if anyone wants to 'call Europe' (in reference to Kissinger's famous question) they should call Van Rompuy, yet Van Rompuy himself declared that in the EU 'there is not one man or one woman who decides. We each have a role' (Kern, 2010). Such comments did little to clarify who actually speaks for Europe, suggesting instead an almost institutionalized confusion.

Such confusion was nowhere more apparent than in the preparations for and subsequent cancellation of the EU–US summit. Holding this summit in Madrid had been a goal planned for more than two years, partly to help 'normalize' Spain–US relations following the tensions prompted by Spain's withdrawal of troops from Iraq in 2004 (Sola and Blanco, 2010, p. 5). *Deustche Welle* reported that:

> Barack Obama snubbed the annual EU–US summit after confusion over who[m] he should be meeting. Should it be Van Rompuy or the Spanish president Jose Luis Zapatero? [Should] the meeting [be] in Brussels or Madrid? Even if the Lisbon Treaty now said the duty fell to Van Rompuy, Zapatero was certainly not ready to give up his seat at the summit.[8]

Washington also wanted the inclusion of specific commitments and agreements to avoid rhetorical conclusions and few concrete results, which further hampered negotiations (Sola and Blanco, 2010, p. 5). During the European Parliamentary review of the Spanish Presidency, some MEPs from outside the Socialist group were quite critical of the Presidency's record and, in particular, the aborted summit with the United States.[9]

Economic Agenda and Responding to the Crisis

Spain hoped the EU could agree on a replacement for the long-term growth strategy known as the 'Lisbon Agenda', which had been designed to make Europe the world's most competitive knowledge-based economy by 2010, although governments were under no obligation to comply with its provisions. With this in mind, and as part of the EU 2020 strategy, Zapatero, speaking ahead of the formal inauguration of Spain's EU Presidency, proposed binding goals for all EU Member States in order to improve international competitiveness: 'Our main aim is to introduce a qualitative leap in our economic union by means of new common policies. It is absolutely necessary for the 2020 Economic Strategy [. . .] to take on a new nature, a binding

[7] *EurActiv*, 23 June 2010.
[8] *Deutsche Welle*, 30 June 2010.
[9] *Europolitics*, 7 July 2010.

nature'.[10] The Spanish proposal was based on a carrot and stick approach, with penalties for non-compliance taking the shape of cutbacks in EU subsidies to offending members.

Amongst Spain's European partners this provoked less than enthusiastic reactions, not least because the Spanish economy was still in contraction, with unemployment reaching 20 per cent in 2010 (double the EU average). Rainer Brüderle, Germany's economics minister, argued that 'their only impact would be to create even more bureaucratic structures, what the EU members need to do now is seek co-ordinated approaches for reducing their debts'.[11] Indeed, the German press attacked Zapatero for 'presenting a spectacular firework of ideas that won't achieve anything apart from securing him a moment of glory'.[12] The article suggested that a little more modesty would be appropriate from Zapatero in view of his own country's negative economic data, for if his proposals were put into practice Spain itself would face sanctions. During the European Parliamentary review, Timothy Kirkhope, leader of the British Conservatives in the European Parliament, remarked that:

> with a budget deficit over 11 percent perhaps they felt a good reason to avoid international scrutiny. With a large deficit and timed reform plan for the own economy at home, they were in no position to offer Europe leadership or to set an example. So the historic opportunity from being the first Presidency following the Lisbon Treaty has been lost. (European Parliament, 2010)

Spain sought via the EU 2020 strategy to rebalance the asymmetry in the EU's economic and monetary union, which established a European Central Bank (ECB), but left the EU with insufficient power to co-ordinate national economic policies. The European Economic Recovery Plan (EERP), which encouraged Member States to incur public sector deficits in order to alleviate the worst effects of the economic crisis on aggregate demand in the EU, not only undermined one of the key aspirations of the Stability and Growth Pact, but also generated major concerns about the sustainability of sovereign debt levels, with a resultant impact on the euro. Thus, the EU 2020 strategy sought to introduce economic, social and environmental sustainability as well as reforming the supervisory arrangements for the financial system.

Perhaps surprisingly, then, Molina (2010, p. 4) judges the outcome of the Presidency with regards to economic decisions as 'outstanding'. Such a judgement is based on how both the Greek crisis and the Spanish economy were managed.

[10] *EU Observer*, 8 January 2010.
[11] *Der Tagesspiegel*, 11 January 2010.
[12] *Der Tagesspiegel*, 11 January 2010.

> Many member states, in particular Spain, have seen clearly during this Presidency the new, direct link that has been established between the creation of the new fund, rigorous application of the deficit limits of the Stability and Growth Pact and the adoption of economic reforms encouraged by Brussels in areas that, in principle, fall outside EU jurisdiction: the labour market, savings banks, pay for civil servants and retirement ages and pensions. (Molina, 2010, p. 5)

However, despite being a main goal of the Spanish EU Presidency, approval of the EU 2020 strategy went almost unnoticed amidst the climate of economic urgency. In March and June, the European Council approved a broad outline of a new more productive model for the entire EU. In regard to banks, which were at the heart of the origins of the financial crisis, Zapatero underlined the importance of the agreement by the Council, at the request of the Spanish Presidency, for the results of the stress tests performed on the credit entities of each Member State to be published during the second fortnight of July (Ausseill, 2010). Indeed, Zapatero pointed to Madrid's proposal to make bank stress tests public – which he said would be 'fundamental' to restoring calm in the markets – as an example of the success of the Spanish Presidency (Ausseill, 2010).

The paradox of a country experiencing major economic difficulties trying to take the lead over plans for Europe-wide growth and recovery was nowhere better encapsulated than by Celestino Corbacho, Minister for Work and Immigration. In describing the Spanish Presidency as a 'resounding success', Corbacho highlighted a series of events, conferences and meetings organized by his department to discuss topics such as new skills for new jobs in a more competitive Europe; the co-ordination of social security regimes; the integration of immigrants as a driving force for development and social cohesion; worker displacement and labour rights; and corporate social responsibility and the social economy. The adoption of the EU 2020 Strategy by the European Council was 'a great achievement', with Corbacho delineating five quantifiable objectives that came together to make Europe 'a competitive knowledge-based economy', placing growth and job creation 'at the heart of our crisis exit strategies'. 'Intelligent, sustainable and inclusive' growth would achieve:

- 75 per cent of the population between 20 and 64 years old having a job in 2020;
- 3 per cent of GDP in the EU to be invested in research and development;
- reaching the 20-20-20 energy targets (20 per cent reduction in energy consumption, for 20 per cent of energy to come from clean and renewable sources and to increase energy efficiency by 20 per cent);

- a school dropout rate lower than 10 per cent and at least 40 per cent of young people having completed higher education; and
- taking 20 million people out of risk of poverty.

As with previous EU-wide growth strategies, such aspirations were understandably met with some scepticism, particularly given the difficulties experienced in Greece, Ireland and Portugal.

Another key part of Spain's Presidency was the push for a 'Europe of Knowledge' – an integration initiative targeted at the further development of the European Research Area (ERA). The project emphasized researcher mobility and the role of science in economic recovery. However, this was not necessarily particularly innovative as it mirrors national flagship strategies built around the 'knowledge economy' in cities such as Barcelona, which have yet to show significant returns even at this smaller urban scale. Indeed, any discussion of knowledge-based competitive cities as the engines of growth for Europe references the knowledge economy.

Foreign Affairs: Establishing Europe as a Global Responsible and Supportive Player

The new Lisbon Treaty effectively strips the Presidency of any role in representing the EU abroad, and therefore Spain's role in this area was a transitional one, involving more diplomatic input than will be the case for future Presidencies. A significant institutional achievement during the Spanish Presidency was the establishment of the European External Action Service (EEAS), agreed in Madrid on 21 June and ratified in Brussels on 20 July. The accord creating the service calls for the deployment of more than 6,000 people in over 130 diplomatic missions around the world over the next five years.

During the European Parliamentary review of the Spanish Presidency in July 2010, the Socialist & Democrats Group leader Martin Schulz highlighted the Spanish Presidency's 'decisive contribution' to the final phase of the negotiations of the EEAS.[13] It was observed that Spain maintained a formal and clear relationship with Van Rompuy and Ashton as far as external political affairs were concerned, but on national interests, concerning the Mediterranean and Latin America, Spain took a more forthright role. This had led to a mixing of Presidential and national priorities (Sola and Blanco, 2010). Whilst the Spanish government tried to make a legitimate – albeit complicated – connection with its major goals in domestic and foreign policy, it

[13] 'Spanish Presidency: Zapatero: Two Main Objectives Achieved', *European Information Service*, 7 July 2010.

could be argued that it paid insufficient attention to the institutional limits that rotating Presidencies have always faced and the fact that the Treaty of Lisbon imposes even more limits as it lowers even further the political profile of these six-month stints in power (Molina, 2010, p. 8).

Zapatero had said that the Spanish EU Presidency would be characterized as 'a Euro–American presidency', paying special attention to the relationships between the EU, Latin America and the Caribbean. However, an area of contention emerged when Spain tried to change the 1996 Common Position on Cuba (Molina, 2010). It is likely that the death of Cuban dissident Orlando Zapata in February torpedoed Spain's bid to get the EU to soften its stance towards the communist island.[14] For his part, Van Rompuy claimed he had 'little time to think about Cuba' since taking office (Kern, 2010). Nonetheless, one triumph for the Spanish Presidency was the signing of a free trade agreement between the South American trading bloc Mercosur and the EU (Ignjatović, 2010). Spain brokered a comprehensive trade agreement, covering in particular manufactured products, agriculture goods, services, investment and trade rules, which is expected to generate an additional €5 billion (US$6.2 billion) in exports per year.

Despite being snubbed by President Obama, Spain helped arrange the Open Sky II and 'Swift' agreements between the EU and the United States. Signed in Luxembourg on 24 June 2010, the second stage agreement builds on the benefits of the ground-breaking EU–US Open Skies agreement of 2007. It generates new commercial opportunities and strengthens the framework of co-operation on issues such as the environment, social protection, competition and security. The full implementation of the first and second stage agreements is expected to give the economy a €12 billion boost as well as create up to 80,000 new jobs. The Swift agreement, meanwhile, permits the transfer of information on international bank transfers to American counterterrorism authorities. It was signed in Brussels on 28 June after Spain accepted demands from MEPs for changes to the text concerning the bulk transfer of data, the creation of an EU counterpart to the American Terrorist Finance Tracking Programme (TFTP) and EU oversight of TFTP data-processing on American soil.

In other areas, the Spanish Presidency recommended that the EU review Serbia's application to join as soon as possible, with Moratinos looking to make progress with the integration of the Western Balkans. As regards the Mediterranean region, the Presidency decided to postpone the regional summit that was due to take place in June in light of the ongoing conflicts in the area. Regarding further issues of EU expansion, some progress was made

[14] Zapata was a political dissident jailed in 2003, who died following a hunger strike.

in the negotiation process with Croatia, the opening of a new chapter with Turkey, and talks with Iceland were also constructive.[15] However, a summit with Morocco, held in Granada, was not considered a success.

A Europe of Rights

An important aspiration of the Spanish Presidency was to encourage greater citizen participation and security in the EU:

> Thanks to the European popular legislative initiative, included for the first time in the Treaty of Lisbon, Member State citizens may urge the Commission to formulate legislative proposals on matters they consider should be regulated at the European level. The Spanish Presidency will work to make this instrument of direct democracy a reality as soon as possible. (Spanish Presidency, 2010, p. 14)

Pressure from the Spanish Presidency led to a draft of the European Citizens' Initiative being presented a month ahead of time, which will allow citizens to propose legislative reforms directly to the Commission if they collect a million signatures in the space of a year from a third of the Member States.

In the area of protection of human rights and justice and internal affairs, the Presidency fulfilled the technical goals of approving the Action Plan of the Stockholm Programme, as well as a number of other initiatives.[16] It also sought to innovate in regard to gender equality and the fight against violence targeted at women (Molina, 2010). Measures included the creation of a European Observatory against Gender Violence, approved in early March at the Employment and Social Affairs Council. Despite opposition from the Commission, a European-wide restraining and protection order for women was approved. Domestic violence can be punished either in civil or criminal proceedings, depending on the country, and this sensitive issue has provoked a fierce legal battle between the Council, which can take initiatives in matters of criminal justice, and the Commission, which has competence over civil matters. At the Justice Council, in early June, Madrid concluded that it had obtained a mandate for negotiations with the European Parliament, which Commissioner Reding disputed.[17] The matter was referred to the Parliament, with the hope that it would be resolved under the Belgian EU Presidency.[18]

[15] See Whitman and Juncos in this volume.
[16] On the Stockholm Programme, see Monar's contribution in this volume.
[17] Europolitics 3991.
[18] *Europolitics*, 16 July 2010.

Conclusions

In practice, and unsurprisingly, the Spanish Presidency was overshadowed by the economic and financial crisis that dominated headlines throughout the period. That the Spanish government was persistently seen as on the verge of bankruptcy and in likely need of an EU bail-out hardly helped raise its credibility as the driver of a new programme for growth. Nonetheless, there were a number of positive achievements during this first Presidency under the terms of the Lisbon Treaty – not least some genuine progress in each of its four priority areas. The key lesson of the Spanish Presidency, though, remains the fact that a common currency and a European central bank are insufficient instruments to manage the heterogeneity of the EU's national economies: until that central challenge is addressed in a credible way, the role of the EU Presidency Trio is likely to be seen as ever more irrelevant compared to the continued significance and influence of Berlin and Paris in particular. It was in the German press where greatest scorn was heaped upon the Spanish Presidency, and a respectable record of achievements is unlikely to alter the perception that Spain's ambitions outstripped its capacity.

References

Arteaga, F. (2002) 'The Balance of the Spanish Presidency of 2002 with Regard to Justice and Home Affairs of the European Union'. Paper delivered at the conference on the Spanish Presidency of the European Union, Foresight Centre, University of Liverpool, 12 October.

Ausseill, P. (2010) 'Spanish EU Presidency Marred by Economic Crisis'. *Agence France Presse*, 24 June.

Barber, T. (2010) 'The Appointments of Herman Van Rompuy and Catherine Ashton'. *JCMS*, Vol. 48, s1, pp. 55–67.

Dinan, D. (2010) 'Institutions and Governance: A New Treaty, a Newly Elected Parliament and a New Commission'. *JCMS*, Vol. 48, s1, pp. 95–118.

Elcano Royal Institute (2009) *Spain and the G20: A Strategic Proposal for Enhancing Its Role in Global Governance* (Madrid: Real Instituto Elcano).

European Parliament (2010) 'Review of the Spanish Presidency', 6 July. Available at: «http://www.europarl.europa.eu/sv/media-professionals/content/20100706SHL80785/html/Review-of-the-Spanish-Presidency-71420».

Hodson, D. (2010) 'The EU Economy: The Euro Area in 2009'. *JCMS*, Vol. 48, s1, pp. 225–42.

Ignjatović, D. (2010) 'Inauspicious Spanish EU Presidency Draws to a Close'. *IHS Global Insight Daily Analysis*, 30 June.

Kern, S. (2010) 'Spanish Presidency of the EU: High Hopes, Low Expectations'. *European Dialogue*, 13 February. Available at: «http://www.eurodialogue.org/osce/Spain-s-EU-Presidency-Greeted-With-Skepticism».

Molina, I. (2010) *'Innovating Europe' in Troubled Times: A First Assessment of Spain's EU Presidency in 2010*. ARI 115/2010 (Madrid: Real Instituto Elcano).

Sola, N.F. and Blanco, A.S. (2010) *La UE en el mundo: actuaciones y limitaciones de la presidencia española 2010*. ARI 82/2010 (Madrid: Real Instituto Elcano).

Spanish Presidency (2010) *Innovating Europe* (Madrid: Ministerio de Asuntos Exteriores y Cooperación, Secretaría de Estado para la Unión Europea).

JCMS 2011 Volume 49 Annual Review pp. 91–102

Ceci n'est pas une présidence: The 2010 Belgian Presidency of the EU*

EDITH DRIESKENS
Leuven University and Clingendael Institute

Introduction

What initially sounded like a recipe for disaster has become a model for success: a country assuming the EU Presidency with a caretaker government for the complete duration of its term. Following the federal elections of 13 June 2010, international commentators showed nervousness at the prospect of long coalition talks and questioned Belgium's capacity to assume the EU Presidency. However, when Belgium passed the torch to Hungary, those commentators agreed about the Belgian stint being successful and wrote that the lack of government was a determinant factor for success.

This article explains why the potential impact of domestic problems on the Belgian Presidency should not have been exaggerated in the first place, pointing towards the importance of timing, experience, preparation and consensus. Also, it argues that the role of the federal government in the management of the EU Presidency diminished in 2001 when regional authorities became fully involved. The Lisbon Treaty eroded its role even further, introducing new foreign policy actors and formalizing the trio Presidency format.

This contribution not only discusses the context that defined Belgium's priorities and achievements in 2010 and the Belgian performance, it also presents some initial indications of the EU's functioning in the post-Lisbon era, in particular of the role of the rotating Presidency.

* The author wishes to thank the diplomats and civil servants who were willing to share their views on working for/with the Belgian Presidency.

I. Belgian Context

When Herman Van Rompuy was appointed the first permanent President of the European Council in November 2010, his fellow Christian Democrat (and predecessor as Belgian prime minister) Yves Leterme replaced him as prime minister of Belgium. On 22 April, after only five months in office, the government collapsed. Elections were organized a few weeks later and won by two parties with opposing views on the Belgian state and its reform. The New Flemish Alliance (Nieuw Vlaamse Alliantie; N-VA) won in the northern (Dutch-speaking) part of the country and aims for a gradual evolution towards an independent Flanders. By contrast, for the Socialist Party (Partie Socialiste; PS) that won in the southern (French-speaking) part, Belgium remains the point of reference. Importantly, the two parties also have different views on socio-economic policy.

The prospect of a long and cumbersome processs of Cabinet formation raised questions about Belgium's capacity to assume the EU Presidency, especially on the part of the international media.[1] However, the government did not collapse until late in the preparation process and assumed a caretaker role. The team had not only prepared itself for running the Presidency, it was also experienced with assuming leading roles in foreign policy, as various members of the cabinets and administration had been involved in Belgium's 2006 chairmanship of the Organisation for Security and Co-operation in Europe (OSCE) and its 2007–08 membership of the United Nations (UN) Security Council. The formation of a new government and N-VA participation would not have altered the pro-European consensus or Belgian position. Yet, the party's limited diplomatic experience could have been a complicating factor for holding the Presidency.

An important reason why the doom and gloom scenario did not come true is that the federal government was not the only government involved in the management of the Presidency.[2] Foreign policy in Belgium is conducted on the basis of the *in foro interno, in foro externo* principle, with the Communities and Regions having full foreign policy powers for those issues for which they are domestically competent. The implementation of that logic gives the federated entities a prominent role in the EU Presidency as holders of both the Presidency and Belgian chairs in ministerial meetings.[3]

[1] For instance, the *Financial Times* wrote that the collapse of the federal government would 'threaten' the Presidency (*Financial Times*, 23 April 2010). Likewise, the *New York Times* argued that the elections of 13 June 'injected a new element of uncertainty into Europe' (*New York Times*, 13 June 2010).

[2] For an authoritative account of the role of the federated entities in Belgium's EU policy-making and decision-making, see Beyers and Bursens (2006).

[3] The 2001 Belgian EU Presidency was the first to introduce the full participation of Regions and Communities; see Kerremans and Drieskens (2002).

Importantly, the detailed rules that determine co-ordination and representation were approached with a touch of pragmatism for the 2010 stint, allowing for continuity, notably within the new trio format (see below), and for actors to choose their seats in function of desired impact and exposure (Drieskens *et al.*, 2010, pp. 37–8). However, as explained below, the role of the federal government was not only eroded from below, but also from above, with the 2010 Presidency being the first for Belgium under Lisbon rules.

II. European Union Context

Various authors indicated that the Lisbon Treaty introduced the most far-reaching changes to the rotating Presidency to date, entrusting the EU's external representation on issues of common foreign and security policy to a permanent President of the European Council and a High Representative for Foreign Affairs and Security Policy.[4] As a result, the country holding the rotating Presidency no longer chairs the European Council or the Foreign Affairs Council, except when the latter covers issues falling under the common commercial policy.[5]

The starting point for the planning and preparation of the Belgian Presidency was that the entry into force of the Lisbon Treaty had occurred before Belgium took over from Spain.[6] Taking no risks, however, the budget also included the costs of representing the EU externally. That cautiousness paid off: the Belgian Presidency turned out to be a transitional one. Its external representation role was diminished rather than abolished. Unlike President Herman Van Rompuy, High Representative Catherine Ashton was not always able to take over, partly because the European External Action Service (EEAS) was not launched until 1 December. The reality of institutional change explains why Belgium's foreign minister (Steven Vanackere) was more visible than its prime minister (Yves Leterme), besides the fact that nine out of ten Council configurations remain the responsibility of the rotating Presidency, including the General Affairs one.

The Belgian team decided to lead by example, setting the right precedents and aiming for full implementation by the end of the term. Confirming Belgium's reputation as defender of the EU interest, it aimed to ensure smooth sailing for Van Rompuy and Ashton, especially as some of its successors appeared to be less supportive of the transition of the capital-based

[4] See Dinan in this volume and Barber (2010).

[5] Not all CFSP-related meetings are chaired by the High Representative or the EEAS; the rotating Presidency still chairs COREPER II and some working groups.

[6] On the Spanish Presidency, see Heywood's contribution to this volume.

system of external representation into a Brussels-based one.[7] Critical voices about a lack of ambition were silenced by the answer that 'Belgium's ambitions for the EU were high' (Vanackere, 2010a) and that 'a Presidency being able to promise 20 priorities and 30 objectives' (Vanackere, 2010b) was a thing of the past.

Importantly, the Lisbon Treaty also codified the format of trio co-operation. That format was elaborated by the Council in 2006 with the aim of strengthening the continuity between successive Presidencies. For the Belgian team, co-operation with Spain and Hungary was especially relevant in the preparatory stages, encouraging an early start (Belgische Senaat en Kamer van Volksvertegenwoordigers, 2008; Drieskens *et al.*, 2010, pp. 48–53). Horizons were broadened and networks established. However, it was also a complicating factor and it did not transform the Presidency into a collective responsibility. Unlike their predecessors, the trio did not send their individual programmes to the Council Secretariat for integration, but jointly drafted a programme. Yet, beyond a shared agenda, co-operation remained limited to symbolic measures like a common logo and website.

III. Priorities and Realizations

Belgium assumed the role of a 'sheepdog whose task is to ensure that the herd moves forward together' (Vanackere, 2010b) and aimed to pass as much legislation through the Council as possible. Mirroring the strategic and operational programmes that were drafted with Spain and Hungary, as well as the Commission's Working Programme, the work centred on five axes: a socio-economic axis (aimed at re-establishing sustainable growth and competitiveness); a social axis (aimed at stimulating social progress); an environmental axis (aimed at transitioning into a green economy); an internal security axis (aimed at deepening and finalizing the European Freedom, Security and Justice Area); and, an external action axis (aimed at increasing the attractiveness of the EU as a global force for peace and security) (Belgian Presidency, 2010a).

The Belgian Presidency made clear from the start that it wanted to be judged on 'concrete realisations', not by 'pre-set expectations' (Vanackere, 2010a). Obsessed with legislative output, the team presented a list of 51 achievements at the end of its mandate, ranging from the approval of the 2011 budget to the formal opening of accession negotiations with Iceland (Belgian Presidency, 2010b). Yet calculating its final grade is rather complex because

[7] On the pro-integration consensus among Belgium's political elite, as well as on the permissive consensus that still characterizes the public at large, see Drieskens *et al.* (2010, pp. 16–24).

it inherited dossiers at various stages of completion. Some of them, like the adoption of the budget for 2011, required intense discussion and negotiation; others, like the Icelandic one, only needed some finishing touches. The Lisbon Treaty also complicates the evaluation of the Belgian touch since it increased the top-down character of the proceedings and the number of actors involved (see below).

That said, close observers identified a number of success stories including approval of the 2011 budget, agreement on the financial and staff regulations of the EEAS and on its 2010 budget, adoption of a comprehensive financial supervision package, amendment of the directive on alternative investment fund managers, approval of a new regulation on credit rating agencies, introduction of the European semester, closer co-operation regarding the EU patent, agreement on the European citizen's initiative, signing of a free trade agreement with South Korea, a compromise on future membership for Serbia, common positions for the biodiversity and climate change conferences in Nagoya and Cancún, and agreement on reforming the Eurovignette directive.[8] In other words, the main results were achieved in the socio-economic, environmental and external action sphere. By contrast, Belgium found limited support for its social policy ambitions; the caretaker nature of its government may have complicated progress on asylum and migration.

In the following sections, we discuss the achievements in more detail. Even if they do not provide a complete picture of the Belgian Presidency, their discussion provides important insights into its focus and approach. It illustrates that economic and financial governance were high on the EU's agenda and that fighting the crisis resulted in the formulation of common answers, in turn increasing the role of the EU and its institutions. Importantly, initiatives like the reform of the Stability and Growth Pact are not discussed because they did not originate from the Belgian Presidency, but from the European Council and its President. The latter's role in the preparations and his political affiliation without doubt facilitated access and co-operation (see above). However, as he had to establish his position and profile, it did not imply free gifts.

The discussion also shows that one of Belgium's most successful instruments was the trilateral dialogue or *trialogue* – that is, the informal negotiations between Commission, Parliament and Council. The Belgian Presidency represented the latter and worked behind the scenes in search of reconciliation and compromise. Where possible, it aimed for legislative texts to be adopted

[8] See, for instance, Van Hecke and Bursens (2011), Ricardi (2010), Beke (2011) and Vos (2011). For an early evaluation, covering the first four months, see Drieskens *et al.* (2010).

after *first reading*. Maintaining good and close relations with the various institutions was thus crucial for success.

Financial Supervision Structure

Building upon the advice of an expert group chaired by Jacques de Larosière, the Commission suggested the creation of a new financial supervisory structure in September 2009. In order to narrow down the differences between the Council and the Parliament, the Belgian Presidency organized various trialogues during the summer. Belgium's approach proved successful: the Economic and Financial Affairs Council (Ecofin) reached agreement on 7 September; the Parliament endorsed it on 22 September (Council, 2010a). The European Parliament managed to bring the decision closer in line with the Larosière Report, after the Commission and the Council tried to tone down the language on the powers of the new bodies.

Three European supervisory authorities (ESAs) were created with the aim of ensuring oversight of banks, markets, insurance and pensions: the European Banking Authority (EBA, based in London), the European Securities and Market Authority (ESMA, based in Paris) and the European Insurance and Occupational Pensions Authority (EIOPA, based in Frankfurt).[9] Those agencies, established in January 2011, are to work together with the national services and the European Systematic Risk Board (ESRB). The ESRB was created as part of the same package. It is located in Frankfurt and chaired by the president of the European Central Bank (ECB) in the five first years. Taking a macroeconomic perspective, it is responsible for overseeing the risks that arise from macroeconomic developments and from developments within the financial sector as a whole.

Investment Funds and Credit Rating Agencies

Also in the realm of enhancing supervision, the Belgian Presidency secured an agreement on a directive on alternative investment fund managers, concluding a year of heavy debate, notably between France and the United Kingdom (Council, 2010b). Following a series of trialogues, draft proposals and position papers, the Council reached a consensus on 19 October. The Parliament approved the compromise on 11 November. As a result of the measure, fund managers, including managers of hedge and private equity funds, will face stronger capital and disclosure requirements from 2013 onwards. To increase investor protection, a so-called 'passport'

[9] Technically speaking, the authorities were established by transforming existing committees.

will be introduced for funds operating throughout the EU, even if registered outside the EU.

Likewise, the rules for credit rating agencies were strengthened during the Belgian term. Following the approval of a draft regulation by the European Parliament on 15 December, such agencies must comply with higher standards and are subject to direct ESMA supervision (see above).[10]

European Union Budget and European Semester

The adoption of the EU's 2011 budget, the first to be adopted under the Lisbon Treaty, required a tour-de-force performance by the Belgian Presidency. The team found itself sandwiched between a maximalist Parliament, which favoured an increase with 6.2 per cent, and minimalist countries like the Netherlands and the United Kingdom, which advocated budgetary restraint. The Conciliation Committee failed to reach an agreement before the deadline of 15 November. As a result, the Commission had to come up with a new draft, leaving little time for the Belgian Presidency to achieve success.

A breakthrough was announced at the eleventh hour. A trialogue meeting on 6 December paved the way for endorsement of the second draft by both the Council (on 10 December) and the Parliament (on 15 December). The latter supported a limited increase of the budget with 2.91 per cent (a number suggested by David Cameron at the European Council meeting in October) in exchange for political guarantees from the next four Presidencies – Hungary, Poland, Denmark and Cyprus – on involvement in the discussions on the next multi-annual financial framework (2014–20) (Council, 2010c). Without an agreement before the end of the year, a system of provisional twelfths would have been applied.[11]

Concerning national budgets, Ecofin finalized Spain's work on the European semester of policy co-ordination and amended the code of conduct of the Stability and Growth Pact on 7 September. As a result, Member States have to submit their annual budget plans for joint review in the first semester of the year (Council, 2010a).

European Union Patent

The icing on the Belgian cake would have been an agreement on the creation of the Community patent. The Belgian Presidency failed to reach consensus, but a significant step was made in the direction of enhanced co-operation. Searching for agreement, it visited the Member States opposing a

[10] *Bulletin Quotidien Europe*, 16 December 2010, p. 9.

[11] In this case, every month one-twelfth of the budget appropriations for the previous financial year are to be spent.

three-language regime for translation of patents and faced tough questions in Rome and Madrid. Countries like the Czech Republic, Cyprus and Poland also expressed their doubts. No agreement was reached despite marathon sessions in Brussels and intense lobbying in Paris and Berlin. Faced with deadlock, a group of 11 Member States formally requested to proceed by enhanced co-operation (Council, 2010d). Their letter to the Commission was answered positively on 14 December, adding the dossier to the list of Belgian Presidency successes.

European External Action Service

The Belgian Presidency was responsible for negotiating the instruments necessary for the functioning of the EEAS – that is, for its staffing, financing and budget. A political agreement on the EEAS was reached on 21 June under the Spanish Presidency. Thanks to the agreement, the Belgian team was given a head start. However, like its predecessor, it would meet a rather assertive European Parliament.

The Parliament endorsed the agreement that was reached in Madrid on 8 July; the Council did so on 26 July after the Commission had given its consent on 10 July. Yet it was only after the Parliament adopted the staff, financial and budget regulations on 20 October and the Council approved the revised regulations on 18 November that the new diplomatic service could formally start on 1 December – exactly one year after the entry into force of the Lisbon Treaty (Council, 2010e).

The Belgian team worked equally hard in the absence of agreement as it did to consolidate agreement; it chaired working groups, even Council meetings, and represented the EU externally. However, it did not represent the EU in the general debate of the UN General Assembly. In fact, the EU did not speak at all, but merely distributed a statement. The majority of the UN membership had not responded positively to its request for additional rights and privileges that would have allowed Van Rompuy to address the meeting. For its part, the Belgian Presidency was unable to force a breakthrough – not even by introducing amendments that would have opened the door for granting other regional actors similar rights and privileges.

Citizen's Initiative and Comitology

As regards the implementation of the Lisbon Treaty, the Belgian Presidency aimed to make progress on the implementation of another two novelties: the citizen's initiative and the new rules on comitology.

The citizen's initiative aims to strengthen the involvement of citizens in EU policy-making, giving the right to petition the Commission to consider legislative proposals. The most difficult question in the discussions was that of identification – that is, whether or not identity card numbers are required to exercise that right. A compromise was reached in trialogue on 30 November, allowing the Member States to make their own decision (Council, 2010f). The Council endorsed the agreement on 14 December; the Parliament followed one day later.

Less visible but even more important, that same week, the Presidency managed to conclude in first reading another agreement necessary for the operationalization of the Lisbon Treaty. On 16 December, the Parliament approved a regulation on comitology, aligning, for instance, the common commercial policy (notably the anti-dumping/subsidy measures) with the comitology framework (Commission, 2010).

Serbia and South Korea

While its role has turned inwards, it would be a misunderstanding to say that the Lisbon Treaty removed the rotating Presidency from the EU's external action. The following examples illustrate its continuing presence.

The Belgian Presidency finalized negotiations on the free trade agreement with South Korea. It convinced Italy to lift its veto in return for a six-month delay of implementation.[12] As a result, the agreement was signed on 6 October, in the margins of the eighth Asia–Europe Meeting, the largest international event hosted by the Belgian Presidency.

Belgium also found an acceptable modus vivendi on EU membership for Serbia. The Netherlands previously blocked any decision in that direction as Serbia avoided full co-operation with the International Criminal Tribunal for the Former Yugoslavia. Other countries, however, wanted to reward Serbia for its constructive attitude on Kosovo in the UN context. A compromise was suggested and accepted, introducing a staged approach in which every step requires a unanimous decision. Following the agreement, the Council invited the Commission on 25 October to submit an opinion on the membership application of Serbia (Council, 2010e). The Dutch government was offered a second concession: the Commission would not submit its opinion before the second part of 2011.

Nagoya, Cancún and Eurovignette

Drawing lessons from the Copenhagen debacle, the Belgian Presidency worked towards common positions for the biodiversity and climate change conferences in Nagoya (18–29 October) and Cancún (29 November–10

[12] *Bulletin Quotidien Europe*, 7 October 2010, p. 4.

December) (Council, 2010g). The Belgian Presidency was quite pleased with the outcome of both conferences, but experienced a hardening of the Commission's position on external representation. An ad hoc formula of representation was used in Nagoya, yet the Belgian Presidency managed to leave for Cancún with an agreement on an integrated delegation for the EU. In fact, for Cancún, the main (and for the press, most visible) question was if a federal or regional minister would head the Belgian delegation.[13]

On road use charges for heavy goods vehicles, and thus related to the climate theme, the Belgian Presidency reached a political agreement at Council level on 15 October. Ending two years of deadlock, the Belgian Presidency managed to conclude an agreement on revision of the Eurovignette directive, but left the successful conclusion in second reading for the Hungarian Presidency (Council, 2010h).

Conclusions

In the second semester of 2010, Belgium assumed the rotating Presidency for the twelfth time. The entry into force of the Lisbon Treaty provided a different context to Belgium's previous tenures. The Belgian Presidency decided to play a facilitating role, ensuring full implementation of the new rules and procedures by the end of the term. It would bring the EU closer again to Brussels, to its structures and method. However, the Lisbon reality was only a partial reality when Belgium took over. In consequence, like René Magritte's iconic painting *La Trahison des Images*, Belgium's Presidency was modelled as a post-Lisbon interpretation of the rotating Presidency, but often showed characteristics of a pre-Lisbon one.[14]

As the country of surrealism, Belgium managed the Presidency with a caretaker government for the complete duration of the term. Yet the impact of the domestic crisis remained limited. Its experience confirmed that the rotating Presidency remains a crucial actor in EU decision-making, chairing most Council configurations, including formations like Ecofin, which gained importance following the EU's renewed focus on financial and economic governance. Its suggests that the Lisbon Treaty may have diminished the external role of the rotating Presidency on paper, but increased its internal representation and co-ordination roles in practice, bringing it closer to how it was conceptualized in the early years of integration.

[13] De Morgen, 25 October 2010.

[14] Belgian surrealist artist René Magritte pictured a pipe and added the text *Ceci n'est pas une pipe*, i.e. *This is not a pipe*.

References

Barber, T. (2010) 'The Appointments of Herman Van Rompuy and Catherine Ashton'. *JCMS*, Vol. 48, s1, pp. 55–67.

Beke, M. (2011) 'Review of the Belgian Rotating Presidency: From Political to Administrative Leadership'. *Analysis of the Real Institute Elcano* (*ARI*), 16/2011. Available at: «http://www.realinstitutoelcano.org/wps/portal/rielcano_eng/Print?WCM_GLOBAL_CONTEXT=/wps/wcm/connect/elcano/Elcano_in/Zonas_in/ARI16-2011».

Belgian Presidency (2010a) 'Belgisch voorzitterschap-programma. Samenvatting – versie 16 juni 2010'. Post-briefing item, 16 June.

Belgian Presidency (2010b) 'Joining Forces for a Europe in Action: An Assessment of the Belgian Presidency of the Council of the European Union (1 July–31 December 2010)'. Post-briefing item, 20 December.

Belgische Senaat en Kamer van Volksvertegenwoordigers (2008) 'Voorbereiding van het Belgisch voorzitterschap van de Europese Unie in 2010. Verslag namens het Federaal Adviescomité voor de Europese Aangelegenheden uitgebracht door Mevrouw Delvaux (S) en de Heer De Croo (K)'. 4-986/1 Senaat – 52 1676/1 Kamer, 9 December.

Beyers, J. and Bursens, P. (2006) 'The European Rescue of the Federal State: How Europeanization Shapes the Belgian State'. *West European Politics*, Vol. 29, No. 5, pp. 1057–78.

Commission of the European Communities (2010) 'Comitology: new rules for the Commission's implementing powers'. IP 17876/10 (PRESSE 349), 14 December.

Council of the European Union (2010a) '3030th Council Meeting: Economic and Financial Affairs'. 13161/10 (PRESSE 229; PR CO 14), 7 September.

Council of the European Union (2010b) 'Hedge Funds: Council Sets Out Its Position with a View to Consulting Negotiations with the Parliament'. 15095/10 (PRESSE 280), 19 October.

Council of the European Union (2010c) 'Council Approves New Draft EU Budget for 2011'. 17764/10 (PRESSE 343), 10 December.

Council of the European Union (2010d) '3057th Council Meeting: Competitiveness'. 17668/1/10 REV 1 (PRESSE 339; PR CO 45), 10 December.

Council of the European Union (2010e) '3040th Council Meeting: General Affairs'. 15349/10 (PRESSE 285; PR CO 28), 25 October.

Council of the European Union (2010f) 'Council Approves Compromise with Parliament on European Citizen's Initiative'. 17876/10 (PRESSE 349), 14 December.

Council of the European Union (2010g) '3030th Council Meeting: Environment'. 14825/10 (PRESSE 276; PR CO 24), 14 October.

Council of the European Union (2010h) '3037th Council Meeting: Transport, Telecommunications and Energy'. 14826/10 (PRESSE 277; PR CO 25), 15 October.

Drieskens, E., Van Hecke, S. and Bursens, P. (2010) 'The 2010 Belgian Presidency: Driving in the EU's Back Seat'. *Swedish Institute for European Policy*

Studies (*SIEPS*) 2010:2op. Available at: «http://www.sieps.se/sites/default/files/2010_2op.pdf».

Kerremans, B. and Drieskens, E. (2002) 'The Belgian Presidencies of 2001', *JCMS*, Vol. 40, s1, pp. 49–51.

Ricardi, F. (2010) 'Results and Lessons from Belgian Presidency of the Council of the EU'. *Bulletin Quotidien Europe*, No. 10283, 23 December, p. 3.

Vanackere, S. (2010a) 'Belgian Presidency of the Council of the European Union: Press Conference, 25 June 2010'. Press conference by Steven Vanackere, Brussels, 25 June.

Vanackere, S. (2010b) 'België voorzitter van de Europese Unie'. Radio interview with Steven Vanackere in De Ochtend (Radio 1), 1 July.

Van Hecke, S. and Bursens, P. (2011) 'The EU, Belgium and the 2010 Presidency: Back to Basics'. Available at: «http://www.euractiv.com/en/future-eu/eu-belgium-and-2010-presidency-back-basics-analysis-500710».

Vos, H. (2011) 'The Belgian Presidency of the European Union in Retrospect'. Available at: «http://www.boell.de/downloads/The_Belgian_Presidency_of_the_European_Union_in_Retrospect.pdf».

JCMS 2011 Volume 49 Annual Review pp. 103–121

Governance and Institutions: Implementing the Lisbon Treaty in the Shadow of the Euro Crisis

DESMOND DINAN
George Mason University and European University Institute

Introduction

The word 'crisis' is much used and abused in the rhetoric of European integration. The rejection by French and Dutch voters of the Constitutional Treaty in 2005, and then by Irish voters of the Lisbon Treaty in 2008, seemingly threw the European Union (EU) into crisis. The crisis was both issue-specific – how to ensure ratification of a Treaty that had been painstakingly negotiated (and renegotiated) over a number of years – and chronic – how to close the yawning gap between the governed and the governing in the EU. The successful outcome of the second Irish referendum on the Lisbon Treaty resolved the former crisis but not the latter, of which the ratification difficulties were a symptom rather than a cause. The Lisbon Treaty itself contained a number of innovations that sought to address the chronic crisis of EU legitimacy – notably the citizens' initiative and a role for national parliaments as guardians of subsidiarity. Like many other parts of the multifaceted new Treaty, these innovations will take some time to affect EU governance.

In the meantime, the period of post-Lisbon Treaty consolidation – the lengthy Treaty implementation stage – was overshadowed by another crisis, this one potentially more serious than the narrowly defined ratification crisis. The global financial crisis was already simmering at the time of the first Irish referendum on the Lisbon Treaty. Indeed, the acceleration of the financial crisis and its impact on Ireland may have been decisive in convincing a majority of voters in the second referendum, in October 2009, to approve the

Treaty (see Dinan, 2010). By that time, however, the financial crisis was stoking the sovereign debt crisis in Greece that soon escalated into a broader crisis for the eurozone and for the EU as a whole. As a result, the emerging eurozone crisis, together with ongoing implementation of the Lisbon Treaty, dominated governance and institutional affairs in the EU in 2010.

The European Council exists in part as a crisis management mechanism. That was its original *raison d'être*. If the European Council had not existed in 2010 – a fanciful notion, given the development of European integration since the origin of the European Council in the mid-1970s – it would have had to have been invented. Who else but the national leaders had the stature and authority to confront the eurozone crisis? At the same time, the European Council was undergoing an important institutional reform. Instead of being chaired by the head of state or government of the country in the rotating Presidency, under the terms of the new Treaty the European Council acquired its own, full-time President, elected for a period of two-and-a-half years, renewable once. Herman Van Rompuy, a former prime minister of Belgium, became the first full-time European Council President on 1 December 2009, as soon as the Treaty came into effect (see Barber, 2010). The combination of the new presidential system and the seriousness of the eurozone crisis put the European Council under a brighter than usual spotlight in 2010.

The EP (European Parliament) was another institution that attracted significant attention in 2010 for reasons related to implementation of the Lisbon Treaty rather than the eurozone crisis. As was the case with previous Treaty reforms, the Lisbon Treaty greatly enhanced the EP's legislative, budgetary and oversight authority. Also following past practice, the EP lost little time instrumentalizing its new authority. In some cases, the EP leveraged provisions in the Lisbon Treaty to influence the outcome of institutional matters in which, according to the Treaty, it should have had only a marginal role. Such was the case with the EEAS (European External Action Service), one of the most striking innovations in the Lisbon Treaty, with potentially important policy implications. The establishment of the EEAS was a key development for the EU in 2010. Regardless of how well or badly the EEAS fares, the story of its coming into being sheds an interesting light on inter-institutional dynamics and on institutional and national prerogatives within the EU.

This article on EU governance and institutions in 2010 highlights implementation of the Lisbon Treaty in light of the eurozone crisis, with particular reference to the functioning of the European Council. It also examines the new position of High Representative of the Union for Foreign Affairs and Security Policy and Vice-President of the Commission, as well as the establishment of the EEAS. Other noteworthy governance and institutional developments in 2010 include the diminution in political importance of the rotating

Council Presidency; the decline of the General Affairs Council; the corresponding rise of Ecofin (the Economic and Financial Affairs Council) and especially of the Eurogroup (the informal Council of eurozone finance ministers); the ongoing erosion of the Commission's political influence, though not its procedural and technical importance; and the relentless march of the EP, well illustrated by the story of the EEAS and the new Commission–Parliament Framework Agreement which, according to the Council, exceeds the terms of the Lisbon Treaty and upsets the EU's institutional balance.

I. The Post-Lisbon European Council

Institutions matter, as do the people who run them. The first incumbents of new institutions are especially influential in shaping the institutions themselves. Herman Van Rompuy seemed the ideal choice for the first full-time President of the European Council – a job that amounts to 'herding cats', as Richard Corbett, a member of Van Rompuy's private office, described it (European Policy Centre, 2011). The feline analogy highlights the individualistic nature of the European Council – a body consisting of highly ambitious, often egotistical politicians, who are paramount on the national political stage. In contrast to the image of a hard-charging national leader, Van Rompuy appears avuncular and unassuming. Nevertheless, he has vast experience of national politics and is ambitious for high office. Having already, as prime minister of Belgium, been a member of the European Council, he knew what to expect as the institution's first standing President.

Van Rompuy's leadership style is open and informal. He frequently speaks publicly about his job and about developments in the EU; he is accessible to the media. In January 2011, Van Rompuy produced the first of a new series of annual reports, *The European Council in 2010*, covering the institution's activities during the previous calendar year. Although glossy and apparently superficial, it is a useful publication that gives a flavour of Van Rompuy's disarming manner. Thus, he described the 7 May summit at which eurozone leaders agreed to establish a mechanism to preserve financial stability as having unexpectedly become 'one of those decisive dinners which seem to be the secret of the Union's success' (European Council, 2011a, p. 6).

Much to the dismay of Commission President José Manuel Barroso, the European Council Presidency soon upstaged the Commission Presidency in Brussels and beyond. A striking example of this was the decision of eurozone leaders at their special summit in March on the eve of the regularly scheduled European Council meeting to 'ask the President of the European Council to establish, in co-operation with the Commission, a Task Force with representatives of the Member States, the rotating Presidency and the ECB (European Central Bank), to present to the Council, before the end of this year, the measures needed to [remedy the eurozone crisis], exploring all options to reinforce the legal framework' (Council, 2010). The new body therefore became the 'Van Rompuy Task Force' – not the 'Barroso Task Force'.

Van Rompuy did not feel threatened by Barroso because he knew that he (Van Rompuy) was in the ascendant. At Van Rompuy's suggestion, the two Presidents agreed to get together once a week to discuss EU affairs. They also agreed upon a set of 'Practical Arrangements between President Van Rompuy and President Barroso Regarding External Representation of the European Union at Presidential Level'. The arrangements refer specifically to EU participation in international summits such as the G8 and G20: both Presidents would participate but, depending on the topic, only one would 'state the position of the EU' (CEPS *et al.*, 2010, pp. 76, 78–9). This would appear to fly in the face of the Lisbon Treaty's goal of streamlining the EU's external representation, and may well bemuse or befuddle the EU's international interlocutors.

Playing second fiddle to Van Rompuy emphasized the extent of Barroso's limited strategic influence within the EU generally. Owing to a combination of personal and political developments during the past 20 years, the Commission Presidency has lost much of its effectiveness within the European Council. Casting covetous eyes at Van Rompuy's prominence, Barroso may well have thought about making a bid to become the next European Council President. Hailing from a small, southern European Member State would be advantageous, although being a Christian Democrat like Van Rompuy might not (European socialists will want one of their own to succeed Van Rompuy). From the perspective of 2010, however, it was impossible to gauge Barroso's intentions or prospects.

Upon becoming President, Van Rompuy sought to set his stamp on the post-Lisbon European Council by calling for an extraordinary meeting in early February, in the picturesque setting of the Solvay Library in Brussels, to discuss Europe 2020, the new strategy for growth and jobs. Inevitably, the mounting debt crisis in Greece dominated the discussion, just as the broader eurozone crisis overshadowed every meeting of the European Council in 2010. Altogether, the European Council met six times during the year: five times formally and once informally (in February). There were also two meetings of the leaders of the eurozone, which Van Rompuy chaired: one in March, just before a formal meeting of the European Council; the other held separately in May (European Council, 2011a, p. 5).

Van Rompuy's relations with national leaders are complicated. He is their peer but also their servant. He knows from experience in the European Council that the 27 national leaders are equal, but two – the president of France and chancellor of Germany – are more equal than the others. Moreover, Van Rompuy owes his position to President Nicolas Sarkozy and Chancellor Angela Merkel, who blocked the appointment of Luxembourg Prime Minister Jean-Claude Juncker, the preferred candidate of most of the other national leaders. Understandably bitter, Juncker has been exceptionally critical of Merkel's and Sarkozy's bilateral initiatives and behaviour within the European Council with regard to the eurozone crisis. He is also critical of what he sees as Van Rompuy's passivity as European Council President. 'If I had become President of the European Council', Juncker said in January 2011, 'it might have exacerbated the conflict [over the eurozone crisis] within the EU. I wouldn't have been content merely summarizing the views of the other heads of state and government. Although I come from a small Member State, I like to say what I think. I see myself as a driving force rather than a follower' (*Spiegel*, 2011).

It would be hard for a European Council President from a small Member State, even someone as forceful as Juncker, to be a 'driving force' in that institution. Fear that a President coming from a big Member State might indeed become a driving force fuelled misgivings among the small Member States during the protracted Treaty reform process about the proposed new position. Similarly, the unwillingness of the big Member States to risk having one of their own become a driving force as European Council President, possibly to the detriment of many of the big Member States, led them to support only candidates from the small Member States. With the possible exception of Juncker, none of the national leaders want the European Council President to be a driving force. At most they are hoping for a good conductor: someone capable of bringing out the best in a large and unwieldy orchestra.

It has been difficult for Van Rompuy to conduct the European Council successfully in the presence of two headstrong soloists, Merkel and Sarkozy, whose own relationship is rocky. Despite deep personal differences between them and the divergent policy preferences of their respective governments, Merkel and Sarkozy had little choice in 2010 but to act together in response to the eurozone crisis. At first they seemed far apart. Taking a characteristically French position, Sarkozy advocated a form of economic governance that privileged the role of national leaders of the eurozone Member States and implied a degree of political interference in the functioning of the ECB. Taking an equally characteristic German position, Merkel dismissed the idea of new institutions, especially regular meetings of eurozone national leaders, and fiercely defended the independence of the ECB. As for the immediate crisis, Sarkozy favoured an exclusively EU bail-out for Greece, whereas Merkel at first recoiled from the idea of a bail-out of any kind. Little wonder that Valéry Giscard d'Estaing and Helmut Schmidt, nostalgic about their duopoly in the early days of the European Council, publicly appealed to Merkel and Sarkozy in May 2010 to strengthen Franco–German ties and 'pursue the direction taken by their predecessors to preserve the security of the euro' (Giscard d'Estaing and Schmidt, 2010).

Apart from the disapproval of such august former leaders, Merkel drew considerable scorn from fellow EU leaders for her initial hands-off approach to the mounting Greek crisis. The chancellor seemed stunned by the enormity of Greece's debt and unaware of its implications for German creditors as well as for the stability of the eurozone. Merkel was highly sensitive to domestic opinion, which grew increasingly critical of economic and monetary union and censorious of Greece. She was equally concerned about the constitutionality of a bail-out, given the critical tone of recent rulings by the German Constitutional Court on EU issues. Merkel's position struck many EU leaders as excessively cautious and even irresponsible. When, eventually, she decided to act, Merkel insisted on IMF (International Monetary Fund) involvement in any bail-out, on assistance to Greece only as a last resort, and on reform of the SGP (Stability and Growth Pact). Merkel was in a strong position to get her way: without Germany – Europe's largest contributor to any potential EU rescue fund – a bail-out would be impossible.

The manner in which Merkel pushed her proposal was typical of the dynamics of the Franco–German relationship and of the European Council. First she convinced Sarkozy, who had opposed IMF involvement because it appeared to imply that the EU was unable to act independently and because it would boost the profile of IMF Director Dominique Strauss-Kahn – a potential rival in the 2012 French presidential election. Merkel and Sarkozy then presented their plan, drawn in part from ideas already floated by others but now packaged as an exclusively Franco–German initiative, to fellow eurozone leaders at a pre-European Council summit on 25 March. Finally, the European Council approved what was, in effect, a fait accompli: the already agreed-upon proposal of the eurozone leaders for a Greek rescue package. Nevertheless, the episode left a bitter aftertaste and cast Merkel as domineering and unyielding; as someone with a narrow national perspective, lacking European vision and uninterested in solidarity among Member States.

Merkel's behaviour, and the forcefulness of the Franco–German tandem, emboldened other national leaders to take a stronger stand. Matters came to a head at the European Council in October, at which national leaders were due to discuss a permanent funding mechanism to succeed the European Financial

Stability Facility, set up in May 2010 and due to expire in 2013. Shortly before the summit, Merkel and Sarkozy met in the French town of Deauville and issued a declaration that they fully expected the European Council subsequently to endorse. Even at the Deauville meeting, Merkel did not have things entirely her own way. Initially she supported the Commission and some of the more fiscally responsible national governments in wanting fines to be imposed automatically on countries that failed to abide by the terms of the SGP. She conceded to Sarkozy that fines need not be automatic but could, instead, be at the discretion of national finance ministers. In return, Sarkozy supported her idea of assigning some of the liability for future financial crises to banks and other private sector creditors. Sarkozy also supported Merkel's call for SGP offenders to lose their voting rights in the Council – an idea that infuriated the governments of the Member States most likely to suffer that sanction. Understandably, those governments would hardly approve revising the Lisbon Treaty to make such a sanction possible.

At the ensuing meeting of the European Council, Merkel therefore dropped her demand concerning the loss of voting rights but won agreement from the other leaders to include a minor change to the Lisbon Treaty authorizing the establishment and possible use of a permanent bail-out mechanism. The thought of changing the Lisbon Treaty and fighting new ratification battles, even for such an apparently benign purpose, filled most EU leaders with dread. Nonetheless, Merkel was adamant: given the Treaty's no-bail-out rule for eurozone members, a Treaty amendment authorizing a permanent bail-out mechanism was essential in order to assuage German public opinion and prevent an unfavourable ruling from the ever-vigilant Constitutional Court.

The details were worked out before and during the December meeting of the European Council. There, national leaders agreed unanimously to amend the Lisbon Treaty in order to establish the ESM (European stability mechanism), including a provision that the mechanism would only 'be activated if indispensable to safeguard the stability of the euro area as a whole' (European Council, 2011b). Who would decide when and if activation was 'indispensable'? At the risk of giving a hostage to fortune, EU leaders had acquiesced in Merkel's demands. Although the proposed amendment would be made using the fast-track reform procedure included in the Lisbon Treaty – on the grounds that the amendment would not increase the Union's competence – ratification was by no means assured. A government could argue, legally, that a referendum was unnecessary for ratification purposes precisely because the amendment did not increase the Union's competence. Yet such an argument would be politically risky for governments to make. And in view of recent experiences with the

Constitutional and Lisbon Treaties, the outcome of any ratification referendum, however technical or seemingly insignificant the proposed Treaty changes, was bound to be uncertain.

Still, given the extent to which national governments dithered and disagreed over their response to the escalating eurozone crisis, it was remarkable that they decided in 2010 first to establish the (temporary) European Financial Stability Facility, then to establish the (permanent) ESM. Van Rompuy was right to assert that 'the decisions we have taken [in the European Council], notably in May, October and December, constitute the biggest reform of the economic and monetary union since the euro was created' (Council, 2011a, p. 6). The political salience of these decisions required action at the top of the EU executive pyramid, in the European Council. Yet Merkel's preponderant influence, initial indecisiveness and subsequent assertiveness irritated other leaders. Her close collaboration with Sarkozy, despite a myriad of differences between them, signalled the centrality of the Franco–German partnership in EU politics and policy-making. David Cameron, the new British prime minister, who attended his first meeting of the European Council in June 2010, may be personally closer to Merkel, but his country's history of EU involvement and position outside the eurozone negate the possibility of a vibrant Anglo–German axis rivalling, let alone supplanting, the essential Franco–German axis.

The other governments' resentment at what looked to them like Franco–German high-handedness, and the fractiousness among national leaders over the eurozone crisis, demonstrated the difficulty of managing the European Council, notwithstanding the reforms in the Lisbon Treaty intended to improve the institution's efficiency. Even so, judged by its handling of the crisis, the European Council was better off with a permanent President rather than the rotating Presidency. Van Rompuy could not stand up to the headstrong leaders of France and Germany, any more than the prime ministers of Spain and Belgium – the countries in the Presidency in 2010 – could have done so. Moreover, the Spanish prime minister's Presidency of the European Council would have been handicapped to some extent by his country's wobbly financial situation, just as the Belgian prime minister's Presidency would have been handicapped by his country's inability to form a new government after the June 2010 parliamentary elections. At least Van Rompuy provided continuity and gave the work of the European Council the appearance of seamlessness and flow at an unexpectedly challenging time. Having become the first holder of a potentially important position during an unprecedented economic and political crisis, Van Rompuy may well grow in office and bequeath to his successor a strong platform on which to influence policy-making at the highest level.

II. The High Representative and the EEAS

Whereas Van Rompuy seemed the ideal choice as the first ever full-time President of the European Council, Catherine Ashton appeared ill-suited as the inaugural High Representative of the Union for Foreign Affairs and Security Policy (see Barber, 2010). Unlike Van Rompuy, whose position was entirely new, Ashton filled a position that already existed, in part, under the pre-Lisbon Treaty regime: that of High Representative for the CFSP (common foreign and security policy). Javier Solana was the sole incumbent of that position, from 1999 to 2009. The contrast between Solana and Ashton at the time of their EU appointments was striking. Solana had been the Spanish foreign minister from 1992 to1995 and Secretary-General of Nato from 1995 to 1999. He had vast experience of Cabinet-level government, of participating in the General Affairs (Foreign Ministers) Council, and of dealing with tricky intra-European and transatlantic security issues under the auspices of Nato. By contrast, Ashton had been in the British Cabinet only from 2007 to 2008, as leader of the House of Lords, and in the Commission only from 2008 to 2009, as a replacement for Peter Mandelson, with responsibility for trade policy. Ashton's year in Brussels was the extent of her international experience.

National leaders were well aware of Ashton's curriculum vitae when they appointed her in November 2009 to the newly elevated position of High Representative. In addition to being responsible for carrying out the CFSP, as Solana had been, Ashton would also have to preside over the Foreign Affairs Council and would be a Commission Vice-President. The fact that the European Council entrusted these heavy responsibilities to someone with little international and Cabinet-level experience suggests that EU leaders had either soaring confidence in Ashton's ability or low expectations of her performance. In fact, EU leaders may not have thought much about the matter. In the usual way of high-level EU appointments, the decision was not considered carefully. Having chosen Van Rompuy – a centre-right politician from a small Member State – as European Council President, it seemed appropriate to choose as the new HR/VP (High Representative and Commission Vice-President) a centre-left politician from a big Member State, and ideally a woman. By common consent it was Britain's turn to make the next high-level appointment. None of the other EU leaders objected when Prime Minister Gordon Brown nominated Ashton. A number of MEPs (Members of the EP) questioned Ashton's suitability at the time of her hearing as Commissioner-designate in January 2010, but the EP as a whole did not object to her appointment.

Not surprisingly, Ashton soon faltered. Her new position was certainly onerous. In some cases it required her, literally, to be in more than one place at the same time. Ashton's early performance cast doubt on the soundness of the Lisbon Treaty's provisions for the HR/VP – how could any one person be expected to do what the Treaty required? – and on the appropriateness of the initial incumbent – surely someone with more experience could do better? Despite their grumbling, it was hard to avoid the conclusion that many national leaders and foreign ministers were pleased to see Ashton flounder – not least because they feared that a strong HR/VP would threaten the preponderance of national players and positions or risk becoming too influential on the European and global stages. One EU leader seemed positively pleased with Ashton's predicament: Commission President Barroso. Already overshadowed by Van Rompuy, Barroso did not want to become subordinate politically to Ashton, who after all was a Commission *Vice*-President.

Apart from the incumbent's qualifications and qualities, the success of the HR/VP and of the Lisbon Treaty's external relations provisions would depend in large part on the EEAS. Considering the potential importance of the EEAS both for the conduct of EU foreign policy and the EU's institutional architecture, the Treaty's stipulations about the new Service are surprisingly short. Article 27(3) TEU simply states that:

> In fulfilling [her] mandate, the High Representative shall be assisted by a European External Action Service. This service shall work in co-operation with the diplomatic services of the Member States and shall comprise officials from relevant departments of the General Secretariat of the Council and of the Commission as well as staff seconded from national diplomatic services of the Member States. The organisation and functioning of the European External Action Service shall be established by a decision of the Council. The Council shall act on a proposal from the High Representative after consulting the European Parliament and after obtaining the consent of the Commission.

Although the EEAS emerged out of the Constitutional Convention of 2002–03, there was little public discussion among EU politicians and officials about its establishment until after the successful Irish referendum on the Lisbon Treaty, in October 2009. No sooner was ratification of the Treaty secure, however, than first the EP, followed closely by the Swedish Council Presidency, produced reports on the putative EEAS (Council, 2009; European Parliament, 2009). The fact that both reports appeared so quickly and so close together, and differed significantly on aspects of the Service's organization and composition, suggested that an inter-institutional dispute was brewing.

Yet the Council failed to appreciate the extent of the EP's likely involvement in the issue. After all, the Treaty required only that the Council *consult* the EP with respect to setting up the EEAS – a notoriously weak obligation. The Council had long resisted the EP's efforts to become involved in the CFSP and national governments were careful, when drafting the Lisbon Treaty, not to extend the EP's external relations prerogatives, with the notable exception of trade policy.

Nevertheless, experience should have taught the Council that the EP is adroit and persistent in the pursuit of greater power – in this case much to the benefit of the EEAS. The EP wanted the new Service to be lodged within the Commission so that the EP would have extensive oversight of it. Even if the new Service was separate from the Commission, the EP would have some leverage over the Council on the question of the EEAS because changes to the Staff Regulation and Financial Regulation are subject to co-decision. Whereas the Council viewed such changes as mere technicalities, the EP linked them to concessions on substantive aspects of the new Service. The EP's leverage was not without limit, however, as the EP wanted the new Service established sooner rather than later and did not want to be blamed for delaying unduly an important institutional innovation for the improvement of EU foreign policy.

In its input into Ashton's proposal for the EEAS, the Council largely ignored the EP, as did the Commission. The High Level Group advising Ashton on the formulation of her proposal comprised representatives of the Council Presidency Trio (the current, preceding and succeeding Presidency countries), the Council Secretariat and the Commission. The EP was not included. No sooner did Ashton present the proposal for a Council Decision in March 2010 than influential MEPs denounced it. Clearly, the lines were drawn for an inter-institutional battle over the EEAS, with the EP pitted against the Council, and the Commission standing on the sidelines.

The ensuing negotiation took the form of a 'quadrilogue', with the four parties being delegates of the HR/VP and representatives of the Commission, the Spanish Council Presidency and the EP. The EP's representatives included Elmar Brok, a veteran MEP with immense experience of intergovernmental conferences, and Guy Verhofstadt, a former Belgian prime minister with immense experience in the European Council. Having such formidable negotiators greatly strengthened the EP's position. The Spanish Presidency finally brokered an agreement at a meeting in Madrid on 21 June. This amended the HR/VP's original proposal in a number of important respects and appended to it a declaration on political accountability and a statement on the basic organization of the EEAS. The two appendices were the most obvious concessions to the EP, which had insisted not only on a degree of political accountability but also on an equal distribution of posts among the three constituencies identified in the relevant Treaty article – the Council Secretariat, the Commission and national diplomatic services – and respect for geographical balance, meaning that the new Member States should be well represented in the EEAS. The latter point was especially important for EP President Jerzy Buzek, a former Polish prime minister.

The remaining steps in establishing the EEAS were procedural: the EP's approval of the Madrid Agreement, in the form of an overwhelming vote in favour of the Brok-Verhofstadt Report on 8 July 2010; a vote of approval of the HR/VP's amended proposal by the College of the Commission on 20 July; and the formal decision of the General Affairs Council on 26 July legally establishing the EEAS. The final step came on 20 October, when the EP approved the legislative texts necessary to launch the Service. In addition to the Staff Regulation and Financial Regulation, these included the 2010 budget. The EEAS eventually began to operate on 1 December 2010, exactly a year after implementation of the Lisbon Treaty (*EurActiv*, 2011).

What the Council had hoped would have been a swift procedure – a decision based on a proposal from the HR/VP, consultation with the EP and the Commission's consent – had turned into a protracted affair. The EP had not succeeded in attaching the EEAS to the Commission. Instead, the EEAS was a 'functionally autonomous body [. . .] separate from the General Secretariat of the Council and from the Commission' (Council, 2010a). The Swedish Presidency report of October 2009 had called the putative EEAS '*sui generis*' – a phrase that did not appear in the Council Decision but that accurately describes the new body. The EEAS is an institution in the political sense, but not within the meaning of the Lisbon Treaty. Nor is it analogous to a Commission service, the Council Secretariat, Coreper (the Committee of Permanent Representatives) or an EU agency (Van Vooren, 2010, pp. 11–13). It is something new entirely.

The Council Decision resolved key political and organizational questions, but did not end jockeying among the institutions or among the Member States over appointments in the upper echelons of the Service, a number of which remained unfilled by the end of 2010. Some politicians complained that Ashton took much too long to fill key positions and that, lacking foreign policy experience, she depended too much on the British Foreign Office. Others complained that the management system of the EEAS, with a Secretary-General under the HR/VP, favoured the French administrative model. Indeed, Pierre Vimont, previously the French ambassador to the United States, became the first Secretary-General. His two deputies were a German and, much to Jerzy Buzek's delight, a Pole. But the fourth member of the top leadership team may prove to be the most influential: Chief

Operating Officer David O'Sullivan, a former Secretary-General of the Commission.

The Commission was uncharacteristically reserved during the negotiations surrounding the EEAS perhaps because it knew that its institutional weight would ultimately prevail in shaping the organizational culture of the new Service. National diplomats would bring their own cultures and styles into the Service, but these would be too numerous and too disparate to have a decisive impact on the Service itself. In keeping with their institution's ethos, officials of the Council Secretariat would be too self-effacing to put their stamp on the EEAS. That would leave the field open to the Commission officials who moved to the new Service, whose working methods would remain firmly set in the mould of their home institution. Unfortunately for the EEAS, those methods are characterized by excessive bureaucratization and a lack of political flair. Under the circumstances, it is difficult to imagine the EEAS becoming a sharp, flexible instrument of EU foreign policy.

In a move that brought the EEAS 'fully [. . .] into being' on 1 January 2011, over 1,600 permanent officials were transferred from the Commission and Council Secretariat to the new Service. These included a majority of staff from the Commission's DG External Relations, which then ceased to exist, and part of DG Development. The remainder of DG Development was merged with DG External Co-operation Programmes into the new DG Development Co-operation (Rapid, 2010a). Earlier, Barroso had shifted responsibility for the European Neighbourhood and Partnership Instrument out of DG External Relations and into DG Enlargement, which he renamed 'Enlargement and European Neighbourhood Policy' in order to emphasize the Commission's continued involvement in external relations issues. Together with the appointment of his former Chief of Staff, João Vale de Almeida, as Head of the EU Delegation in the United States, just before such an appointment would have been subject to the new EEAS regime, Barroso's reconfiguration of the Directorates-General demonstrated his protectiveness of the Commission's prerogatives in the face of major institutional change.

The EEAS, comprising the Brussels headquarters and 137 Union Delegations in third countries and international organizations, will take a few years to become fully staffed and operational. According to the Council Decision, in 2013 EEAS positions will be open to officials from other EU institutions, including the EP. The HR/VP will review the organization and functioning of the EEAS and may submit a proposal for a revision of the Decision, to be adopted by the Council no later than the beginning of 2014 (Council, 2010a). In the meantime, the world will not stand still and the EEAS will have to prove its worth by helping to strengthen the coherence and effectiveness of

EU foreign policy. That is a tall order, given the nature of the EU and the nature of the EEAS, as the story of its negotiation and formation clearly shows.

The proliferation of foreign policy-related portfolios in a College of one Commissioner per Member State, and the growing external dimension of other portfolios, such as competition and the environment, will continue to pose a challenge for the external action of the EU. In April 2010, as part of an effort to improve co-ordination within the Commission, the College approved the formation of a 'Group of Commissioners' on external relations chaired by Ashton and including not only Piebalgs (Development), Füle (Enlargement and Neighborhood Policy), Georgieva (International Co-operation, Humanitarian Aid and Crisis Response), but also De Gucht (Trade) and Rehn (Economic and Monetary Affairs), with the possible association of others at a later stage (for a full list of Commissioners in the second Barroso Commission, see Dinan, 2010). The Groups of Commissioners are intended to ensure better internal organization and the effective preparation of key initiatives. In the case of external relations, Ashton is the lead Commissioner, whose group acts on the basis of a mandate from Barroso setting out its purpose and the 'products' to be delivered (Commission, 2010).

On the Council side, Ashton has more autonomy and authority. Whereas Solana was a servant of the Council, Ashton is in charge (she presides over the Foreign Affairs Council). The foreign minister in the Council Presidency has therefore lost a key responsibility, while continuing to preside over the General Affairs Council, which co-ordinates other aspects of EU policy. Under the terms of the Lisbon Treaty, foreign ministers no longer automatically attend meetings of the European Council, whereas Ashton is a non-voting member. To compound matters for the foreign ministers, the seriousness of the eurozone crisis elevated the importance of Ecofin, the Economic and Financial Affairs Council, and especially the Eurogroup, the Economic and Finance Ministers whose countries are in the eurozone, at the expense of the General Affairs Council.

III. Institutional Balance

In the traditional analysis of inter-institutional relations, the Commission and the EP were allies, lined up on the supranational side against the Council, which exemplified intergovernmentalism. Such a perception, never entirely accurate, is completely anachronistic, not least because the Council is a central part of the EU's supranational framework. As for institutional balance, the EP's leadership now sees the Commission neither as a partner nor a rival, but as a lesser entity in a new political landscape dominated by the Council and the EP, locked in a conflictual relationship. Despite ritualistic calls for a strong Commission, EP leaders have been chipping away at the Commission's political influence and institutional authority ever since the Santer Commission resigned, in 1999, under pressure from the EP.

The year 2010 produced more evidence of the EP's relentlessness towards the Commission, especially during the hearings for the second Barroso College and the contemporaneous negotiation of the new Commission–EP Framework Agreement. The performance of the Commissioners-designate before their respective parliamentary committees in January 2010 varied greatly amongst the carry-overs from the outgoing team as well as the new nominees. The EP pressed for the removal of the Bulgarian Commissioner-designate, who performed poorly at her hearing and against whom there were allegations of conflict of interest. Fortunately for Barroso, the Bulgarian government did not stand by the beleaguered nominee, who soon withdrew. Fortunately also, her replacement, Kristalina Georgieva, performed well at her hearing in early February. That paved the way for the EP to approve the new Commission, by 488 to 137 votes, with 72 abstentions, on 9 February (*EurActiv*, 2010). Nevertheless, the EP had secured a scalp, signalling to the Commission, just as it had five years previously, that the hearings and approval process could not be taken for granted.

Immediately before voting on the new Commission, the EP voted on and approved the substance of a new Framework Agreement between the two institutions (European Parliament, 2010). The timing was not coincidental. Framework Agreements on working relations between the Commission and the EP have existed since 1990 and are updated every five years. Ordinarily the negotiations for the 2010 update would not have begun until the middle of the year. By negotiating the new Agreement six months early, however, and implicitly linking approval of the Commission and approval of the Agreement, the EP greatly strengthened its leverage over Barroso. Having decided on the substance of the Agreement by February, the Commission and EP negotiators finalized the text in June. The Presidents of the two institutions signed the Agreement in October, giving it the legal standing of a non-legislative act (European Union, 2010).

The new Agreement needed to take account of the Lisbon Treaty, which enhanced the EP's budgetary, legislative and oversight roles. Yet the EP seemed to have wrung concessions from the Commission that went beyond the arrangements required to ensure that the new Treaty provisions worked smoothly. The Council certainly thought so. In August 2010, at the request of Coreper, the Council's Legal Service reviewed the draft Framework Agreement. Coreper discussed the resulting report in September and October, and agreed with the Legal Service that the Council should not accept the proposed Agreement because of its institutional, political and legal shortcomings. Coreper therefore recommended that the Council adopt a statement expressing concern about the potential impact of the Agreement, which the Council did, as an 'A' item (meaning without discussion), on 21 October, the day after Barroso and Buzek signed the Agreement (Council, 2010b, c).

In its statement, the Council claimed that 'several provisions of the Framework Agreement have the effect of modifying the institutional balance set out in the Treaties, according the European Parliament prerogatives that are not provided for in the Treaties and limiting the autonomy of the Commission and its President'. The Council was particularly concerned about the provisions on international agreements, infringement proceedings against Member States and transmission of classified information to the EP. The statement concluded forcefully that 'the Framework Agreement cannot be applied to the Council. The Council will submit to the Court of Justice any act or action of the European Parliament or of the Commission performed in application of the provisions of the Framework Agreement that would have an effect contrary to the interests of the Council and the prerogatives conferred upon it by the Treaties' (Council, 2010c).

The Council's statement was a remarkable rejoinder, especially as the Commission considered that the Agreement was 'in full respect of the balance between the institutions as defined by the Treaties' (Rapid, 2010b). From the Council's perspective, the Commission seemed to have acquiesced, in the Commission–EP Framework Agreement, in its own emasculation. By contrast, the EP saw the new Agreement as a fair reflection of the EU's institutional balance. Officially the Commission concurred with the EP, but there were internal murmurings of discontent. Yet overviews of the institutional balance – or imbalance – should not disguise the fact that, in the everyday give and take of inter-institutional relations in 2010, the Commission often held its own. Or that in the gradual emergence of an EEAS organizational culture, the Commission's influence might well predominate. In the grand scheme of the EU's inter-institutional dynamics, however, the impression of Commission subservience to the EP and placement at the bottom of the Commission–Council–EP triangle is difficult to refute.

Conclusions

Events in 2010 once again demonstrated that the European Council – an official EU institution that exists outside the traditional Commission–Council–EP triangle – plays a crucial role in the EU decision-making system.

If nothing else, the ongoing eurozone crisis revealed clearly where the real centre of power in the EU lay. Thus, the crisis put the European Council front and centre of the EU and emphasized the centrality of the Franco–German partnership in tackling highly complex, politically contentious problems. At the same time, the performance of the Franco–German partnership was far from optimal and tended to exasperate other national governments. Apart from its implications for the stability of the eurozone and economic governance in the EU, the euro crisis therefore revealed serious divergences among Member States and rifts among national governments that are bound to make the conduct of EU institutions and governance even more challenging in the years ahead.

Unrelated to the eurozone crisis, 2010 was a year of institutional reform and innovation for the EU due to implementation of the Lisbon Treaty. Thanks to the crisis, however, the usefulness as well as the limitations of the standing European Council Presidency became fully apparent. The EP continued to rise politically in the post-Lisbon institutional framework, most obviously with respect to the Commission during the negotiation of the new Framework Agreement and the Council with respect to the establishment of the EEAS. The coming into being of the EEAS, regardless of the machinations behind it, was the most striking institutional development in the EU in 2010. Despite its rocky start due to predictable internal rivalries and unexpected external challenges, the EEAS represents a major step forward for the conduct of EU external relations. Having finally begun to function, it remains to be seen in 2011 if the much-anticipated EEAS will live up to expectations.

References

Barber, T. (2010) 'The Appointments of Herman van Rompuy and Catherine Ashton'. *JCMS*, Vol. 48, s1, pp. 55–67.

CEPS, Egmont and EPC (2010) *The Treaty of Lisbon: A Second Look at the Institutional Innovations* (Brussels: CEPS, Egmont and EPC). Available at: «http://www.ceps.eu/book/treaty-lisbon-second-look-institutional-innovations».

Commission of the European Communities (2010) Note d'information de M. le President, *SEC*(2010)475, 16 April. Available at: «http://ec.europa.eu/transparency/regdoc/rep/10060/2010/FR/10060-2010-1914-FR-3-0.Pdf».

Council of the European Union (2009) Presidency Report to the European Council on the European External Action Service, 14930/09, Brussels, 23 October.

Council of the European Union (2010a) Decision 2010/427/EU of 26 July establishing the organization and functioning of the European External Action Service, OJL 201/30, 3 August. Available at: «http://eur-lex.europa.eu/LexUriServ/LexUriServ.do?uri=OJ:L:2010:201:0030:0040:EN:PDF».

Council of the European Union (2010b) Note from the General Secretariat to Coreper, 'Framework Agreement on relations between the European Parliament and the Commission', 15018/10, Brussels, 18 October. Available at: «http://register.consilium.europa.eu/pdf/en/10/st15/st15018.en10.pdf».

Council of the European Union (2010c) Press Release, 3039th Council meeting, Employment, Social Policy, Health and Consumer Affairs, Luxembourg, 21 October. Available at: «http://europa.eu/rapid/pressReleasesAction.do?reference=PRES/10/282&format=HTML&aged=0&language=EN».

Dinan, D. (2010) 'Institutions and Governance: A New Treaty, a Newly Elected Parliament and a New Commission'. *JCMS*, Vol. 48, s1, pp. 95–118.

EurActiv (2010) 'The New European Commission', *EurActiv*, 16 March. Available at: «http://www.euractiv.com/en/future-eu/new-european-commission-linksdossier-188498».

EurActiv (2011) 'The EU's New Diplomatic Service', *EurActiv*, 8 March. Available at: «http://www.euractiv.com/en/future-eu/eus-new-diplomatic-service-linksdossier-309484».

European Council (2010) 'Statement by the Heads of State or Government of the Euro Area, 25 March 2010'. Available at: «http://www.consilium.europa.eu/uedocs/cms_data/docs/pressdata/en/ec/113563.pdf».

European Council (2011a) *The European Council in 2010* (Luxembourg: Publications Office of the European Union).

European Council (2011b) 'European Council 16–17 December 2010 conclusions', Brussels, 25 January. Available at: «http://www.consilium.europa.eu/uedocs/cms_data/docs/pressdata/en/ec/118578.pdf».

European Parliament (2009) Committee on Constitutional Affairs, Institutional aspects of creating a European Service for External Action (Brok Report), 2009/2133 INI, 20 October.

European Parliament (2010) 'Framework Agreement on relations between the European Parliament and the Commission', 9 February. Available at: «http://www.europarl.europa.eu/sides/getDoc.do?pubRef=-//EP//TEXT+TA+P7-TA-2010-0009+0+DOC+XML+V0//EN».

European Policy Center (2011) The Implementation of the Lisbon Treaty: One Year On, Report, 12 January. Available at: «http://www.epc.eu/events_rep_details.php?cat_id=6&pub_id=1214».

European Union (2010) 'Interinstitutional Agreements: Framework Agreement on relations between the European Parliament and the European Commission', *Official Journal*, L 304/47, 20 November. Available at: «http://eur-lex.europa.eu/LexUriServ/LexUriServ.do?uri=OJ:L:2010:304:0047:0062:EN:PDF».

Giscard d'Estaing, V. and Schmidt, H. (2010) 'L'appel de Giscard et Schmidt', *Le Point*, 27 May. Available at: «http://vge-europe.eu/public/Appel_Giscard-Schmidt.pdf».

Rapid (2010a) 'A New Step in the Setting-Up of the EEAS: Transfer of Staff on 1 January 2011', press release, IP/10/1769, Brussels, 21 December. Available at:

«http://europa.eu/rapid/pressReleasesAction.do?reference=IP/10/1769&format=HTML&aged=0&language=en&guiLanguage=en».

Rapid (2010b) 'Commission and Parliament Sign Revised Framework Agreement', press release, IP/10/1358, Brussels, 20 October. Available at: «http://europa.eu/rapid/pressReleasesAction.do?reference=IP/10/1358».

Spiegel (2011) 'Jean-Claude Juncker on Saving the Euro: "It Would be Wrong to Create Taboos" '. *Spiegel*, 1 January. Available at: «http://www.spiegel.de/international/europe/0,1518,741183,00.html».

Van Vooren, B. (2010) *A Legal–Institutional Perspective on the European External Action Service* (The Hague: T.M.C. Asser Instituut Inter-university Research Centre).

JCMS 2011 Volume 49 Annual Review pp. 123–143

Internal Market: Regulating the So-Called 'Vultures of Capitalism'*

JAMES BUCKLEY
European Parliament
DAVID HOWARTH
University of Edinburgh

Introduction

The 2010 internal market legislative agenda was dominated by financial regulation. Nine new European Union directives and regulations, drawn up in the immediate aftermath of the financial crisis in late 2008 and 2009, were adopted during the year and progress was made on several more. The focus on financial services reflects the strong political and populist backlash in many EU Member States against financial institutions, and banks in particular. Governments individually and collectively – at both the EU and the international levels – looked to the reinforcement and creation of mechanisms that would decrease the risk of systemic collapse and the future burden of bank failures upon governments and taxpayers. From a non-transparent past, dominated by European and national civil servants and lobbyists (see Mugge, 2011), EU financial regulation took centre stage in EU-level policy-making. Tackling national and international financial instability became high politics (see also Hodson's and Marsh's contributions to this volume). The increased political salience of financial services also came with its own dangers – notably rushed and badly designed legislation. Yet, despite the intensity of political will, the complexity of EU-level legislation and fundamental disagreements among Member States meant delays to the adoption of most

* The authors would like to thank Tim Haughton for his helpful comments. James Buckley has contributed to this article in a personal capacity. From 2009 to 2011, James worked in the European Parliament as Assistant to an S&D MEP, who was a member of the Economics and Monetary Affairs Committee and focused most of his work on financial regulatory matters.

major pieces of legislation. The impressive legislative activity at the EU level in the area of financial services regulation yielded surprisingly limited results in 2009, with marginal likely impact upon the activities of financial sector institutions (Buckley and Howarth, 2010).

This negative assessment must be somewhat modified for the EU legislation adopted or developed in 2010. After a brief overview of the legislation adopted or developed during the year, the focus of this article will be on the legislative process surrounding the new directive covering hedge funds and private equity firms: the Alternative Investment Fund Mangers Directive (AIFMD), adopted in late 2010. AIFMD merits study as the first effort to create an EU legal framework for increasingly important and controversial elements of several Member State financial systems. This directive also provides a good case study of the difficulties that the politicization of highly technical financial legislation can bring – notably in terms of poorly designed draft legislation. Further, the adoption of AIFMD merits study as an example of the impact of intense industry lobbying at the EU level – despite the determination of several powerful Member State governments and many Members of the European Parliament (MEPs) to adopt far-reaching legislation. Industrial associations, bolstered by the British government, were able to bring about the adoption of a directive that was reworked significantly from previous versions to diminish the additional constraints and costs imposed on AIFM.

I. Overview of EU Legislative Developments

The supervision package, consisting of seven pieces of legislation adopted on 24 November, ranks as one of the more important legislative achievements adopted in 2010.[1] Three regulations focused on the creation of the European System of Financial Supervisors (ESFS) consisting of the European Supervisory Authorities (ESAs): the European Banking Authority (EBA), the European Securities and Markets Authority (ESMA) and the European Insurance and Occupational Pensions Authority (EIOPA). These Authorities replaced the weaker pre-existing supervisory Committees. An additional regulation created the European Systemic Risk Board (ESRB) and another assigned powers to the European Central Bank (ECB) in relation to the ESRB.[2] An

[1] See also Amtenbrink's contribution on legal developments in this volume.

[2] Regulation (EU) 1092/2010 of the European Parliament and of the Council of 24 November 2010 on European Union macro-prudential oversight of the financial system and establishing a European Systemic Risk Board; Regulation (EU) 1093/2010 of the European Parliament and of the Council of 24 November 2010 establishing a European Supervisory Authority (European Banking Authority), amending Decision 716/2009/EC and repealing Commission Decision 2009/78/EC; Regulation (EU) 1094/2010 of the European Parliament and of the Council of 24 November 2010 establishing a European Supervisory Authority

omnibus directive was adopted to provide the legal framework for the ESAs to operate.

The three new Authorities were to oversee supervision in the banking, securities and insurance markets, but day-to-day oversight of individual companies would remain the responsibility of national supervisors. The ESAs would have the power to draw up harmonized technical standards for national supervisors to apply and they would mediate in the event of disputes between national regulators. The EBA was assigned a significant role on stress-testing EU banks and resolution issues for cross-border systemically important financial institutions (SIFIs). The ESAs were not, however, to supervise financial institutions directly;[3] this was left to national authorities and, in some cases, to cross-border 'colleges' created for specific large banks and insurance companies with a strong international presence. Further, subject to the request of Member States, the Authorities could be assigned greater powers in the event of an 'emergency' situation. The ESRB would be chaired by the President of the ECB and include representatives of national central banks. Its task would be to monitor the build-up of risk at the level of the financial system. There was a significant clash between the European Parliament and the Council and among Member States on the powers of the new Authorities over national supervisors, with notably the United Kingdom opposed to any transfer of powers to the new ESAs (Buckley and Howarth, 2010). While the creation of the Single Rulebook on technical standards for national supervisors can be considered to be potentially significant, the creation of the Authorities was more headline-grabbing than significant in reality. The actual contribution of these bodies to financial stability in the EU remained to be seen. It was unclear how emergency powers over national supervisors would work and very unlikely that they would be used. Further, there were outstanding staffing issues. The ESRB came into existence on 16 December and the ESFS began operation at the start of January 2011.

(European Insurance and Occupational Pensions Authority), amending Decision 716/2009/EC and repealing Commission Decision 2009/79/EC; Regulation (EU) 1095/2010 of the European Parliament and of the Council of 24 November 2010 establishing a European Supervisory Authority (European Securities and Markets Authority), amending Decision 716/2009/EC and repealing Commission; Directive 2010/78/EU of the European Parliament and of the Council of 24 November 2010 amending Directives 98/26/EC, 2002/87/EC, 2003/6/EC, 2003/41/EC, 2003/71/EC, 2004/39/EC, 2004/109/EC, 2005/60/EC, 2006/48/EC, 2006/49/EC and 2009/65/EC in respect of the powers of the European Supervisory Authority (European Banking Authority), the European Supervisory Authority (European Insurance and Occupational Pensions Authority) and the European Supervisory Authority (European Securities and Markets Authority); Decision 2009/77/EC; Council Regulation (EU) 1096/2010 of 17 November 2010 conferring specific tasks upon the European Central Bank concerning the functioning of the European Systemic Risk Board.

[3] One exception is credit rating agencies which will be directly supervised by the ESMA. The ESMA is also likely to be given direct supervisory powers over trade repositories as a result of the Over-the-Counter Derivatives (EMIR) regulation (see below), but this has met resistance from the British government.

The AIFMD, covering managers of hedge funds, private equity firms, real estate and potentially other investment funds, was adopted by the European Parliament on 11 November following a unanimous agreement on a final draft in the Council on 19 October.[4] AIFMD was a controversial directive that split the Council and, to a lesser degree, the Parliament between those wanting stronger restrictions on the activities of AIFM (led by France, Germany and, in the Parliament, the Socialists and Democrats and Greens) and those wanting to maintain a lighter touch regulatory framework (the United Kingdom, Nordic Member States and, in the Parliament, the Alliance of Liberals and Democrats and the European Conservatives and Reformists). It was pushed by the Commission (ordered by Commission President José Manuel Barroso himself) in response to French and German demands. The Commission's stated objective was to create robust and harmonized regulatory standards for all AIFM, and to enhance the transparency of the activities of AIFM and the funds they manage towards investors and public authorities. The Commission argued that 'this would enable Member States to improve the macro-prudential oversight of the sector and to take co-ordinated action as necessary to ensure the proper functioning of financial markets' and 'help to overcome gaps and inconsistencies in existing regulatory frameworks at the national level and to provide a secure basis for the development of the internal market' (FSA, 2010). The AIFMD is considered further below.

The latest amendment to the Capital Requirement Directive (referred to widely as 'CRD3') was adopted on 10 October.[5] In terms of actual impact upon financial institutions, CRD3 is the most significant legislative development agreed during the year. It adopts several agreements reached or anticipated under the Basel III international agreement on guidelines on bank capital requirements which was adopted two months later. Thus, most elements of the directive should not be seen as an EU achievement per se. CRD3 sets the rules on the amount of capital banks must set aside for transactions on their trading books. However, CRD3 went beyond the Basel III provisions subsequently agreed by including provisions on the remuneration of bank staff and the delegation of decision-making powers on remuneration issues to the EBA. Member States and the Parliament and the Council clashed on these rules and the powers assigned to the new EBA, with the British government pushing for more relaxed rules and limited delegation. The Parliament sought

[4] *COM* (2009) 207 final, 'Proposal for a Directive of the European Parliament and of the Council on Alternative Investment Fund Managers', COD/2009/0064. The European Commission published its proposal for the directive on 29 April 2009. A revised proposal was accepted at a meeting of the Economic and Financial Affairs Council (Ecofin) on 19 October 2010.

[5] *SEC* (2009) 974 / 975 final, 'Directive of the European Parliament and of the Council amending Directives 2006/48/EC and 2006/49/EC as regards capital requirements for the trading book and for re-securitisations, and the supervisory review of remuneration policies'.

to transfer clearer monitoring powers to the new EBA to ensure implementation and wanted tighter rules on bonuses, so that these would include less cash and more shares, to be held for at least three years, which conformed to international (G20) guidelines. The Parliament also sought to include rules on claw-backs for long-term underperformance of share price (European Parliament, 2010).

A range of additional legislation was proposed and debated in 2010. The first concerns Investor Compensation Schemes (ICS).[6] This would be a minimum harmonization directive creating an EU framework for the compensation that investors can expect for asset manager/depository failure or malpractice. There appears to be no particular Member State driver. Rather the ICS legislation was pushed by the Commission in response to the heterogeneity of national ICS and in response to issues resulting from the Bernard Madoff scandal.[7] There was general support among Member States for the proposals but concern in certain states where Commission compensation limits would be lower than existing national ones (including the United Kingdom).

Another directive was proposed on Deposit Guarantee Schemes (DGS), a minimum harmonization directive for DGS for bank failure, including cross-border banks.[8] This was a controversial piece of legislation considered necessary to respond to issues emerging in the single market in banking during crises. The DGS directive was driven by the Commission, ostensibly in order to restore consumer confidence in cross-border banks. It was also motivated by the conflict created in late 2008 by differing national practice and unilateral Member State action to prevent bank runs, and more specifically by the failure of Icesave and its impact on British and Dutch account holders. The British and French accepted most elements of the proposed directive, except for Commission requirements that the DGS be pre-funded (the existing scheme in the United Kingdom is post-funded). There were also debates as to how much should go into the DGS fund, how long banks would have to build up the fund, and how it would be administered and utilized. The directive has been resisted by Germany due to the impact on the variety of schemes already in place across its three-tier banking structure. German MEPs had a strong presence on the Parliament's Economic and Monetary Affairs Committee, and the proposed directive's Rapporteur and shadows from the major party

[6] *COM*(2010) 371 final, Proposal for a 'Directive of the European Parliament and of the Council, amending Directive 97/9/EC of the European Parliament and of the Council on investor compensation', 2010/0199 (COD), *SEC*(2010) 845, *SEC*(2010) 846.

[7] Bernard Madoff's wealth management fund amounted to the largest 'Ponzi-scheme' in history that defrauded thousands of investors of billions of dollars, including many based in the EU.

[8] *COM*(2010)368 final, 'Proposal for a Directive of the European Parliament and of the Council on Deposit Guarantee Schemes', 2010/0207 (COD), *COM*(2010)369, *SEC*(2010)835, *SEC*(2010)834.

groups were German. The likely outcome remains uncertain. The strong German resistance to changes to its 'mutual' schemes will probably result in the preservation of existing systems but with EU rules requiring more transparency.

The Commission proposed the Over-the-Counter (OTC) Derivatives (also known as EMIR) regulation which involves shifting where possible OTC derivatives trading to central clearing, the creation of rules for establishing a central counter party (CCP) and EU supervision of trade repositories.[9] EMIR is considered a critical piece of legislation by the Commission and Member States in order to meet G20 commitments and ensure convergence with new American rules. It has been driven by the Commission with support from Germany and France. The British government is broadly in favour, but has opposed certain elements of the proposed regulation, seeking to curtail the role and powers of the ESMA. The British have also opposed the inclusion of any specific reference to CCPs having access to central bank liquidity and attempts to prohibit the interoperability of CCPs. The British government has also been concerned with the impact on pension funds and insurers of collateral requirements for central clearing of derivatives contracts. The main debates in the European Parliament have centred on the definition of OTC derivatives, interaction with the Markets in Financial Instruments Directive (MIFID) from 2004, the role of ESMA in the authorization and operational supervision of CCPs, and risk mitigation requirements.

The European Commission also adopted a draft regulation requiring additional transparency and disclosure requirements for short-selling activities, seeking powers to enable Member States to outlaw temporarily short-selling and impose severe restrictions on 'naked short-selling' (the process of selling a financial instrument that is neither owned nor borrowed by the vendor) and specifically naked credit default swaps (CDS), particularly for sovereign debt.[10] This has been a particularly controversial piece of legislation. It is not part of any G20 agreement. Rather it has been driven by the belief, widespread in the European Parliament and certain Member States, that the eurozone debt crisis was caused by 'Anglo-Saxon speculation', especially naked short-selling. The regulation has been strongly supported by Germany – which in May 2010 imposed a unilateral temporary ban on the naked short-selling of sovereign debt – France, and some Member States with real or potential solvency issues – notably Greece and Spain. It has been strongly

[9] *COM*(2010)484, 'Proposal for a Regulation of the European Parliament and of the Council on OTC derivatives, central counterparties and trade repositories', *SEC*(2010)1059.

[10] *COM*(2010) 482 final, 'Proposal for a Regulation of the European Parliament and of the Council on Short Selling and certain aspects of Credit Default Swaps', 2010/0251 (COD), *SEC*(2010) 1055, *SEC*(2010) 1056.

resisted by the British government as unnecessary on the grounds that short-selling was not connected to the financial crisis and is an insignificant cause of the sovereign debt crisis. The regulation is likely to be passed against the preferences of the United Kingdom, with some compromise on banning naked CDS due to the impact of a ban on the ability of sovereigns to raise funds.

II. Tackling the 'Vultures of Capitalism': The Alternative Investment Fund Mangers Directive

Hedge funds and private equity firms, although frequently criticized by many EU Member State governments, were not major culprits of the financial crisis. Thus the push to regulate these industries at the EU level must be understood in largely political terms (Buckley and Howarth, 2010). Prior to 2009, Charlie McCreevy, the Internal Market Commissioner, repeatedly expressed hostility to the regulation of these industries at the EU level. The proposal to initiate discussions on the need for EU regulation came from the Commission President, José Manuel Barroso, rather than from the Council or Directorate-General Internal Market (DG Internal Market senior official, 2010).[11] Some observers see the directive in terms of Barroso's bid to secure French, German and European Parliament support for his second term as Commission President.[12] Many MEPs wanted tough legislation on hedge funds and private equity firms. In 2008, the head of the European Socialists group, former Danish prime minister Poul Nyrup Rasmussen, had produced a very strong and damning own initiative report on private equity funds in the Parliament which was considered a key driver for the legislation – at least among Socialists.[13] Some see AIMFD as a knee-jerk reaction to the losses suffered by many EU citizens through hedge funds that channelled money to the American financier Bernard Madoff.[14] Officially, the Commission justified the move in terms of the need for EU regulation given the cross-border dimension of risks posed by these funds and the need to remove obstacles to the cross-border marketing of these funds in the EU.[15]

German and French governments have long been critical of hedge funds and private equity firms as embodiments of 'vulture capitalism' and fundamentally contradictory to the German system built on 'patient' capital

[11] See also *Financial Times*, 14 April 2010 and 16 May 2010.
[12] *Financial Times*, 14 April 2010.
[13] *European Voice*, 29 May 2008. Available at: «http://www.europeanvoice.com/article/imported/private-equity-firms-fear-risk-rules/60959.aspx».
[14] *Financial Times*, 13 May 2010.
[15] *Financial Times*, 14 July 2009.

(Engelen, 2005) and France's 'managed' capitalism (Schmidt, 2002). Many politicians from across the political spectrum saw the need for a new directive to crack down on financial activities that were purely speculative or had no economic or social benefit, like 'naked short-selling' that 'destabilized' the financial system or buy-out funds that loaded companies with debt.[16] Hedge funds and private equity groups were roundly criticized by German politicians in the mid-2000s after cutting thousands of jobs at Gröhe, a German tap maker, and for their campaign against Deutsche Börse, the Frankfurt stock exchange group.[17] The French and Germans had sought reinforcement of EU-level regulation and international guidelines on AIFM for several years on the grounds that only international action could be effective since most of these firms were based abroad. For several EU Member States, the AIFMD also offered a mechanism to bolster their own fledgling asset management industries. Once implemented, the directive would give approved EU-based managers the right to market their funds across the 27-country bloc – a feature that could increase the attractiveness of having an onshore presence in Europe. The Commission launched a consultation on the need for EU regulation on these industries in December 2008 (Commission, 2008). While a small majority of Member State governments accepted unilateral EU action if necessary (Quaglia, 2011), most governments and industry respondents to the consultation preferred the development of international guidelines on these industries. The development of the draft directive was rushed, without the usual preparatory work, from industry consultations to impact assessments, resulting in a highly flawed initial draft.[18]

In June 2009, the European Commission adopted its proposal for the draft directive on AIFM.[19] The proposed directive introduced a European passport for AIFM; an EU authorization and supervisory regime for all AIFM above a certain size; capital, governance and transparency requirements; and the introduction of a three-year transition period during which AIFM would not be able to market throughout the EU funds domiciled in third countries (though Member States could continue to allow them to operate via national private placements). Following this period, these funds could be marketed only if their country of domicile complied with the conditions set out in the OECD Model Tax Convention and other requirements.

The British government and most of the AIFM sector were opposed to the draft directive and then led efforts to dilute its most constraining elements. As

[16] *Financial Times*, 16 May 2010.
[17] *Financial Times*, 2 September 2008.
[18] Interview with a DG Internal Market senior official, June 2010. See also *Financial Times*, 14 April 2010 and 16 May 2010.
[19] *COM*(2009) 207, final.

host to 80 per cent of EU fund managers, the United Kingdom sought to maintain the international competitiveness of its financial sector with light-touch regulation, which also reflected the British Liberal Market Economy (LME) (Quaglia, 2011). The AIFMD was the subject of a considerable lobbying effort on the part of targeted industries – principally hedge funds and private equity funds, but also funds that invest in venture capital, property and commodities. Other institutional investors and pensions funds, while not directly covered by the directive, expressed their concern that it would increase their costs and reduce their choice as investors.[20] Further, there was concern that the draft AIFMD cast its regulatory net so wide that it captured other investment vehicles, including long-established and publicly quoted investment trusts that were already subject to regulation at the national and EU level (Rothschild, 2010). Despite their hostility to most of the specific elements of the directive, associations representing AIFM were broadly supportive of the 'EU passport' which created an opportunity for many firms, helping them to market their services to the 'conservative' pension funds in Member States such as Germany and France.

Under the Swedish Council Presidency during the second half of 2009 some of the more controversial elements of the directive were removed (including the introduction of a leverage cap on the funds) or watered down (including a measure that would have required AIFM to deposit funds only in large European banks – widely opposed as protectionist) (Manvatkar, 2009). In November 2009, the Parliament's Economic and Monetary Affairs Committee agreed 130 changes to the draft directive. Some of the modifications adopted, however, sparked further controversy. Notably, the Parliament sought the removal of '*de minimis*' rules, which would have allowed very small private equity funds and companies relying on these funds to escape the regulation, on the grounds that there would be attempts to get around thresholds, and the addition of new guidelines on proportionality that would spare private equity funds that posed few risks.[21] There remained major divisions in the European Parliament, generally between left and right, with much of the left continuing to call for tighter leverage rules and a complete ban on short-selling.

In 2010, the debate on the proposed directive focused upon the following elements: the requirements for government authorization including conduct standards, new rules for how 'third-country' funds and managers based outside the EU could access investors inside the bloc, rules on disclosures to regulators and investors, capital requirements, a limit on total borrowing

[20] *Financial Times*, 13 May 2010.
[21] *Financial Times*, 2 December 2010.

(depending on fund type), the independent valuation of fund assets, the need for AIFM funds to be held by depository banks that would be held liable in case of problems, constraints on remuneration policies, and disclosure rules for firms with fund investors on financial performance and strategy. Some of the proposals were relatively basic and were already required by most national regulators. Others – notably the third-country and remuneration rules – were controversial. A further matter of debate concerned the extent to which national governments and regulators should have discretion over how to implement parts of the regulation. The Spanish Council Presidency of the first half of 2010 failed to reach a compromise on the directive at the March European Council.[22] Qualified Majority Voting applied on the directive. However, the Spanish Presidency heeded the request by British Prime Minister Gordon Brown, who pleaded for a delay in voting until after the United Kingdom general election in May.

Politicians in some Member States argued that the draft directives in circulation in 2010 were already too tame and did not do enough to rein in funds.[23] At the same time, the British and American governments and mostly British-based AIFM stepped up their lobbying efforts to water down the legislation further. In a letter to MEPs in May, three major British financial sector associations – the Investment Management Association (IMA), the National Association of Pension Funds (NAPF) and the Alternative Investment Management Association (AIMA) – argued that the proposals were 'unworkable', warned of 'scope creep' and called for a 'pragmatic and workable solution'.[24] The British Private Equity and Venture Capital Association argued that the directive threatened the United Kingdom's national strategic interest: 'It is the same as an attack on manufacturing in Germany or farming in France'.[25] The Association also pointed out that the lack of legal certainty discouraged investors that were vital to future European economic growth and that it was already having a negative impact on AIFM. For example, it was argued that legal uncertainty hit the ability of the hedge fund industry to become a dominant force in the expanding area of alternative undertakings for collective investment in transferable securities (Ucits) better known as 'Newcits'.[26] We focus below on three issue areas of particular controversy: 'third-country' access, depository rules and remuneration.

[22] On the Spanish Presidency, see Heywood in this volume.
[23] *Financial Times*, 13 May 2010.
[24] *Financial Times*, 13 May 2010.
[25] *Financial Times*, 15 March 2010.
[26] *Financial Times*, 9 May 2010.

Third-Country Access

Much of the debate in 2010 on the directive focused on the so-called 'third-country' issue: the scope of rules according to which non-EU-based funds could obtain the 'EU passport' to market to professional investors throughout the Union. The French government in particular sought to restrict the ability of funds based in low tax jurisdictions to access its market and argued that the passport should be granted only to non-EU fund managers domiciled in jurisdictions with equivalent regulatory regimes.[27] Many in the European Parliament, and in particular the Socialists, were in favour of similarly tough rules. Drafts of the directive circulating during the first half of 2010 addressed the issue in different ways. One was to reserve access for EU-based funds, while allowing individual states more say in whether professional investors could access funds managed outside the bloc. Another was to allow outside funds to sign up to EU principles as long as their home country met basic rules on transparency, tax and money laundering. The British and American governments, amongst others, and the fund management industry challenged these proposals as protectionist.[28] The Spanish Presidency's compromise text in March also failed. This proposed allowing access, provided that there were 'appropriate co-operation arrangements for the purpose of systemic risk oversight and in line with international standards [. . .] in place between the competent authorities of the Member State where the fund is marketed and the competent authorities of the AIFM'.[29]

The American administration made very public its opposition to the 'third country' element of the proposed directive and its perception of EU efforts to dictate the global regulatory landscape. The United States Securities and Exchange Commission stated that it would be unlikely to be able to comply with the equivalent criteria suggested in AIFMD drafts, which would have closed the EU market to American-based funds (Harris, 2010). A 1 March letter from Timothy Geithner, the American Secretary of the Treasury, to Michel Barnier, the Commissioner for Internal Market and Services and the Spanish Chair of the Ecofin Council, was leaked to the press and published in full in the *Financial Times*, as was a 5 April letter from Mr Geithner to the British chancellor of the Exchequer and the German, French and Spanish finance ministers enjoining them to support a reconsideration of the AIFM.[30] In the 1 March letter, Mr Geithner notes:

[27] *Financial Times*, 14 April 2010.
[28] Reuters, 10 November 2009; *Financial News*, 17 September 2009.
[29] *Financial Times*, 15 March 2010.
[30] *Financial Times*, 11 March 2010 and 6 April 2010.

> I believe we agree that [it] is essential to fulfil our G-20 commitment to avoid discrimination and maintain a level playing field. In this context, we are concerned with various proposals that would discriminate against US firms and deny them the access to the EU market that they currently have. We strongly hope that the rule that you put in place will ensure that non-EU fund managers and global custodian banks have the same access as their EU counterparts. You will see that our approach in the US maintains full access for EU fund managers and custodians to our market.[31]

The American administration stopped short of threatening retaliatory action. However, if the third-country rules of the directive were not significantly watered down, EU-based fund managers could face reprisals in the United States Congress. Senior EU officials responded to American concerns by insisting that the proposed directive was in line with G20 guidelines to improve transparency in the financial system and noted that Mr Barnier sought to work with the American administration to ensure 'robust standards'.[32] The British Labour government joined forces with the Obama administration to water down the demands imposed on third-country funds. Many British AIFMs ran funds that were based outside the EU for tax purposes. The British sought a regime that allowed non-EU funds to be marketed across the EU provided the jurisdiction in which they were based had 'equivalent' regulatory standards, with a relaxed set of criteria to determine 'equivalence'. Ireland, the Czech Republic, Malta, Sweden and Austria adopted a similar position.

Industry associations echoed the concerns of the American Treasury Secretary to the third-country proposal, warning of retaliatory action in non-EU jurisdictions which would damage EU-based financial services.[33] The uncertainty also hit offshore centres, including the Cayman Islands, which had already lost funds to onshore locations in Europe. The percentage of hedge funds domiciled in the Cayman Islands dropped from 40.1 to 37.3 per cent from the end of 2008 to early 2010, with Ireland and Luxembourg seeing their share jump by 60 per cent to 7.3 per cent.[34] For the first time, the Channel Islands of Jersey and Guernsey established a diplomatic mission in Brussels reflecting their governments' fears that their financial services industries could be damaged by new EU regulations.[35] Half of Jersey's economy consisted of financial services.

[31] *Financial Times*, 11 March 2010.
[32] *Financial Times*, 12 March 2010.
[33] *Financial Times*, 13 May 2010.
[34] *Financial Times*, 2 May 2010.
[35] *Financial Times*, 3 July 2010.

With the failure to reach a compromise deal on the third-country issue at the March European Council, MEPs went ahead with their own efforts to produce a more acceptable draft. Surprisingly, the Economic and Monetary Affairs Committee responsible for the directive shifted its views. The AIFMD Rapporteur, the French conservative MEP Jean-Paul Gauzès, put forward compromise solutions more popular in the United Kingdom than in his home country.[36] The Committee organized discussions of a possible transitional arrangement on the issue, during which national rules would continue to apply. Mr Gauzès proposed that after a five-year period, the EU should recognize which third countries had 'equivalent' regulatory standards and funds/fund managers based there should have access to the EU market. Mr Gauzès also proposed a 'two-tier' approach to the registration of third-country funds. His proposal suggested that funds managed within an EU Member State but domiciled outside could be eligible for a passport provided the country of domicile met four conditions: that the foreign regulator supplied the EU regulators with the information they required; that the foreign jurisdiction allowed European funds to be sold there; that regulation to prevent money laundering and funding terrorism was in place; and that an acceptable tax agreement existed. If a jurisdiction fell short of some of these four standards, the funds might still be able to seek country-by-country marketing approval. But if a jurisdiction fell short of all of them, the funds would be barred from marketing in the EU. Funds both domiciled and managed outside the EU would have to meet a higher standard – to obtain a passport they would have to show that their home jurisdiction had 'equivalent' regulation to the EU. While this compromise appeared to lower the hurdle for third-country access, many investor and industry groups remained concerned by the definition of 'equivalent'. Critics also noted that funds investing in emerging markets would find it hardest to comply, making it more difficult for EU investors to back fund managers in African and other countries, with negative implications for growth in the developing world.[37]

Depository Rules

One of the most contentious elements of the draft AIFMD required fund assets to be independently valued and kept by a depository bank that would be held liable in case of problems. The French and Spanish governments championed the depository rules to ensure investor protection: many of their investors suffered major losses in the Bernard Madoff fraud. Initial Commission proposals in the wake of the financial crisis stated that depositories

[36] *Financial Times*, 4 April 2010.
[37] *Financial Times*, 13 May 2010.

would be liable for the loss of AIFM assets 'no matter what'. Depositories came out in opposition arguing that unlimited liability would lead to 'unintended consequences', including potentially increased costs for investors and the possible growth of systemic risks due to sector consolidation.[38] Unqualified protection was subsequently watered down, reflecting the productive lobbying exercise of depositories in Brussels. United Kingdom-based funds and investors viewed the proposed rules as prohibitively expensive and argued that the rule would make it harder to start up new funds. Private equity funds sought and – in the Parliament's draft of the directive in May – received an exemption from the depository rule.

The revised directive provisions on depository rules were more acceptable to depositories and 'custodians' and brought clarity to their role. The legislation provided a European definition of 'safe keeping', clearly laying out the extent of the fiduciary duties for depository banks. Previously, different national interpretations of safe keeping were loose and resulted in different legal outcomes on cases of asset losses.[39] The AIFMD eventually adopted outlines the duties of depository banks in great detail including: monitoring cash flows (making sure subscription monies arrive in accounts); safekeeping assets (providing traditional custody for financial instruments); subjecting third-party sub-custodians to prudential supervision to make sure assets exist and set limits to rehypothecation (where banks reuse collateral posted by clients to back their trades); and ensuring accurate and timely valuation of assets. The hedge fund industry broadly supported AIFMD provisions that enabled a sub-custodian to take liability under contract, instead of the custodian and depositories which would be able to avoid untenable levels of liability.

Other elements of the final directive adopted were more problematic for industry – notably the strict liability rule, which established in the case of asset loss the rule that banks would immediately make good the loss by replacing the lost instruments with similar ones or through cash compensation. This created potentially limitless liabilities for depositories. Strict liability could also have a potentially significant impact on the kinds of investments that firms would be able to make.[40] Notably, investments in emerging markets or riskier EU Member States like Greece and Ireland would be discouraged because of the lack of a suitable sub-custodian or depository to which to delegate. Funds specializing in emerging markets previously paid around 8–12 basis points for custody depending on the size of the fund. The risk was this would double under the AIFM directive.[41] The result would be to drive some investment

[38] *Financial Times*, 15 December 2010.
[39] *Financial Times*, 15 December 2010.
[40] *Financial Times*, 12 December 2010.
[41] *Financial Times*, 12 December 2010.

offshore. The directive also reversed the 'burden of proof', which means that depositories would have to prove that they had no responsibility in case of lost assets, which would be more time-consuming. Previously, investors had to prove there had been fault on the part of the custodian.[42] Despite the lack of clarity as to the impact of the new liability rule, industry was reconciled to the directive's liability provisions in part because all EU Member States would be required to state clearly how they would implement them, thus contributing to harmonization and a level playing field. Industry saw the drawbacks to a lack of harmonization as in the 1986 Ucits Directive, the interpretation of which differed markedly among Member States.[43]

Many outstanding issues remained in the application of the rules which would come into effect only after consultation with the investment industry in 2011. The bankruptcy of the sub-custodian continued to be treated differently in the Member States. There also remained the issue of whether prime brokers would accept the delegation to them of contractual obligations. The transfer of responsibility for the restitution of assets was welcomed by hedge funds, but prime brokers were less pleased. The AIFMD would also add to the burden on transaction banking imposed by the Basel III framework with its toughening of capital, liquidity and leverage standards.[44]

Constraints on Remuneration Policies

Industry was concerned that EU rules to regulate bank bonuses set in CRD3 might also apply to hedge funds.[45] A key clause in the directive created confusion on the matter: '[T]he principles recognise that credit institutions and investment firms may apply the provisions in different ways according to size, internal organisation, complexity of activities [. . .] In particular it may not be proportionate for investment firms to comply with all the principles'. Thus, although hedge funds were caught within the ambit of CRD3, Member State regulators could interpret the degree to which remuneration rules would be applied. It was unlikely that the British Financial Services Authority (FSA) would apply the CRD3 rules to asset managers. Nonetheless, industry sought clarification on the matter in the AIFMD and the adoption of more appropriate guidelines. The debate initially went against industry: rules on remuneration were added to the Commission's original draft of the AIFMD that mirrored CRD3 rules for credit institutions allowing only 30 per cent of any bonus for bankers and fund managers to be paid straight away in cash and only 20 per cent

[42] *Financial Times*, 12 December 2010.
[43] *Financial Times*, 12 December 2010.
[44] *Financial Times*, 12 December 2010.
[45] *Financial Times*, 1 July 2010.

for large bonuses. At least half of the bonus would have to be deferred, to be paid in shares and securities, with the aim of increasing the manager's commitment to the strength of the institution. Individual Member States would be left to decide precisely the percentage of the bonus to be staggered. Industry expressed its concern that these rules would have a deleterious impact upon hedge funds and private equity firms, which operated differently than banks.

AIFMD remuneration rules were subsequently modified. However, they remained surprisingly detailed, rarely seen within European regulation: itself a reflection of the importance many MEPs and some Member States attached to remuneration issues. The directive introduces procedures and limits on pay and 18 remuneration principles that fund managers would be expected to follow. Industry associations were generally hostile and expressed their fear that funds would move offshore.[46] They also feared the rules could 'leak' into the retail market in the context of the Commission's review of the existing Ucits Directive, starting in December 2010, to align it with the AIFMD rules on depositories. Industry associations accused the Commission of attempting to transpose remuneration rules set for large credit institutions onto fund managers. One principle, for example, called for AIFM 'senior management and risk takers' to invest 50 per cent of variable compensation in their fund and the obligation that managers would have to provide aggregate information on remuneration with performance monitored over 'a multi-year framework appropriate to the life-cycle of the [fund]'.[47] Industry expressed concern over the level of detail in the directive but hoped that Member State regulators would take a more 'proportionate' approach in implementation. The new European Securities and Markets Authority (ESMA) would produce guidelines on remuneration in 2011. These would take into account the size of the firms and its funds, and the scope and complexity of their activities. The British FSA announced that it was prepared to extend a relaxed version of CRD3 rules on remuneration to AIFM.[48]

Other Issues

There were major disagreements on a range of other issues. Industry associations argued that capital requirements in the AIFMD would make it harder to start new funds. The draft directive also included reporting requirements for companies (mostly small and medium-sized, SMEs) that had private equity or venture capital investors. A group of these SMEs expressed their concern in an open letter sent to MEPs that they would be negatively affected

[46] *Financial Times*, 5 December 2010.
[47] *Financial Times*, 5 December 2010.
[48] *Financial Times*, 5 December 2010.

by proposed rules that they disclose their financial performance, capital structure, research spending and strategy. These companies feared that they would be placed at a disadvantage in relation to their multinational competitors.[49] The exemption threshold of 50 employees was also seen as too low.[50]

The Final Deal

The most controversial provisions of the draft directive were substantially scaled back. The British FSA played an important role in negotiating a compromise on third-country funds and managers.[51] Non-EU funds would be able to apply for the 'EU passport' if they demonstrated regulatory 'equivalence'. The policy on 'equivalence' ended up reflecting policy already established in international financial forums. The home jurisdiction of the non-EU funds applying for the 'EU passport' would have to comply with International Organization of Securities Commissions' (IOSCO) standards on hedge fund oversight, which include compliance with international tax and anti-money laundering agreements. It was very likely that the United States and other key markets would be deemed appropriately regulated jurisdictions.[52] The Parliament's proposed tandem approach was adopted allowing the current system of individual market application to continue until 2015 (Griffiths, 2010). Industry was positive about the adopted version of the directive.[53] The French government's hard-line position on third-country funds lost support from other Member States.

AIFMD can be seen very much as a British government victory in the Council and a lobbying victory for industry. The most controversial proposals, including plans to impose fixed caps on leverage and capital requirements, were either removed or watered down significantly. AIFMD required fund managers to appoint a separate custodian for hedge fund assets and provide independent portfolio valuations, but this provision reflected what was already standard industry practice for most funds operating in the EU. Questions remained over the power of ESMA in relation to national authorities in the authorization of AIFM, particularly those based in third countries, following the completion of the five-year transition period. The reporting requirements imposed unwelcome, albeit limited, compliance costs on funds and some SMEs, but their existing business practices were not affected in any significant way.

[49] *Financial Times*, 19 April 2010.
[50] *Financial Times*, 16 May 2010.
[51] *Financial Times*, 12 December 2010.
[52] *Wall Street Journal*, 31 October 2010.
[53] *Financial Times*, 17 October 2010.

The AIFMD adopted broadly aligned with developments in the G20, which called for a set of unified best practices, to be left in the hands of private sector bodies (Helleiner and Pagliari, 2009).[54] AIFMD provisions on registration and reporting were similar to existing British practice which already required the registration of managers with the FSA and voluntary reporting through the Hedge Funds as Counterparties Survey (HFACS), although the reporting requirements were now to become compulsory. The new directive was also largely aligned to existing American legislation adopted in the aftermath of the financial crisis which observers have described as not onerous or likely to restrict existing business activities (Brown *et al.*, 2010). The Dodd-Frank Wall Street Reform and Consumer Protection Act of July 2009 requires all hedge funds above a minimum size to register with the SEC, imposes minimal reporting requirements, and subjects funds to periodic SEC examinations and inspections.

Conclusions

Even in the post-financial crisis world of politicized financial regulation, the industry lobby and its allies were able to shift EU policy on AIFM significantly. The result was the adoption of a directive that led one major financial newspaper to announce: 'Hedge funds win big in Brussels'.[55] The era of industry largely designing EU legislation on the financial sector as described by Mugge (2011) was over, at least in the short to medium term. At the same time, as the AIFMD and other EU-level legislation since the financial crisis showed, industry continued to undertake considerable effort at both the national and EU levels to direct legislation. Financial industries were forced to invest more in their lobbying activities in national capitals and in Brussels, where there had been a significant expansion in their presence since 2008.[56] This increased effort was a response to more than just the increased number of draft directives and regulations which forced industry into rearguard action. There are claims of an end to easy access to senior Commission officials and a greater need to court European parliamentarians.[57] Further, the increased presence of the financial lobby in Brussels, both major trade associations and individual banks seeking to protect company specific interests, made influence more difficult, despite attempts at building a common front.

[54] In June 2009, IOSCO established voluntary guidelines for funds based on industry 'best practice' (IOSCO, 2009).

[55] *Wall Street Journal*, 31 October 2010; see also *Hedgeweek* (2010).

[56] *Financial News*, 8 February 2010. Available at: «http://www.efinancialnews.com/story/2010-02-08/investment-banks-gear-up-lobbying-in-brussels».

[57] *Financial News*, 8 February 2010.

Banks and other financial services were forced to make greater use of public affairs businesses in Brussels. Yet there remained the suspicion that some top bankers and industry officials continued to enjoy privileged access to senior officials in DG Internal Market.[58]

A number of factors explain industry's success in the case of the AIFMD, which might not be replicated on other directives. First, the position of the affected industries was largely homogeneous. Second, it had a determined champion in the British government, with the United Kingdom home to 80 per cent of the EU's AIFM. Third, the strong opposition of the American administration to the third-country element of the directive and possibility of retaliation strengthened industry's hand further. Fourth, the ideologically inspired push by the European Parliament and the German government against AIMF did not hold sway in the face of entrenched interests. The French government persisted in their demand for tighter rules. However, the French became increasingly isolated as the Commission, Parliament and German government accepted the need for a compromise.

A glance at the EU legislative agenda for 2011 suggests that the Annual Review piece on the internal market for this year will, yet again, be focused on financial regulation. 2011 should see the adoption of directives on Investor Compensation Schemes (ICS) and Deposit Guarantee Schemes (DGS) and the regulation on Over-the-Counter Derivatives, despite the lingering disagreements among Member States on specific elements of these pieces of legislation. However, an entrenched battle continues on naked short-selling and another looms on CRD4 – the draft legislation for which was to be presented in 2011.[59] CRD4 was expected to be a combination of a regulation and a directive on capital requirements, leverage ratios and dynamic provisioning, and effectively the EU's legislative proposal for implementing Basel III. Alongside the Commission's plans for recovery and resolution schemes for cross-border banks, CRD4 was considered the most critical piece of post-crisis legislation. It was also highly controversial in a number of Member States due to their banks' high leverage ratios: several, including Germany, Austria, France, Italy and Denmark placed significant pressure on the Commission to allow for 'European specificities' in the implementation of Basel III. Several – notably Germany and Italy – were particularly concerned about the definition of tier-one capital. On the other side, the United Kingdom, supported by Spain and the Netherlands, pushed very hard for non-deviation from Basel III on the grounds that this was necessary to restore confidence in

[58] *Financial News*, 8 February 2010.

[59] See «http://ec.europa.eu/internal_market/bank/regcapital/index_en.htm» for further information.

European banks. The European Parliament was expected to side with those Member States fighting for the consideration of 'European specificities'. The Rapporteur and key shadows in the Economic and Monetary Affairs Committee on CRD4 were all German or Austrian. The Commission was expected to give some leeway on the quality of capital, but to stick as much as possible to G20/Basel III commitments. Unlike the AIFMD, the battle over CRD4 would not involve a largely unified financial lobby and national positions would align with the positions of their banks.

References

Brown, S. *et al.* (2010) 'Hedge Funds, Mutual Funds, and ETFs'. In Acharya, V. *et al.* (eds) *Regulating Wall Street: The Dodd-Frank Act and the New Architecture of Global Finance* (Hoboken, NJ: John Wiley & Sons).

Buckley, J. and Howarth, D. (2010) 'Internal Market: Gesture Politics? Explaining the EU's Response to the Financial Crisis'. *JCMS*, Vol. 48, s1, pp. 119–41.

Commission of the European Communities (2008) 'Consultation paper on hedge funds', 18 December.

Engelen, K. (2005) 'Blinking Left, Driving Right'. *International Economy*, Spring, pp. 56–63.

European Parliament (2010) 'Draft Report', Committee on Economic and Monetary Affairs, 2009/0099 (COD), Rapporteur: Arlene McCarthy, 2 March.

Financial Services Authority (FSA) (2010) 'Alternative Investment Fund Managers Directive'. Available at: «http://www.fsa.gov.uk/pages/About/What/International/pdf/AIFM%20(PL).pdf».

Griffiths, T. (2010) 'EU Reaches Agreement on Directive Text'. *HFM Week*, 26 October.

Harris, J. (2010) 'SEC says US Unable to Meet EU Equivalence Criteria'. *Hedge Funds Review*, 10 June. Available at: «http://www.hedgefundsreview.com/hedge-funds-review/news/1653845/sec-us-unable-meet-eu-equivalence-criteria».

Hedgeweek (2010) 'EU Ministers Agree Third-Country Compromise on AIFM Directive'. *Hedgeweek*, 20 October.

Helleiner, E. and Pagliari, S. (2009) 'Towards a New Bretton Woods? The First G20 Leader Summit and the Regulation of Global Finance'. *New Political Economy*, Vol. 14, No. 2, pp. 275–87.

International Organization of Securities Commissions (IOSCO) (2009) *Elements of International Regulatory Standards on Funds of Hedge Funds Related Issues Based on Best Market Practices* (Madrid: IOSCO).

Manvatkar, R. (2009) *AIFM Directive Update Draft Gauzes Report, Revised Swedish Proposal and European Parliament's Impact Assessment* (London: Linklaters). Available at: «http://www.linklaters.com/pdfs/LinklatersAIFMDirectiveupdate_December09.pdf».

Mugge, D. (2011) 'Limits of Legitimacy and the Primacy of Politics in Financial Governance'. *Review of International Political Economy*, Vol. 18, No. 1, pp. 52–74.

Quaglia, L. (2011) 'The "Old" and "New" Political Economy of Hedge Funds Regulation in the European Union'. *West European Politics*, Vol. 34, No. 4, forthcoming.

Rothschild, J. (2010) 'Europe is Getting It Wrong on Financial Reform'. *Financial Times*, 20 April.

Schmidt, V.A. (2002) *The Futures of European Capitalism* (Oxford: Oxford University Press).

JCMS 2011 Volume 49 Annual Review pp. 145–164

Justice and Home Affairs

JÖRG MONAR
College of Europe/University of Sussex

Introduction

The year 2010 marked a new start for the JHA (justice and home affairs) domain: it was the first year of the application of the – in this domain extensive – Lisbon Treaty reforms; the first year of the 2010–14 Stockholm Programme, which saw tensions between the Commission and the Council over the implementation of the Programme; and the first year of a new European Union (EU) 'Internal Security Strategy', which revealed problems of the new administrative splitting of the JHA domain between 'home affairs' and 'justice' in the Commission. The Greek asylum crisis highlighted again the deficits of EU policy in this field, but the establishment of the new Asylum Support Office offered some new perspectives, and the Commission also made new proposals in the difficult field of legal migration. The border agency Frontex saw a new expansion of its activities, and some legislative progress was made in both the civil and the criminal justice fields. The total annual output of the JHA Council dropped slightly from 121 adopted texts the year before to 114 texts,[1] indicating a slow start to the implementation of the Stockholm Programme. In this article, we will examine developments in each of the main JHA policy areas and then conclude with a look at the plans for the further implementation of the Stockholm Programme.

[1] Lists of texts provided by the General Secretariat of the Council and author's own calculations.

JCMS: Journal of Common Market Studies © 2011 Blackwell Publishing Ltd, 9600 Garsington Road, Oxford OX4 2DQ, UK and 350 Main Street, Malden, MA 02148, USA

I. Developments in Individual Policy Areas

Asylum Policy

While the overall number of asylum applications in the EU slightly decreased during the year, the disparities between the Member States continued to vary enormously: for the second quarter of 2010, for instance, Cyprus had a total of 775 applications per 1 million inhabitants whereas Portugal had only 5 (Eurostat, 2010). Being geographically amongst the most exposed of the EU Member States, Greece continued to face major problems in endeavouring to ensure adequate asylum procedures and reception conditions. This posed a direct challenge to the possibility of EU Member States and associated Schengen countries under the 2003 Dublin II Regulation to return asylum seekers to Greece if they had entered first through that country. In response to repeated warnings from the United Nations High Commissioner for Refugees (UNHCR) and the European Council on Refugees and Exiles (ECRE) about the situation of asylum seekers in Greece as well as an increasing number of rulings of national courts (especially in Austria, France, Hungary, Italy, Poland, Romania, Sweden and Spain) against transfer decisions back to Greece, more and more Member States and associated Schengen countries took the decision to suspend transfers back to Greece. At the end of the year these included: Austria, Belgium, Denmark, Finland, Iceland, the Netherlands, Norway, Switzerland and the United Kingdom (UNHCR, 2010, 2011).

The suspension of Dublin transfers by some countries could not stop an avalanche of legal cases being brought against transfer decisions to Greece that had already been made. In addition to several preliminary ruling cases brought by higher courts in Germany, Ireland and the United Kingdom pending before the Court of Justice of the European Union (CJEU), at the end of the year more than 600 cases were pending before the European Court of Human Rights (ECtHR) (UNHCR, 2011). The legal challenges to the EU asylum system culminated in *MSS* v *Belgium and Greece* (no. 30696/09) before the ECtHR – a case heard in September and decided by Grand Chamber judgment on 21 January 2011. It concerned an Afghan national who, travelling via Iran and Turkey, had entered the EU through Greece but applied for asylum in Belgium. Under the applicable rule of the Dublin II Regulation, the Belgian authorities decided to send him back to Greece. The applicant appealed twice in vain against this transfer decision, and was sent back to Greece. There, according to his own reports, he was immediately placed in detention in a building adjacent to the airport, where, according to his reports, he was locked up in a small space with 20 other detainees where access to the toilets was restricted, they were not allowed out into the open air, were given very little to eat and had to sleep on dirty mattresses or on the bare floor. Following his release and issuance of an asylum seeker's card he had to live in the street with no means of subsistence.

In its ruling, the ECtHR concluded that there had been a violation by Greece of Article 3 ECHR (prohibition of inhuman or degrading treatment or punishment) because of the applicant's detention and living conditions in Greece, and also of 13 ECHR (right to an effective remedy) taken in conjunction with Article 3 ECHR because of the risk of the applicant's expulsion to Afghanistan without adequate examination of the merits of his asylum application and without access to an effective remedy. Belgium was condemned for a violation of Article 3 ECHR both because of having exposed the applicant to the deficiencies in the asylum procedure in Greece and because of having exposed him to detention and living conditions in Greece that were in breach of Article 3, as well as for a violation of Article 13 ECHR because of the lack of an effective remedy against the applicant's expulsion order. EU emergency assistance measures to Greece, topped up in December by a further €9.8 million to improve accommodation assistance and further provision of expert assistance on reforming the national asylum system (Commission, 2010a), came too late to avert what amounted to a highly embarrassing condemnation of the functioning of the EU asylum system. The ruling of the Strasbourg Court could hardly have exposed in clearer terms the unsustainability of the EU's claim that all Member States provide equal access to protection to justify the 'Dublin system' of rendering one Member State responsible for deciding on an asylum application for the whole of the EU.

Given this background the progress of the negotiations on the six 'second-phase' legal instruments of the common European asylum system (CEAS) – which would at least in part address the current deficiencies – appeared rather slow. Proposed by the European Commission in several steps from 2007 to 2009, all proposals encountered serious difficulties in the Council where a range of Member States were concerned about the likely higher financial and administrative burdens the proposed improvements to procedural rights and reception conditions of asylum seekers are likely to entail as well as insufficient provisions regarding potential abuses of their asylum systems. In the European Parliament, the proposed recasting of the Eurodac Regulation regarding electronic comparison of fingerprints of asylum seekers encountered significant opposition because of the foreseen access to law enforcement authorities to the system. In October, the Commission submitted a new proposal not providing for such access, but this led to negative reactions in the Council (Council, 2010a).

Although the Belgian Presidency of the second half of the year made progress on the CEAS legislative package a priority of its programme, in the end it could only secure a political agreement on the extension of the scope of the long-term residence directive to beneficiaries of international protection, meaning that those falling into this group who are long-term residents will enjoy equality of treatment with citizens of the Member State of residence with regard to a wide range of economic and social matters (European Parliament, 2010a). Yet this was arguably the least controversial of the second-phase CEAS instruments, and at the end of the year the original deadline for the adoption of the package set by the Hague Programme was missed without any decisive breakthrough on the other proposed legislative acts. In response to the difficulties within the Council, EU Commissioner Cecilia Malmström announced the submission of amended legislative proposals regarding the Asylum Procedures and Reception Conditions Directives during 2011, which led the ECRE to raise concerns about a potential watering down of the improved procedural safeguards and higher reception conditions standards that had been proposed earlier (ECRE, 2010).

Nevertheless, the year saw at least one significant element of progress in the field of asylum with the adoption on 19 May of the Regulation establishing the European Asylum Support Office (EASO) for the purpose of facilitating, co-ordinating and strengthening practical co-operation between Member States and improving the implementation of the CEAS (European Parliament/Council, 2010a). The Regulation provides for the EASO to promote the identification and pooling of best practices between Member States (Article 3); the gathering of relevant, reliable and up-to-date information on countries of origin of asylum seekers; the drafting of reports on these countries as well as the development of a common format and a common methodology for using country of origin information and the 'fostering of convergence of assessment criteria' (Article 4). It also has to support the relocation of asylum seekers if Member States are faced with 'disproportionate pressures' on their asylum and reception systems (Article 5), and develop general or specific training modules regarding asylum matters for members of national administrations, courts or tribunals (including specific issues such as the handling of applications for vulnerable persons, interview techniques and the use of medical reports) as well as a 'European asylum curriculum' (Article 6). The Office is, finally, also expected to support the external dimension of the CEAS, to which effect it may co-operate with the authorities of third countries as regards, for instance, capacity building and the implementation of regional protection programmes (Article 7).

The list of tasks of the EASO, whose seat the Council established at Valetta Harbour in Malta, is a daunting one, and it seems clear that the Office will need quite a bit of time to grow into those tasks. The Member States have taken care not only of keeping the EASO under their direct control – its Management Board, which has wide-ranging powers including the appointment of the Office's Executive Director, is composed of one member per Member State and two members from the Commission – but also to prevent the Office from exercising any directing or controlling function with regard to national authorities. The Regulation explicitly excludes, for instance, the tasks of the EASO as regards country of origin information leading to 'instructions' to Member States about the granting or refusal of applications (Article 4(e)).

However, it has been given an operational co-ordination role similar to that of Frontex in the field of EU external border management. On the proposal of the EASO Executive Director, the Management Board is to define the number and profiles of national experts to be made available for an 'Asylum Intervention Pool', which will form the basis for the potential deployment of 'asylum support teams' if a Member State subject to particular pressures requests the EASO for assistance (Articles 13 and 15). While the home Member States retain autonomy with regard to the number, profiles and duration of deployment of their experts, the decision of deployment is left to the EASO Executive Director on the basis of an operating plan agreed with the requesting Member State (Articles 16–18), which gives the new Office clearly a certain leadership function. As Member States are expected to make their experts available for free and all operational costs of the deployment of the support teams (travel, subsistence, insurance, technical equipment, etc.) being covered out of the EU-funded budget of the EASO, the establishment of the Office – which held its first Management Board meeting in November and is expected to become fully operational by June 2011 with an initial annual budget of €8.0 million – constitutes a further step towards solidarity in the CEAS.

Migration Policy

In its first annual report on immigration and asylum submitted to Parliament and Council in May, the European Commission arrived at an overall positive assessment of the progress made in the domain of migration, highlighting, in particular, the 2009 Blue Card Directive, the range of new initiatives on the facilitation of integration and progress on the side of return of illegal migrants through agreements with third countries and the activities of Frontex. Yet the report also indicated a number of deficits at the national level, such as insufficient numbers and effectiveness of inspections at workplaces in sectors where there is a particular risk of exploitation of illegally staying workers and thus far only limited use of the opportunities for fostering voluntary departure offered by the Returns Directive. In several fields covered by the report the Commission expressed its dissatisfaction with the level of factual information provided by Member States – which certainly makes it difficult to come to an adequate EU-wide assessment of progress and challenges in the migration domain. The deficits of information appeared to be particularly obvious in the case of the estimated size of the illegally staying population in the EU where the Commission was only able to refer to the results of a research project of the 6th Framework Programme from 2008, covering only 15 Member States and estimating this size with a rather large margin of between 1.5 and 3.3 million (Commission, 2010b).

In its 'Europe 2020 Strategy' presented in March the European Commission defined a comprehensive labour migration policy able to respond 'in a flexible way to the priorities and needs of labour markets' as a key element of a necessary modernization of labour markets in the EU in view of the objectives of raising employment levels and 'ensuring the sustainability of our social models' (Commission, 2010c). On 13 July, the Commission presented two legislative proposals which were fully in line with this strong emphasis on the facilitation of skill-selective labour immigration into the EU which had already guided the proposal for the EU Blue Card Directive adopted in 2009.

The first proposal, a Directive on intra-corporate transfers, is aimed at facilitating the temporary secondment of mangers, specialists and trainees from third countries to branches of companies located in EU Member States. It provides for a fast-track entry procedure (30 days for processing of the application with no labour market test being applied), a single application for a combined work and residence permit, the possibility of a legal challenge against decisions rejecting an application with a requirement for the respective authority to justify the rejection, the handling of applications for family reunification in the first country of residence within two months, permission to carry out part of the assignment in a branch of the same group located in another Member State for a period up to 12 months and a range of equal treatment rights with the nationals of the host country. The Commission justified the proposal by arguing that it removes the obstacles to satisfying the needs of multinational companies to allocate specialist know-how flexibly and rapidly across borders. It tried in advance to reduce opposition in the Council by emphasizing that the Directive would not create a right of admission and not affect the Member States' control of volumes of admission (Commission, 2010d).

The second proposal introduced was for a Directive establishing common entry and residence conditions for third country seasonal workers. It provides for a fast-track (30 days) procedure for the admission of third country seasonal workers on the basis of a common definition and common criteria, including the existence of a work contract or a binding job offer that specifies a salary. Seasonal workers would be issued with a visa or a residence permit allowing them to work for a maximum period of six months in any calendar year. In order to facilitate 'circular migration', Member States would have the choice of either issuing up to three seasonal worker permits covering up to three subsequent seasons within one administrative act ('multi-seasonal worker permit') or providing a facilitated procedure for third country nationals who were admitted as seasonal workers and who apply to be admitted again in a subsequent year. The proposal provides for a range of rights regarding residence and working conditions to prevent exploitation, and prospective employers will be required to provide evidence that the seasonal workers will have appropriate accommodation during their stay. The Commission justified the proposal by pointing out the need to create a common framework for addressing structural shortages of low-skilled and low-qualified workers in national labour markets, the need to protect them against exploitation and substandard working conditions, and the advantages the instrument might bring in terms of reducing illegal employment, which is widespread in this sector (Commission, 2010e).

In the midst of the fallout of the financial and eurozone crisis and rising unemployment rates in most Member States, the two proposals aimed at the facilitation of the access to third country nationals to EU labour markets did not come at a particularly favourable time. The most negative reaction came from the European Trade Union Confederation (ETUC): while recognizing the need of taking action against the exploitation of workers from the third countries, ETUC saw in the proposals primarily an attempt by the Commission to further liberalize the internal market and undermine the host country principle, the result of which would be to 'open the door to large-scale organized social dumping and fraud' (ETUC, 2010). The reception of the Directive on intra-corporate transfers in the Council was slightly more positive than that of the Directive on entry and residence conditions of seasonal workers. Yet several ministers emphasized the need to take national labour market considerations into account and have more flexibility regarding the proposed duration of stay and time limits for taking decisions. It was also questioned whether third country nationals should be accorded rights equivalent to those of EU nationals, especially with regard to social security benefits, and whether the regulation by the EU of rules on seasonal workers was in line with the principle of subsidiarity (Council, 2010b).

With regard to the second Directive, the European Commission encountered for the first time significant direct opposition to one of its initiatives from national parliaments under the 'yellow card' procedure newly introduced by the Treaty of Lisbon (Article 6 of the amended Protocol 2 on the Application of the Principles of Subsidiarity and Proportionality). Under this procedure, the Commission can be forced to review its proposal if at least one-third of national parliaments state within eight weeks of the date of transmission of the legislative proposal that they consider that the proposal does not comply with the principle of subsidiarity. A range of national parliaments – including the Austrian, British, Czech, Danish, Dutch and Polish chambers – raised various degrees of concern regarding the proposed Directive to violate the principle of subsidiarity mainly on grounds of interfering with different national labour market needs and policies and running against the right of Member States according to Article 7(5) TFEU to determine volumes of admission of third country nationals for work purposes (see, for instance, House of Lords, 2010). As there were some serious misgivings also in other parliaments – such as the French senate – the threshold for activating the 'yellow card' procedure might in the end have been met if the critical momentum would have had more time to build up than the deadline of eight weeks. Yet the deadline was not met, and as a result, Commissioner Maroš Šefčovič could limit himself in his response to the presidents of the respective parliaments in January 2011 to a measured refutation of the parliaments' concerns and a vague hint at potential 'further improvements' of the text (Commission, 2011). The quite significant intervention of the national parliaments on this occasion not only showed how sensitive EU action on labour immigration issues continues to be at the national level, but also that the deadline imposed on national parliaments for carrying out their subsidiarity checks constitutes a major organizational challenge for them.

Border and Visa Policy

In its report on the situation at the EU's external borders in 2010 Frontex reported for the period January to September a decrease in detections of illegal border crossings on all major entry routes into the Union, with the major exception of the Eastern Mediterranean route where illegal crossings over the Greek–Turkish land border had increased by 372 per cent to over 31,000 in comparison to the previous year, although the migration route to Greece via Albania remained almost as important with over 27,000 taking that route (Frontex, 2010a). This highlighted the continuing major illegal immigration pressure in the southeastern region of the Union, which also partly accounted for the critical asylum situation in Greece (see above). Although there were also prolonged or new joint operations in the Canary Islands region ('EPN-HERA') and at the eastern land borders towards Belarus and Russia ('Unity'), the southeastern region remained a focal point for the activities of Frontex: with a budget of over €1.7 million, the extension of the 2009 'Poseidon' operation on preventing unauthorized border crossings and countering cross-border criminality at southeastern sea borders, which involved the deployment of Greek, Maltese, Polish and Swedish personnel and equipment, remained the financially most important single joint operation of the year (see Frontex website factsheets).

In response to an urgent assistance request from the Greek government, Frontex activated at the end of October for the first time the Rabit (Rapid Border Intervention Team) mechanisms to increase control and surveillance levels at the border between Greece and Turkey. The Member States and associated Schengen countries made available 175 border control specialists and equipment including one helicopter, 19 patrol cars and nine thermovision vans for deployment to Greece (Frontex, 2010b). The guest officers, under the command of the Greek authorities, helped with patrolling, screening and interviewing tasks and contributed during November to a significant diminution of illegal border crossing and the arrest of 13 facilitators (Frontex, 2010c). Yet the Rabit deployment could obviously not change the fundamentals of Greece's particular geographical exposure to illegal migration pressure, and in December it was decided to prolong the operation into the new year.

As Frontex-led sea border joint operations had come under criticism because of the diverging practices of participating national units regarding interception of ships and the respect of the principle of non-refoulement of refugees on the high seas, the Council agreed on 26 April on a Decision establishing a set of rules of engagement for joint operations at sea. These rules provide that no person shall be disembarked in a country in contravention of the principle of non-refoulement, or from which there is a risk of expulsion or return to another country being in contravention of that principle (Council, 2010c). They also provide guidelines for search and rescue operations at sea. Frontex joint operations often have to deal with such missions because of the parlous state of vessels with which migrants and refugees try to reach the shores of EU Member States, although these are formally outside of the legal competence of the EU. The Council Decision, which supplemented the Schengen Borders Code of 2006, indicated the particular legal and operational complexity of sea border protection operations that have become a major part of the EU's external border policy.

While Frontex's operations were focused on making the illegal crossing of EU external borders more difficult, the EU's visa policy made some progress with making the legal crossing easier. On 17 June a visa facilitation agreement was signed with Georgia, and on 8 November two visa waiver agreements were reached with Brazil – one for holders of ordinary passports and one for holders of diplomatic, service or official passports.

On the technical side of the EU's border policy, the preparations for the much delayed entry into operation of the second-generation Schengen Information System (SIS II), with its enhanced data processing capabilities regarding alerts on persons and stolen objects, continued. The main problem remained system capacity. The original specifications anticipated the management of 15 million records, increasing over time to 22 million. Because of the expansion of the number of Member States and Schengen associate countries and intensive use of the system by the competent authorities (mainly border guards and police forces) the existing system contained in January over 31 million alerts. Yet experts estimated that the size of SIS II when going live was likely to be 52 million alerts, with steady increases expected in the future. As a result, it was agreed that the system capacity at the go-live point should be 70 million alerts and that SIS II should be tested to a capacity of 100 million alerts.

After the 'inconclusive' results of a first major test in January, a second 72-hour load test in March resulted in 99.96 per cent of 26,844,897 queries being answered within the service-level agreement time of one second (the majority of the remaining queries were answered in less than three seconds). Although this did still not satisfy three Member States, the test was declared 'passed', which averted the possibility of the SIS II project – to which a total of €95.4 million had been committed – being given up in favour of other potential technical solutions (Commission, 2010f). Further development and testing and then the different phases of migration from the old to the new system will require substantial time, which led the Commission in September to present a new timetable foreseeing the go-live of the system only for the first quarter of 2013 (Commission, 2010g).

Judicial Co-operation

In the field of judicial co-operation in civil matters only one new legal instrument was adopted, but the context in which it was adopted was at least as significant as its content: in order to enhance legal certainty for international couples as to the law applicable to their divorce or legal separation proceedings, the Commission had introduced in 2006 a proposal for the so-called 'Rome III Regulation' regarding jurisdiction and introducing rules concerning the applicable law in matrimonial matters. Numerous objections by a range of national delegations had already made it clear in 2008 that the necessary unanimity would be unattainable, as a result of which a total of ten Member States addressed a request to the Commission to submit a proposal to the Council by January 2009 allowing them to establish 'enhanced co-operation' amongst themselves in the area of applicable law in matrimonial matters. On 24 March, the Commission submitted a proposal to that effect (Commission, 2010h), which was approved by a Council Decision on 12 July (Council, 2010d) and opened the way to an adoption of Regulation 1259/2010 'implementing enhanced co-operation in the area of the law applicable to divorce and legal separation' on 20 December. The Regulation offers spouses four choices of applicable law in the case of divorce or separation (law of the state where the spouses are habitually resident, or of the state where they were habitually resident, or of the state of nationality of either spouse or of the state where the court is seized) and provides rules for deciding on the applicable law in case of disagreement or absence of choice (Council, 2010e).

With only Austria, Belgium, Bulgaria, France, Germany, Hungary, Italy, Latvia, Luxembourg, Malta, Portugal, Romania, Slovenia and Spain eventually agreeing to participate, the Rome III Regulation represents the first ever case of 'enhanced co-operation' since the mechanism of differentiated integration was introduced by the Treaty of Amsterdam in 1999. The prescribed minimum number of Member States (nine) was comfortably met, although Greece added a special twist of 'flexibility' to this instrument of flexibility by first asking to participate and then withdrawing from the projected enhanced co-operation on 3 March. While the Regulation clearly constitutes a further advance of EU civil justice co-operation and while it is quite possible that other Member States might decide to join the group of 14 at a later stage, it creates a precedent for further legal differentiation within the EU's 'area of freedom, security and justice' (AFSJ) which has already its fair share (and problems) of differentiation because of the Schengen opt-outs.

In the field of judicial co-operation in criminal matters there was also only one new substantive piece of legislation adopted which, from an institutional perspective, had the rare and doubtful distinction of emerging from competing proposals. In July 2009 the European Commission proposed a Framework Decision on the right to interpretation and to translation in criminal proceedings that aimed at making progress at least on these judicial rights after a more comprehensive proposal had completely failed in the Council in 2007. In October 2009 the Council had reached a 'general approach' on the initiative which – unsurprisingly under the then still applicable unanimity requirement – led to several restrictions of the scope of the obligation of Member States, such as the exclusion of proceedings regarding minor sanctions not imposed by a court (for example, traffic offences), the exclusion of documentary evidence from the list of 'essential' documents to be translated and the exclusion of the need for a separate legal review mechanism regarding compliance with the translation obligations.

With the entry into force of the Lisbon Treaty on 1 December 2009 both the instrument and the procedure had to be 'Lisbonized', meaning that the text had to be turned into a Directive and the ordinary legislative procedure with qualified majority voting and co-decision by the European Parliament became applicable. In order not to have the main lines of compromise already reached in the Council put at risk by a new Commission proposal and co-decision by the Parliament, the Council's General-Secretariat managed to get a group of 13 Member States to make a proposal on the basis of the general approach previously reached (Council, 2009). The Commission, however, could not resist the temptation to try to save most of its original proposal under the changed procedural rules by reintroducing it on 9 March largely unchanged as a Directive proposal of its own (Commission, 2010i). This led to a letter from the President of JHA Council, Francisco Caamaño, to the new EU Commissioner for Justice, Vivianne Reding, in which the Council expressed its 'regret' about the competing initiative introduced by the Commission, the 'confusing message' it may convey to national parliaments and the outside world, and the delays it could mean for decision-making (Council, 2010f). However, mainly thanks to the flexible approach of the European Parliament, which agreed to merge in its first reading the two proposals including compromises agreed on in the inter-institutional 'trilogue', the Directive was adopted on 20 October.

In terms of substance, the new Directive establishes detailed rules regarding the right to interpretation and to translation of essential documents together with measures to ensure the quality of both. It applies to persons suspected or accused of having committed a criminal offence for the entire duration of the criminal proceedings or proceedings for the execution of a European arrest warrant (European Parliament/Council, 2010b). It can be regarded as an important first step in addressing the persisting deficit in commonly defined judicial rights in EU criminal justice co-operation which continues to affect negatively the mutual trust necessary for the cross-border recognition of judicial decisions. Yet it may be asked whether a Council looking a bit less only at the cost side of judicial rights and a new Justice Commissioner slightly less keen on leaving her mark on a point of principle might not have spared the Union the complex institutional game of competing proposals with their avalanche of paperwork in all official languages – which most of the EU citizens might have had difficulties understanding (and taxpayers may have preferred not to have paid for).

Although the most widely used instrument of mutual recognition in criminal matters, the execution of European arrest warrants (EAWs), continues, it is still frequently affected by differences between the procedural rules and practices of Member States. As a result of a new round of mutual evaluations regarding the application of the EAW, the Council adopted on 3 June conclusions on the recommendations made by the evaluating EAW experts which placed a major emphasis on a common time limit for the submission of a language-compliant EWAS (six days), revised guidelines for compliance with the proportionality requirement and better information (through a new form) on the progress of EAW procedures (Council, 2010g).

The external side of criminal justice co-operation was developed further with the conclusion on 18 October of an agreement on mutual legal assistance between the EU and Japan. It provides for a range of assistance measures, including taking of evidence, seizing proceeds of crime, obtaining bank information, taking of testimony and hearing by video conference, with the use of the information obtained being restricted to the specific purpose defined in the assistance request. The agreement also provides for certain grounds of refusal (political offence exception, *ne bis in idem* principle, double criminality). Similar to the 2003 mutual assistance agreement with the United States, the EU–Japan agreement explicitly provides that where a request concerns an offence punishable by death, the requested Member State may refuse assistance (Council, 2010h).

Internal Security Co-operation

After the preceding year which had been marked by significant legislative activity in this sphere, the Council focused largely on strategy and programming. The Spanish Presidency of the first half of the year pushed for an early agreement on the first EU 'Internal Security Strategy' (ISS) which, under the heading of 'Towards a European Security Model', was duly adopted by the Council on 25 February. Defining first the main common threats (topped by terrorism, organized crime and cybercrime), the IIS then identified the main instruments of response (including threat anticipation, comprehensive programming, effective use of EU agencies and mutual recognition) and strategic guidelines for action (including a comprehensive and intelligence-led approach to internal security, a comprehensive model for information exchange and a reinforced external dimension). While the document has the merit of integrating the different dimensions of internal security and makes a strong case for a better integrated use of legislative and operational as well as internal and external instruments, it remains rather vague on the substance of the EU 'internal security' model (apart from emphasizing its commitment to fundamental values), does not clarify who should be responsible for achieving what, and fails to establish any details for meeting any of the rather broad objectives (Council, 2010i).

In November the Commission presented a more concrete action plan for the implementation of the ISS, listing a range of timetable-linked measures under the guiding of objectives of disrupting criminal networks, preventing terrorism, raising levels of security in cyberspace, strengthening border management and increasing resilience to crises and disasters (Commission, 2010j). Yet the Commission's action plan had its own questionable aspects as it elevated disaster management to a much bigger priority than in the ISS – which suggested that the Commission was seeking a new additional role for itself in this field – and as it comprised preciously few references to criminal justice measures although these should arguably be part of any comprehensive internal security approach. The latter indicated deficits of interaction between the responsible DG Home Affairs which had been newly separated from the DG Justice as a result of the splitting of the justice and home affairs portfolio between two Commissioners.

Both the ISS and the Commission action plan placed a considerable emphasis on the increased threats posed by cybercrime. In response to those, the Commission introduced on 30 September a proposal for a new Directive on attacks against information systems which should replace the existing one that dates from 2005. The proposal was motivated, in particular, by the new threats posed by 'botnets' – networks of computers that have been infected by malicious software and may be activated to attack information systems. The proposal, which received a positive initial reception in the Council, provides for the criminalization of the making available of devices/tools used for committing such offences, defines additional 'aggravating circumstances', introduces 'illegal interception' as a criminal offence and makes it obligatory for the Member States to collect adequate statistical data on cyber attacks for improved policy responses (Commission, 2010k).

At a more operational level, the Council adopted on 26 April an 'action-oriented paper' regarding the fight against organized crime in West Africa. This paper responded to increasing evidence that the region constitutes a growing internal security threat to the EU not only because of the (traditional) role as a major platform for drug-trafficking, but also because of its importance as a basis and/or transit zone for terrorism, the facilitation of illegal immigration, the trafficking of human beings for sexual exploitation, the counterfeiting of money, piracy, cybercrime, the trade in counterfeited products, mass marketing fraud, and illegal waste or arms trafficking. The paper placed a major emphasis on threat-analysis-based law enforcement capacity-building efforts in the region, early warning mechanisms, more synergy between the national efforts of Member States including co-ordination of their liaison officers, the potential dispatch of Europol liaison officers, and better co-ordination of EU and national technical assistance projects

(Council, 2010j). The frequent references to the need for improved co-ordination in the paper highlighted the basic problem that in the domain of law enforcement, co-operation operational capabilities can only be provided by Member States.

On the external side of EU internal security co-operation, the European Parliament demonstrated its extended powers with respect to agreements in this field after the Lisbon Treaty when it rejected – with an overwhelming majority of 378 to 196 – the SWIFT Interim Agreement between the EU and the United States. This agreement, which was intended to ensure continued access of American law enforcement authorities to the financial messaging data handled by the international SWIFT bank consortium, had already been concluded by the Council and provisionally entered into force on 1 February, which was arguably a rather cavalier way of dealing with the Parliament's newly extended powers of consent. In spite of intense lobbying not only from the Commission and Member States – most of which regarded transatlantic co-operation on financial messaging data of major importance for the fight against terrorist financing – but also from the United States (including Secretary of State Hillary Clinton) for which the agreement was crucial for the Terrorist Finance Tracking Programme (TFTP), the Parliament's LIBE Committee successfully recommended to the plenary a rejection of the agreement on the grounds of inadequate data protection provisions, especially as regards access of the United States to 'bulk' rather than individually targeted data, absence of a judicial authorization requirement, and lack of rules on retention and oversight (European Parliament, 2010b).

This forceful intervention of the Parliament in the external dimension of justice and home affairs, however, lost part of its moral strength when the EP voted through on 7 July the text of a hastily renegotiated definite EU–US agreement that provided only limited additional data protection safeguards, consisting mainly of the data transfers being monitored by 'independent overseers', a limitation of retention to the duration of the specific investigations or prosecutions, and the exclusion of 'data mining' and other types of algorithmic or automated profiling or computer filtering (Council, 2010k). This cleared the way for an entry into force of the agreement on 1 August, but made the EP's earlier stance look like being influenced more by an interest in affirming institutional prerogatives than substantive policy reasons. Nevertheless, the SWIFT saga, which will have as a by-product the development of an EU TFTP system over the next few years, showed that Council and Commission as well as third countries will now have to reckon with the Parliament as an important factor in the external dimension of the AFSJ. During the renegotiation of the SWIFT agreement, the Commission, the Council Presidency and the United States went to great lengths in briefing and communicating with the LIBE Committee – which is likely to set a precedent also for future negotiations.

II. The Implementation of the Stockholm Programme

The first year of implementation of the 2010–14 Stockholm Programme saw progress on some of the most immediate objectives set, such as the adoption of the ISS (see above) and the setting-up of the new Standing Committee on operational co-operation on internal security (COSI), which held its first meeting on 11 March and focused during the following months on ways of further promotion of operational co-operation between the Member States (Council, 2010l). It was up to the Commission to come up with a detailed action plan for the implementation of the Programme, which it did on 20 April. After a general overview, the action plan on 'delivering an area of freedom, security and justice for European citizens' comprises a 58-page timetable with over 250 measures consisting of reports, programmes, legislative proposals and other initiatives. The Plan provides for more proposals in the field of criminal law than in any other field, followed in terms of sheer numbers by civil law, law enforcement co-operation and legal immigration, with rather few elements on asylum and illegal immigration, and some proposals – such as on participation in EP elections and consular protection – that are legally outside of the scope of the AFSJ and partially reflect the fact that EU Justice Commissioner Vivianne Reding has also been given responsibility for citizens' rights (Commission, 2010l).

When the Commission's action plan was discussed by the JHA Council on 3–4 June there was widespread dissatisfaction among the ministers who felt that on many aspects the Commission had gone beyond the Stockholm Programme, while others that had been agreed in the Programme had been omitted. The Commission had, for instance, included a framework for the transfer of protection of beneficiaries of international protection, mutual recognition of asylum decisions, the establishment of a European Public Prosecutor Office and improved financial compensation of consular protection in crisis situations included in the action plan although none of these had been foreseen by the Stockholm Programme, whereas it had not included any measure against abuse and fraud in relations with the right of free movement of persons – an objective that was of major concern to several Member States and figured prominently in the Stockholm Programme. As a result, the JHA Council, in its Conclusions, did not endorse the action plan, 'noted' the discrepancies between action plan and Programme, 'urged' the Commission to take only initiatives that are 'in full conformity' with the Stockholm

Programme in order to ensure its complete and timely implementation and asked for a mid-term review of action taken by June 2012, which should take 'due account' of these Conclusions (Council, 2010l).

This was the first time that a Commission action plan for the implementation of an AFSJ multi-annual programme failed to be agreed by the Council. The Commission was legally not obliged to get the Council's agreement, and did indeed not submit a revised action plan, but the reaction of the Council – as well as the not minor difficulties some of the legislative proposals encountered during the year – does not augur well for an ambitious and rapid implementation of the Stockholm Programme over the next few years.

Key Readings

Calderoni, F. (2010) *Organized Crime Legislation in the European Union: Harmonization and Approximation of Criminal Law, National Legislations and the EU Framework Decision on the Fight Against Organized Crime* (Berlin: Springer).

Guild, E., Carrera, S. and Eggenschwiler, A. (eds) (2010) *The Area of Freedom, Security and Justice Ten Years On: Successes and Future Challenges under the Stockholm Programme* (Brussels: CEPS).

Monar, J. (ed.) (2010) *The Institutional Dimension of the European Union's Area of Freedom, Security and Justice* (Brussels: PIE Peter Lang).

References

Commission of the European Communities (2010a) 'The European Commission provides an additional €9.8 million and further technical support to Greece on asylum and border issues'. Press Release IP 10/10/1719, 15 December.

Commission of the European Communities (2010b) 'First annual report on immigration and asylum'. *COM*(2010) 214, 6 May.

Commission of the European Communities (2010c) 'Europe 2020: A strategy for smart, sustainable and inclusive growth'. *COM*(2010) 2020, 3 March.

Commission of the European Communities (2010d) 'Proposal for a Directive [. . .] on conditions of entry and residence of third-country nationals in the framework of an intra-corporate transfer'. *COM*(2010) 378, 13 July.

Commission of the European Communities (2010e) 'Proposal for a Directive [. . .] on the conditions of entry and residence of third-country nationals for the purposes of seasonal employment'. *COM*(2010) 379, 13 July.

Commission of the European Communities (2010f) 'Report from the Commission to the European Parliament and the Council: Progress report on the development of the second-generation Schengen Information System (SIS II), January 2010–June 2010'. *COM*(2010) 633, 5 November.

Commission of the European Communities (2010g) 'Report on the global schedule and budget for the entry into operation of the second-generation Schengen Information System (SIS II)'. *SEC*(2010) 1138, 21 September.

Commission of the European Communities (2010h) 'Proposal for a Council Regulation (EU) implementing enhanced co-operation in the area of the law applicable to divorce and legal separation'. *COM*(2010) 105, 24 March.

Commission of the European Communities (2010i) 'Proposal for a Directive of the European Parliament and of the Council on the right to interpretation and translation in criminal proceedings'. *COM*(2010)82, 9 March.

Commission of the European Communities (2010j) 'The EU Internal Security Strategy in action: five steps towards a more secure Europe'. *COM*(2010) 673, 22 November.

Commission of the European Communities (2010k) 'Proposal for a Directive [. . .] on attacks against information systems and repealing Council Framework Decision 2005/222/JHA'. *COM*(2010) 517, 30 September.

Commission of the European Communities (2010l) 'Delivering an area of freedom, security and justice for Europe's citizens: Action plan implementing the Stockholm Programme'. *COM*(2010) 171, 20 April.

Commission of the European Communities (2011) 'Commission reply to opinions concerning subsidiarity received from national parliaments on the proposal for a Directive on the conditions of entry and residence of third-country nationals for the purpose of seasonal employment'. *COM*(2010) 379, January.

Council of the European Union (2009) 'Initiative of the Kingdom of Belgium, the Federal Republic of Germany, the Kingdom of Spain, the Republic of Estonia, the French Republic, the Republic of Hungary, the Italian Republic, the Grand-Duchy of Luxembourg, the Republic of Austria, the Republic of Portugal, Romania, the Republic of Finland and the Kingdom of Sweden for a Directive of the European Parliament and of the Council on the rights to interpretation and to translation in criminal proceedings'. 17235/09, 14 December.

Council of the European Union (2010a) 'Common European Asylum System: State of Play'. 15561/10, 29 October.

Council of the European Union (2010b) 'Press Release 3034th Meeting of the Council, Justice and Home Affairs, Luxembourg, 7–8 October 2010', 8 October.

Council of the European Union (2010c) 'Council Decision of 26 April 2010 supplementing the Schengen Borders Code as regards the surveillance of the sea external borders in the context of operational co-operation co-ordinated by the European Agency for the Management of Operational Co-operation at the External Borders of the Member States of the European Union'. OJ L 111, 4 May.

Council of the European Union (2010d) 'Council Decision of 12 July 2010 authorising enhanced co-operation in the area of the law applicable to divorce and legal separation'. OJ L 189, 22 July.

Council of the European Union (2010e) 'Council Regulation (EU) No 1259/2010 of 20 December 2010 implementing enhanced co-operation in the area of the law applicable to divorce and legal separation'. OJ L 343, 29 December.

Council of the European Union (2010f) 'Initiative for a Directive of the European Parliament and of the Council on the rights to interpretation and to translation in criminal proceedings: draft letters to be sent to the Commission and to the European Parliament'. 7598/10, 17 March.

Council of the European Union (2010g) 'Follow-up to the recommendations in the final report on the fourth round of mutual evaluations, concerning the European arrest warrant, during the Spanish Presidency of the Council of the European Union: Draft Council Conclusions'. 8436/2/10 REV 2, 28 May.

Council of the European Union (2010h) 'Agreement between the European Union and Japan on mutual legal assistance in criminal matters'. OJ L 39, 2 February.

Council of the European Union (2010i) 'Internal security strategy for the European Union: towards a European security model'. 5842/2/2010, 23 February.

Council of the European Union (2010j) 'Strategic and concerted action to improve co-operation in combating organised crime, especially drug trafficking, originating in West Africa'. 5069/3/10 REV 3, 25 March.

Council of the European Union (2010k) 'Agreement between the European Union and the United States of America on the processing and transfer of financial messaging data from the European Union to the United States for the purposes of the Terrorist Finance Tracking Program'. OJ L 195, 27 July.

Council of the European Union (2010l) 'Draft Council Conclusions on the Commission Communication "Delivering an area of freedom, security and justice for Europe's citizens: action plan implementing the Stockholm Programme" '. *COM* (2010) 171 final, 9935/10, 19 May (adopted 4 June).

European Council on Refugees and Exiles (ECRE) (2010) *ECRE Memorandum on the Occasion of the Hungarian Presidency of the EU (January–June 2011)* (Brussels: ECRE).

European Parliament (2010a) 'European Parliament legislative resolution of 14 December 2010 on the proposal for a Directive of the European Parliament and of the Council amending Directive 2003/109/EC to extend its scope to beneficiaries of international protection'. P7_TA(2010)0463, 14 December.

European Parliament (2010b) 'Draft Recommendation on the proposal for a Council Decision on the conclusion of the Agreement between the European Union and the United States of America on the processing and transfer of financial messaging data from the European Union to the United States for purposes of the Terrorist Finance Tracking Program', Committee on Civil Liberties, Justice and Home Affairs, Rapporteur: Jeanine Hennis-Plasschaert. PE438.440v01-00, 3 February.

European Parliament/Council of the European Union (2010a) 'Regulation (EU) No 439/2010 [. . .] of 19 May 2010 establishing a European Asylum Support Office'. OJ L 132, 29 May.

European Parliament/Council of the European Union (2010b) 'Directive 2010/64/EU of 20 October 2010 on the right to interpretation and translation in criminal proceedings'. OJ L 280, 26 October.

European Trade Union Confederation (ETUC) (2010) 'Seasonal Work and Intracorporate Transfers: Meeting of the ETUC Executive Committee'. Brussels, 13–14 October.

Eurostat (2010) 'Asylum Applicants and First Instance Decisions on Asylum Applications in Second Quarter 2010'. *Data in Focus*, 42/2010.

Frontex (2010a) *Situation at the External Borders (January–September 2010)* (Warsaw: Frontex).

Frontex (2010b) 'Frontex to Deploy 175 Specialist Border-Control Personnel to Greece'. News Release, 29 October.

Frontex (2010c) 'Frontex Estimates Illegal Border Crossing at the Greek Turkish Border have Diminished by 44% at the End of November'. News Release, 30 November.

House of Lords (2010) *House of Lords, European Union Committee: Subsidiarity Assessment: Admission of Third-Country Nationals as Seasonal Workers, 1st Report of Session 2010–11, 13 October* (London: The Stationery Office).

United Nations High Commissioner for Refugees (UNHCR) (2010) *UNHCR Information Note on National Practice in the Application of Article 3(2) of the Dublin II Regulation in Particular in the Context of Intended Transfers to Greece, 16 June* (London: UNHCR).

United Nations High Commissioner for Refugees (UNHCR) (2011) *Updated UNHCR Information Note on National Practice in the Application of Article 3(2) of the Dublin II Regulation in Particular in the Context of Intended Transfers to Greece, 31 January* (London: UNHCR).

JCMS 2011 Volume 49 Annual Review pp. 165–186

Legal Developments

FABIAN AMTENBRINK
Erasmus University Rotterdam

Introduction

In many regards, 2010 will be remembered as the year in which the Union was preoccupied with dealing with the fallout of the global financial and economic crisis that began in mid-2007. It was the year in which the Union formulated its regulatory response to the turmoil in the global financial markets that hit European financial institutions with full force, while at the same time dealing with the dramatic financial situation of several eurozone Member States. It is therefore these two events that form the main focus of this article.

After years of relatively little progress in terms of the Europeanization of financial market supervision, in 2010 the Union decided to introduce a new and extensive regulatory regime for financial supervision. This is intended to address both micro- and macro-prudential supervisory aspects. At the core of this reform is the introduction of three new supervisory authorities: the European Banking Authority (EBA), the European Securities and Markets Authority (ESMA) and the European Insurance and Occupational Pensions Authority (EIOPA). Moreover, a European Systemic Risk Board (ESRB) has been created that also foresees a role for the ECB (European Central Bank).

The creation of a new financial supervisory regime has not been the only Union response to the crisis. Indeed, the financial situation in several Member States triggered ad hoc measures both by the Member States and the Union that not only turned out to be anything but uncontroversial from a legal point of view, but were also hardly in line with the financial markets' interpretation of the EU legal regime.

Additionally, 2010 has been a year in which the *acquis Union* has further developed through the jurisprudence of the Court of Justice of the European Union (ECJ). Standing out are several judgments in which the Court continues to develop its concept of European citizenship and the free movement of persons, as well as the general principle of age discrimination. Some of the rulings are likely to cause controversy and are therefore also included in this review.

I. The New Regulatory Framework for Financial Market Supervision

The de Larosière Report produced by the expert group charged by the European Commission to advise on the future of European financial regulation and supervision saw the financial and economic crisis as the product of a combination of circumstances such as the precarious macroeconomic developments, a risk management system that failed to detect risks adequately and a regulatory, supervisory and crisis management system that neither prevented the crisis from occurring nor adequately dealt with its consequences.[1] Existing rules were criticized for placing 'too much reliance on both the risk management capabilities of the banks themselves and on the adequacy of ratings' and moreover for paying 'too much attention [. . .] to each individual firm and too little to the impact of general developments on sectors or markets as a whole' (de Larosière Report, 2009, p. 10). Moreover, 'serious limitations in the existing supervisory framework globally, both in a national and cross-border context' were identified with regard to the exchange of information between national supervisors that operate on the basis of different frameworks. Finally, a lack of focus on macro-prudential supervision and systemic risks was noted (de Larosière Report, 2009, pp. 10–11).

In the European context these findings clearly point towards the shortcomings of the Lamfalussy framework of financial supervision.[2] Indeed, already in the mandate for the de Larosière expert group it was recognized that while 'the current national-based organisation of Union supervision lacks a framework for delivering supervisory convergence and limits the scope for effective macro-prudential oversight based on a comprehensive view of developments in financial markets and institutions', the existing Level 3 Committees have not achieved a level of convergence in supervisory practices and procedures

[1] The High-level Group on Financial Supervision in the EU, chaired by J. de Larosière, Brussels, 25 February 2009. See also Buckley and Howarth (2010).

[2] Generally on this framework, see Lastra (2003).

across Member States that has 'allowed the EU to identify and/or deal with the causes of the current financial crisis' (de Larosière Report, 2009, p. 10, Annex I, p. 69). The report recommended the construction of a European system of supervision through the creation of a European system of financial supervision (ESFS) and the establishment of a European body charged with macro-prudential supervision.

To a large extent, the European Commission followed these recommendations by proposing a new supervisory framework for the EU, the contours of which became clear by mid-2009 (see Commission, 2009). At the heart of the new ESFS that passed the Council and the European Parliament (EP) in late November 2010 were three Regulations on the basis of which three new supervisory authorities were established at the European level, including the European Banking Authority (EBA), the European Insurance and Occupational Pensions Authority (EIOPA) and the European Securities and Markets Authority (ESMA).[3] These European Supervisory Authorities (ESAs) effectively replace the previous Level 3 Committees under the Lamfalussy framework, in what has been described as a replacement of the 'comitology superstructure [. . .] by an agency-based superstructure', even if the legal bases of the three new bodies avoid the term 'agency' (Moloney, 2010; see also Chiti, 2009). While the new institutional framework falls significantly short of a centralized European supervisor, the ESFS will not only stand for a closer co-ordination of national supervisors that continue to remain in charge of the day-to-day supervision at the national level, but must also provide for a higher convergence of the rules applicable to financial market participants (single rulebook), as well as provide the ESAs with a set of tools that – in the last instance – will allow them to intervene in individual cases.

As described in the preambles to the legal bases of the three ESAs, the EFSF aims to create an integrated network of national and Union supervisory authorities. In addition to a Management Board and a Board of Appeal, all

[3] Regulation 1093/2010 of the European Parliament and of the Council of 24 November 2010 establishing a European Supervisory Authority (European Banking Authority), amending Decision 716/2009/EC and repealing Commission Decision 2009/78/EC, OJ 2010, L 331/12; Regulation 1094/2010 of the European Parliament and of the Council of 24 November 2010 establishing a European Supervisory Authority (European Insurance and Occupational Pensions Authority), amending Decision 716/2009/EC and repealing Commission Decision 2009/79/EC, OJ L 331/48; Regulation 1095/2010 of the European Parliament and of the Council of 24 November 2010 establishing a European Supervisory Authority (European Securities and Markets Authority), amending Decision 716/2009/EC and repealing Commission Decision 2009/77/EC, OJ 2010, L 331/84. See also Directive 2010/78/EU of the European Parliament and of the Council of 24 November 2010 amending Directives 98/26/EC, 2002/87/EC, 2003/6/EC, 2003/41/EC, 2003/71/EC, 2004/39/EC, 2004/109/EC, 2005/60/EC, 2006/48/EC, 2006/49/EC and 2009/65/EC in respect of the powers of the European Supervisory Authority (European Banking Authority), the European Supervisory Authority (European Insurance and Occupational Pensions Authority) and the European Supervisory Authority (European Securities and Markets Authority), OJ 2010, L 331/120.

three Authorities feature a Board of Supervisors with a rather diverse composition, including not only the heads of the competent national supervisory authorities and the chairperson of the respective ESA, but also including a representative from the European Commission, the ECB, the ESRB and the two other ESAs. Yet only the heads of the competent national supervisory authorities have voting rights. It is this Board of Supervisors that is charged with adopting the measures corresponding to the tasks and powers of the respective ESA as laid down in its legal basis.[4]

The sectors in which the ESAs become active largely correspond to the existing fields of European financial market regulation, including *inter alia* the Capital Requirement Directive,[5] the Depository Guarantees Scheme Directive,[6] the Directive on taking-up and pursuit of the business of insurance and reinsurance,[7] and the regulatory regime applicable to markets in financial instruments and investment services.[8] Additionally, ESMA is given a prominent role in the registration and supervision of CRAs – an activity that had only become subject to regulation for the first time in the EU in 2009.[9]

The ESAs not only develop guidelines, recommendations, and draft regulatory and implementing technical standards,[10] but they are also charged with ensuring that any regulatory and implementing technical standards laid down in directly applicable legislative acts are observed by the financial institutions in the Member States. However, the ESAs only step in if and to the extent that the competent national authorities do not or wrongly apply legislative acts.[11] In emergency situations and based upon a Council decision an ESA can adopt individual decisions to national supervisory authorities requiring them to take necessary measures to ensure orderly functioning and integrity of financial markets or the stability of the whole or part of the financial system in the Union.[12] In case of a refusal of a national authority to act, the EBA, EIOPA

[4] See, respectively, Article 43 of Regulation 1093/2010, Regulation 1094/2010 and Regulation 1095/2010.
[5] Comprising Directive 2006/48/EC relating to the taking up and pursuit of the business of credit institutions, OJ 2006, L 177/1 (as amended) and Directive 2006/49/EC on the capital adequacy of investment firms and credit institutions, OJ 2006, L 177/201 (as amended).
[6] Directive 94/19/EC on deposit-guarantee schemes, OJ 1994, L 135/5.
[7] Directive 2009/138/EC on the taking-up and pursuit of the business of Insurance and Reinsurance (Solvency II), OJ 2009, L 335/1 (as amended).
[8] Directive 2004/39/EC on markets in financial instruments, OJ 2004, L 145/1 (as amended); Directive 2009/65/EC on the co-ordination of laws, regulations and administrative provisions relating to undertakings for collective investment in transferable securities (UCITS), OJ 2009, L 302/32 (as amended).
[9] See Regulation 1060/2009 on credit rating agencies, OJ 2009, L 302/1. See also De Haan and Amtenbrink (2011).
[10] The latter based on a delegation from the European Commission.
[11] See, respectively, Article 17 of Regulation 1093/2010, Regulation 1094/2010 and Regulation 1095/2010.
[12] See, respectively, Article 18 of Regulation 1093/2010, Regulation 1094/2010 and Regulation 1095/2010.

and ESMA can ultimately directly address a decision to a financial institution to take the necessary action to comply with its legal obligations, including the cessation of any practice.

While disagreements between competent authorities in cross-border situations are foreseen to be mediated by the competent European authority in charge of a particular sector, the close co-operation between the three ESAs is supposed to be ensured by the Joint Committee of European Supervisory Authorities. Consisting of the chairs of the three ESAs, this committee is also to ensure cross-sectoral consistency between the three Authorities *inter alia* regarding financial conglomerates, micro-prudential analyses of cross-sectoral developments, risks and vulnerabilities for financial stability, and retail investment products.[13]

In addition to the reinforcement of micro-prudential supervision, the EU regulatory reform has also led to the establishment of the ESRB as part of the ESFS with the task to contribute to the prevention or mitigation of systemic risks to financial stability in the Union that arise from developments within the financial system.[14] The composition of the main decision-making body of the ESRB arguably is even more diverse than that of the aforementioned ESAs, thereby once more reflecting the multi-level nature of financial oversight in Europe. Those members with a voting right include the President and the Vice-President of the ECB, the Governors of the national central banks, a Member of the European Commission, the chairpersons of the three ESAs, the chair and the two vice-chairs of the Advisory Scientific Committee, and the chair of the Advisory Technical Committee. Moreover, high-level representatives of the Member States of the competent national supervisory authorities, as well as the president of the Economic and Financial Committee, participate without a voting right. While this set-up may ensure full participation and input from all government stakeholders in the decision-making process, it is questionable whether the size of the body enhances efficiency in the discussions and decision-making. What is more, decisions that actually matter the most – that is, recommendations to the EU, the Member States or to European or national supervisory authorities and the making public of a warning or recommendation – are subject to a two-thirds majority vote.[15] Indeed, the task of the ESRB is not limited to providing

[13] See, respectively, Article 54 of Regulation 1093/2010, Regulation 1094/2010 and Regulation 1095/2010.
[14] Regulation 1092/2010 on European Union macro-prudential oversight of the financial system and establishing a European Systemic Risk Board, OJ 2010, L 331/1; Council Regulation 1096/2010 conferring specific tasks upon the European Central Bank concerning the functioning of the European Systemic Risk Board, OJ 2010, L 331/162.
[15] Article 10, Regulation 1092/2010.

relevant European and national supervisory authorities with information on risks, but also to actually intervene in the case of the detection of significant risks by issuing warnings and recommendations for remedial action that may also include legislative initiatives.[16]

One aspect of the new ESRB that has already resulted in discussions is the close proximity of the ECB. While the latter has not been put in charge of macro-prudential supervision, the fact that at least for the first five years of operation the ECB president serves as the chair of the ESRB does signal close co-operation. This is not without risks. First of all, a failure of the ESRB to anticipate systemic risks may result in reputational damage and loss of credibility on the parts of the European monetary policy authority. Moreover, the institutional arrangements may blur the accountability not only of the ECB, but also of the ESRB.

Overall, the $64,000 question is whether the new institutional framework does indeed stand for a stronger macro- and micro-prudential supervision in the EU and will reduce risks and improve risk managements.[17] Ultimately the test will be the stability of the EU financial system and – in case of calamity – an effective crisis management at the European level.

II. The Union's (Regulatory) Response to the Eurozone Debt Crisis

The global financial and economic crisis has not only highlighted major flaws in the financial supervisory regime on both sides of the Atlantic, but has arguably also revealed the weakness of the European system of economic governance as laid down in Title VIII TFEU on Economic and Monetary Union (EMU). Indeed, the shortcomings of the system of economic co-ordination both inside and outside of the eurozone have been well documented – not least in several contributions to this journal – and will not be repeated here (for example, Featherstone, 2011). Yet the crisis also revealed the limited sustainability in the face of a crisis of the European rules on government deficit financing.

In the course of 2010 the financial situation in several eurozone Member States had deteriorated to the extent that the quasi-insolvency of one or more of them was no longer unthinkable. At the end of 2010, 24 of the 27 EU Member States were subject to the excessive deficit procedures pursuant to Article 126 TFEU. In fact, only Estonia, Luxembourg and Sweden had not exceeded the government deficit and debt limits introduced by primary Union

[16] Articles 16–18, Regulation 1092/2010.

[17] As aimed at in the de Larosière Report (2009, p. 4).

law.[18] Initially the situation was particularly problematic in Greece, which had to admit the existence of a government deficit and debt that exceeded anything that country had previously reported (Commission, 2010). The consequence was a dramatic loss of confidence by the financial markets and the downgrading of the creditworthiness of that country by all major CRAs to the point where Greek government bonds received junk status. Greece threatened to end up in a debt spiral from which there would be no escaping without outside help.[19]

Despite several endorsements by the Eurogroup,[20] continuing uncertainty in the financial markets forced eurozone Member States, upon the request of Greece, to grant Greece bilateral loans, thereby not only supporting the country but also sending a signal to financial markets. In total, the loan, centrally co-ordinated by the European Commission, amounted to €110 billion in instalments,[21] with strict conditions attached that took the shape of national measures to reduce the (excessive) deficit. Interestingly, these conditions were introduced in the ongoing excessive deficit procedure against Greece and placed on a Council Decision under Article 126(9) TFEU, as well as the post-Lisbon Article 136 TFEU, which allows *inter alia* for the adoption of measures specific to eurozone Member States in order to strengthen the co-ordination and surveillance of their budgetary discipline and to set out economic policy guidelines for them.[22]

Moreover, in the face of the deteriorating financial situation in some other eurozone Member States, the Ecofin Council also agreed to create the European Financial Stabilization Mechanism (EFSM), with an initial volume of maximal €60 billion, complemented by the European Financial Stability Facility (EFSF) – a 'special purpose vehicle'.[23] Next to the EFSM, the EFSF allows eurozone Member States to seek financial support in the form of a loan

[18] Namely by Article 126(1) TFEU and the Protocol on the excessive deficit procedure annexed to the TEU and the TFEU.
[19] See also Hodson in this volume.
[20] Declaration by the President of the Eurogroup Jean-Claude Juncker regarding Greece of 3 March 2010; Statement on the support to Greece by euro area Members States, Brussels, 11 April 2010; Statement on the support to Greece by euro area Members States, Brussels, 11 April 2010.
[21] €80 billion from the Member States and €30 billion from the IMF.
[22] 2010/320/: Council Decision of 10 May 2010 addressed to Greece with a view to reinforcing and deepening fiscal surveillance and giving notice to Greece to take measures for the deficit reduction judged necessary to remedy the situation of excessive deficit, OJ 2010, L 145/6; Communication from the Commission to the Council, Follow-up to the Council Decision of 10 May 2010 addressed to Greece, with a view to reinforcing and deepening fiscal surveillance and giving notice to Greece to take measures for the deficit reduction judged necessary to remedy the situation of excessive deficit, Brussels, 19 August 2010 (*COM*(2010) 439 final).
[23] See Press Release, Extraordinary Council meeting, Economic and Financial Affairs, Brussels, 9/10 May 2010 (9596/10 (Presse 108)).

or credit line. To finance this assistance, the EFSF is authorized to issue financial instruments (debt securities) at very favourable market conditions. The eurozone Member States are not only the shareholders of the EFSF, they also irrevocably and unconditionally guarantee, towards their own contribution, the payment of all amounts payable by the EFSF following the issuance of financial instruments. In total, the eurozone Member States guarantee €440 billion, whereby the burden-sharing is based on the ECB's capital key. The International Monetary Fund (IMF) agreed to participate in the EFSM with a contribution of €250 billion.

Whereas the EFSF is based on an intergovernmental agreement between the eurozone Member States and thereafter set up as a public limited company (*société anonyme*) under Luxembourg law with an initial capital of around €18 million,[24] the EFSM was created through Union legislation in the shape of a Council Regulation.[25] Article 1 of Regulation 407/2010 describes the purpose of the EFSM as 'preserving the financial stability of the European Union'. The EFSM allows the Union to provide financial assistance in the form of a loan or a credit line to a Member State that is experiencing, or is seriously threatened with, a severe economic or financial disturbance caused by exceptional circumstances beyond its control. In December 2010, Ireland became the first country to make use of these new loan facilities.[26]

The Union's handling of the debt crisis in Greece and the subsequent establishment of the EFSM and EFSF raised serious concerns about the legality of the chosen measures under Union law. The background to these concerns – that can only be discussed to a limited extent in the present contribution – is formed by the provisions in the TFEU on government financing (Articles 123 and 124 TFEU), the prohibition on parts of the Union and the Member States taking on the liabilities of another Member State (Article 125(1) TFEU), as well as the seemingly limited possibility to financially assist Member States in financial distress included in Article 122(2) TFEU (for example, Louis, 2010).[27]

[24] EFSF Framework Agreement between Belgium, Germany, Ireland, Spain, France, Italy, Cyprus, Luxembourg, Malta, the Netherlands, Austria, Portugal, Slovenia, Slovakia, Finland, Greece and European Financial Stability Facility, 7 June 2010. Articles of Incorporation of 15 December 2010.

[25] Council Regulation 407/2010 of 11 May 2010 establishing a European financial stabilization mechanism, OJ 2010, L 118/1.

[26] 2011/77/EU: Council Implementing Decision of 7 December 2010 on granting Union financial assistance to Ireland, OJ 2011, L 30/34. Ireland has been granted a loan (in instalments) amounting to a maximum of €22.5 billion, with a maximum average maturity of $7^1/_2$ years for a period of 3 years.

[27] There are also numerous contributions in the German legal literature. See, for example, Nettesheim (2011).

Legal Basis of the Measures

With regard to the legal basis of the rescue measures a differentiation must be made between the ad hoc bilateral loans to Greece and Regulation 407/2010 establishing the EFSM. With regard to the former, the Member States actually acted outside the Treaty framework. The same also applies to the EFSF. Yet, this is not to say that Union law was circumvented. Indeed, it has been pointed out rightly in this context that economic policy is a competence that in principle belongs to the Member States (Nettesheim, 2011). Article 5 TFEU makes clear that the economic policies of the Member States are co-ordinated but not Europeanized.

Yet, while primary Union law may thus not exclude the course of action taken, this is not to say that the latter cannot become subject to a review under Union law. According to the principle of loyal co-operation, Member States are obliged to refrain from any measures that jeopardized the achievement of the objectives of the Union.[28] Although the Member States have chosen not to take action at the EU level, arguably this does not exclude a review of their conduct under Union law. Whether and to what extent the principle of loyal co-operation has indeed been violated by the course of action taken by the Member States depends upon whether these measures are considered to be in breach of Union law. At the same time it remained unclear why Article 122(2) TFEU, which allows for Union financial assistance to a Member State that is in difficulties or is seriously threatened with severe difficulties caused by natural disasters or exceptional occurrences beyond its control, was not applied. This is even more so the case since Council Regulation 407/2010 establishing the EFSM has been based on this provision.

To be sure, the validity of Article 122(2) TFEU as a legal basis for the EFSM is anything but uncontroversial. While there can be little doubt that countries such as Greece and Ireland have been in severe financial difficulties, the question is whether these difficulties have resulted from exceptional occurrences beyond the control of these countries. Proponents of Article 122(2) TFEU as a valid legal basis refer to the dramatic financial situation of these countries resulting from the global financial and economic crisis, resulting from bank bail-outs and the instability of financial markets (for example, Häde, 2009, p. 401).[29] The drafters of Regulation 407/2010 also seem to have had this interpretation of causes and effects in mind when they included in the preamble a reference to 'the unprecedented global financial crisis and

[28] Article 4(3) TEU.

[29] The author also differentiates between effects of the global crisis and those of bad economic policy on the part of the Member States.

economic downturn' that 'has caused serious damage to economic growth and financial stability and a significant deterioration in the deficit and debt position of States has produced'.[30]

It is indeed tempting to assume simply that the serious, if not dramatic, deterioration of the market conditions for government refinancing, particularly in the case of Greece, signified an exceptional occurrence beyond the control of the Member State. It has been rightly pointed out that Article 122(2) TFEU does not require that the situation has not been caused by the Member State concerned (Herrmann, 2010, p. 414). Yet, the passage 'beyond its control' also suggests that the conduct of the Member State is hardly irrelevant in defining the scope of application of this provision. More in line with this latter reading of the law, the phrase 'exceptional occurrences' has been linked to the reference in Article 122(2) TFEU to natural disasters, as it is argued that a similar event that causes a severe economic shock is required (Geelhoed, 2003). Natural disasters are difficult or impossible to predict. Whether the same holds true for the budgetary position of certain eurozone Member States is questionable. In retrospect, Member States could have done much more prior to the global financial and economic crisis to consolidate their budgetary situation and to address any structural shortcomings in the economic sphere. As such, the crisis not only stands for the failure of national governments, but also for the insufficiency of a European system of economic policy co-ordination that has failed to address these problems. Regardless of whether the global economic and financial crisis qualifies for an application of Article 122(2) TFEU, this event has certainly not been the only factor in causing the debt crisis in the euro area.

It is also doubtful whether the scope of Article 122(2) TFEU allows for the adoption of a legally binding act of the magnitude of Regulation 407/2010. Article 122(2) TFEU refers to severe difficulties in a Member State and states that the Union can grant financial assistance to that Member State. It may thus be argued that this provision provides for a legal basis for concrete measures in individual cases. On the contrary, Regulation 407/2010 foresees 'a Union stabilization mechanism to preserve financial stability in the European Union'.[31] Regulation 407/2010 thus introduces a general Union framework for financial assistance to Member States in need. What is more, Regulation 407/2010 does not as such include a provision stating the temporary nature of this mechanism.[32]

[30] Preamble 5, Council Regulation 407/2010.

[31] Preamble 5, Council Regulation 407/2010.

[32] Article 9, Regulation 407/2010, only foresees a regular review of the implementation of the Regulation and on the continuation of the exceptional occurrences that have justified its adoption.

Indeed, the preamble to Regulation 407/2010 confirms that its drafters were primarily concerned about the consequences of a deteriorating financial situation in the eurozone.[33] Concerns about a domino effect within the eurozone and the knock-on effects of a potential restructuring of the debts of some eurozone Member States on the financial sector in other countries were arguably the key motive behind the setting up of the EFSM and EFSF, and also for granting financial assistance to Greece. This view is supported by public statements by members of the European Commission. During a debate in the EP on the EFSM and EFSF, Commissioner Michel Barnier (Internal Market) argued there was no room in this situation for a long (legislative) process.[34] Be that as it may, Article 122(2) TFEU does not necessarily support such practical considerations.[35]

Compatibility of the Measures with Primary Union Law

Mainly the rescue package for Greece, but also the establishment of the EFSM and EFSF and the granting of financial aid to Ireland under this mechanism have raised questions about the actual scope of the Union rules on deficit financing according to market principles expressed in Articles 123–125 TFEU. Article 119(3) TFEU identifies sound public finances as one of the fundamental principles with which Member States (and indeed the EU) must comply. Article 126(1) TFEU further defines this principle by stating that Member States must avoid excessive government deficits.[36] Flanking this obligation are Articles 123 and 124 TFEU, which prohibit the monetary financing of the public sector and privileged government access to financial institutions. In addition, Article 125(1) TFEU states that neither the Union nor other Member States are liable for the commitments of another Member State and, moreover, are not allowed to assume such a liability. In essence, Articles 123–125 TFEU in the past have been interpreted as aiming to ensure that Member States cannot escape their obligation under Union law to conduct sound public finances through monetary financing or by passing on their financial liabilities to the Union and/or other Member States. Member States were to be confronted 'with the financial consequences of a budgetary policy in deficit' (Amtenbrink, 2008, p. 908). In fact, the extent of financial distress which Greece faced at the time it requested assistance from the Union is arguably an example of the severe consequences of a continuous government budgetary policy in deficit.

[33] Preamble 4, Regulation 47/2010.
[34] See the EP debate of 6 July 2010 in Strasbourg.
[35] For the possibility of using Article 352(1) TFEU instead as a legal basis, see Jeck (2010).
[36] This rule is further quantified in the Protocol on the Excessive Deficit Procedure annexed to the TEU and TFEU.

Against this legal background the several rescue measures have been criticized for their incompatibility with Article 125 TFEU.[37] Put in a nutshell, some commentators interpret these measures as a government bail-out (for example, Jeck, 2010; Kube and Reimer, 2010). Yet from a formal legal perspective such a breach of Article 125(1) TFEU cannot be easily constructed based on the measures that have actually been taken. Neither the bilateral loans to Greece nor the loans granted under the EFSM and EFSF amount to a taking on of the liability of the beneficiary country by the Union and/or other Member States. Instead new liabilities have been created. Moreover, the irrevocable and unconditional guarantees by the eurozone Member States for the payment of all sums payable by the EFSF do not amount to a guarantee of the existing liabilities of the beneficiary country (Nettesheim, 2011). To the extent that the scope of the measures may actually escape the prohibition of Article 125(1) TFEU, the measures have also been considered a breach of a general Union principle that prohibits the financial rescue of Member States. Yet regardless of its desirability, from a legal perspective, little hard evidence can be found for the existence of such an enforceable principle in primary Union law. In fact, the very existence of the aforementioned Article 122(2) TFEU, which allows for financial assistance to some extent, provides evidence to the contrary.

Article 125(1) TFEU thus arguably does not rule out voluntary financial assistance. Yet, at the same time, it can be observed that there is a great discrepancy between what can be interpreted as the legal scope of Article 125 TFEU and what the no bail-out rule in primary Union law has been widely perceived to entail. In fact, the European legal framework applicable to EMU has been associated by financial markets with a general ban in Union law to come to the rescue of Member States. Viewed from this perspective, even if no formal violation of the *loi traité* can be constructed, the chosen measures have anything but contributed to the credibility of the current system of economic governance in the Union. Rather the approach taken by the Member States and Union leaves the impression of a changing of the rules halfway into the game. What is more, the current plans to establish a permanent rescue mechanism from mid-2013 in the shape of the European Stability Mechanism (ESM) suggest that the Union is turning away from such a strict interpretation under Union law of the self-responsibility of Member States. Yet at the same time it aims at reinforcement of the legal regime of economic governance in the shape of the reform of the multilateral surveillance and excessive deficit

[37] With regard to the question as to whether the measures can be interpreted as a form of monetary financing in breach of Article 123 TFEU, see Kube and Reimer (2010).

procedure and a new focus on the prevention and correction of macroeconomic imbalances in the eurozone.[38]

III. Development of the *Acquis Union* in the Jurisprudence of the ECJ

While 2010 was dominated by the Union's attempts to deal with the effects of the global financial and economic crisis and a failing system of economic governance, it was unquestionably also a year in which the *acquis Union* was developed further through the jurisprudence of the ECJ. Particularly noteworthy were judgments by the Court relating to Union citizenship and the free movement of persons, as well as to age discrimination. For reasons of space, it is these two areas that this section will concentrate on.

Union Citizenship and Free Movement of Persons

The free movement of persons in the internal market has been subject to judicial interpretation and, some would add, judicial development, for some time. Yet, it is really since the introduction of the wider concept of Union citizenship that the scope of the Union free movement provision and correspondingly the limitations of the national legislators in this regard have come to the forefront. This is not only the case with regard to the extent of the right of residence in another Member State and the equal treatment of EU nationals, but also the issue of nationality itself.

Article 207(1) TFEU states unequivocally that every person holding the nationality of a Member State is a citizen of the Union and, moreover, that citizenship of the Union is additional to and does not replace national citizenship. As Union citizenship is 'destined to be the fundamental status of nationals of the Member States'[39] this status is subject to the recognition by a Member State of the status of an individual as a national of that country. Union citizens enjoy the rights and are subject to the duties provided for in the TFEU. In the past the ECJ has ensured that these rights were not only observed with regard to movement and residence throughout the Union (Barnard, 2010), but also, for example, with regard to democratic

[38] See in this regard the current proposals from September 2010 that envisage amending Regulation 1466/97 on the strengthening of the surveillance of budgetary positions and the surveillance and co-ordination of economic policies (*COM*(2010) 526 final) and Regulation 1467/97 on speeding up and clarifying the implementation of the excessive deficit procedure (*COM*(2010) 522 final); introducing two Regulations on the effective enforcement of budgetary surveillance in the eurozone (*COM*(2010) 524 final) and on enforcement measures to correct excessive macroeconomic imbalances in the eurozone (*COM*(2010) 525 final); and introducing a Regulation on the prevention and correction of macroeconomic imbalances (*COM*(2010) 527 final).

[39] Case C-184/99, *Rudy Grzelczyk* v *Centre public d'aide sociale d'Ottignies-Louvain-la-Neuve* [2001] ECR I-6193, para. 31.

participatory rights such as those raised in *Eman and Sevinger*.[40] Member States are certainly not at liberty to restrict such rights beyond what is objectively and reasonably justified.

In the case *Janko Rottman* v *Freistaat Bayern*, the ECJ had to deal with the question of whether Union law stands in the way of the loss of the status as Union citizen as a result of a withdrawal in one Member State of naturalization acquired by intentional deception, if that results in the statelessness of a person because the person concerned does not recover the original nationality of another Member State.[41] Moreover, the question was raised as to whether Union law requires a Member State to refrain from withdrawing naturalization if that withdrawal would have the legal consequence of loss of citizenship of the Union. In this case, Germany had withdrawn the naturalization of a former Austrian national after it had become apparent that the person in question had failed to mention during the nationalization procedure that he had been prosecuted in Austria and that an arrest warrant had been issued against him.

The judgment of the ECJ is significant in several regards (Kochenov, 2010). First, the Court's statement that 'according to established case-law, it is for each Member State, *having due regard to Community law*, to lay down the conditions for the acquisition and loss of nationality' and the observation that 'the fact that a matter falls within the competence of the Member States does not alter the fact that, in situations covered by European Union law, the national rules concerned must have due regard to the latter'[42] clarify that the nationality laws of a Member State do not fall outside the scope of Union law. Indeed, the Court considers any national measure that can result in the loss of Union citizenship and the rights attached thereto to fall 'by reason of its nature and its consequences, within the ambit of European Union law', whereby it is for the ECJ to adjudicate on such matters.[43]

In reviewing the withdrawal of nationalization under Union law the ECJ comes to the conclusion that the measure in question can be justified as a reason relating to the public interest. In particular the Court considered that 'it is legitimate for a Member State to wish to protect the special relationship of solidarity and good faith between it and its nationals and also the reciprocity of rights and duties, which form the bedrock of the bond of nationality'.[44] As to the consequence of statelessness, referring to the act of deception, the ECJ does not consider such a consequence to be in breach of either Union law or

[40] Case C-300/04, [2006] ECR I-8055.
[41] Case C-135/08, [2010] ECR I-nyp.
[42] Case C-135/08, paras 39, 41 and 46, emphasis added.
[43] Case C-135/08, para. 42.
[44] Case C-135/08, para. 51.

indeed international law, such as the Convention on the reduction of statelessness, the European Convention on nationality or any general principle of international law. The Court's reference to an obligation by the national court to review the proportionality of such a decision withdrawing nationalization cannot distract from the somewhat disconcerting general conclusion that apparently nothing in Union law prevents the emergence of statelessness.[45]

Overall *Janko Rottman* v *Freistaat Bayern* cannot be interpreted to mean that European citizenship has somehow been detached from the nationality of a Member State or that Union law determines nationality. Yet it becomes clear that Member States are subject to review by the ECJ when it comes to the compatibility of their nationality laws with Union law. Moreover, the judgment is likely to further widen the already considerable scope of Union citizenship based on the jurisprudence of the ECJ.

In other developments in 2010, the extensive scope of the free movement provisions and those applicable to the rights of migrant workers were verified in several judgments. In the case of *London Borough of Harrow* v *Nimco Hassan Ibrahim and Secretary of State for the Home Department* a third-country national married to a Danish national who had school-age children of Danish nationality was refused housing assistance in the United Kingdom with reference to the fact that she did not have the right of residence.[46] The plaintiff and her children were dependent on social assistance in the United Kingdom. In the case of *Maria Teixeira* v *London Borough of Lambeth and Secretary of State for the Home Department* a Union citizen with a dependent school-age child was refused housing assistance for homeless persons with reference to the fact that she had not retained her status as a worker.[47]

Legally the question in both cases was whether the right of residence under Directive 2004/38 can be made subject to the access to sufficient resources so as not to become a burden on the social assistance system of the Member State of residence and, moreover, to having a comprehensive sickness insurance cover in that Member State in situations in which the person concerned is a parent caring for a child who is in education in the Member State concerned. In its judgments, the ECJ first made clear that Article 12 of Regulation 1612/68, which remains applicable even after the introduction of Directive 2004/38, gives children of migrant workers an independent right of residence in connection with the right of access to education in the host Member State. The Court went on to observe that linked to this right of the child is a right of residence of the parent who is the primary carer of the child. This right of residence is not subject to having sufficient resources and

[45] On the ethical implications of this, see Kochenov (2010).

[46] Case C-310/08, [2010] ECR I-nyp.

[47] Case C-480/08, [2010] ECR I-nyp.

comprehensive sickness insurance cover in that Member State.[48] What is more, that right of residence does not per se end at the age of majority 'if the child continues to need the presence and the care of that parent in order to be able to pursue and complete his or her education'.[49]

These judgments seem to confirm the more general trend set *inter alia* in *Baumbast*[50] and the approach by that Court to the protection of family life beyond the sphere of (cross-border) economic activities. This trend is further confirmed in the recent 2011 judgment in the case *Gerardo Ruiz Zambrano* v *Office national de l'emploi*[51] in which the ECJ gives wide interpretation to the scope of Union citizenship to include a right of residence and the right to a work permit to a third-country national with minor children, who are Union citizens, arguing that the refusal of such rights by a national authority would deprive the minors 'of the genuine enjoyment of the substance of the rights attaching to the status of European Union citizen'.[52]

Age Discrimination

The ECJ in 2010 handed down several judgments dealing with the compatibility of Union law of national measures which included differential treatment based on age. Directive 2000/78 establishing a general framework for equal treatment in employment and occupation in principle prohibits direct or indirect discrimination based on age such as in relation to conditions for access to employment and employment and working conditions, including dismissals and pay.[53] Member States can, however, justify such a differentiation based on age on grounds of legitimate aims, including *inter alia* legitimate employment policy, labour market and vocational training objectives.[54]

In 2005 the judgment in the case *Mangold* caused considerable controversy.[55] In the view of many commentators the ECJ constructed a general principle of Community law of non-discrimination on grounds of age.[56] As a consequence of this case, a provision in German law on part-time working and fixed-term contracts amending and repealing provisions of employment law, which authorized, in principle without restrictions, the conclusion of

[48] Case C-310/08.
[49] Case C-480/08, para. 86.
[50] Case C-413/99, *Baumbast and R* [2002] ECR I-7091.
[51] Case C-34/09, [2010] ECR I-nyp.
[52] Case C-34/09, paras 42–43.
[53] OJ 2000, L 303/19. See Articles 1 and 4.
[54] OJ 2000, L 303/19, Article 6.
[55] Case C-144/04 *Mangold* [2005] ECR I-9981.
[56] Case C-144/04 *Mangold* [2005] ECR I-9981, paras 74–75. The ECJ in this context simply refers to the preamble to Council Directive 2000/78/EC establishing a general framework for equal treatment in employment and occupation (OJ 2000 L303/16).

fixed-term contracts of employment once the worker had reached the age of 52, was considered incompatible with Community law. The controversy was not only caused by the acceptance by the ECJ of a general principle of age discrimination, but also by the fact that this effectively resulted in the horizontal application of the substance of Directive 2000/78 prior to the expiring of the period fixed for its transposition into national law. This judgment received much attention, mainly from German legal commentators, for its approach to the establishment of a general principle and the effects it assigned to a Directive prior to the expiring of the deadline for its transposition (Hailbronner, 2006; Reich, 2007; Temming, 2008; Gerken *et al.*, 2009).

From its 2010 judgment in the case of *Kücükdeveci* it has become clear that the ECJ does not seem to have any intention to reconsider this approach,[57] despite the fact that even from within the European judiciary concerns have been voiced with regard to the potential effects of such an approach.[58] In *Kücükdeveci*, the plaintiff in essence challenged German law for providing that periods of employment completed before the age of 25 are not to be taken into account in calculating the notice period for the termination of an employment relationship. In the concrete case, the employment relationship was with a private employer. While the implementation period of Directive 2000/78 had expired, the conferring German Higher Labour Court considered that the relevant provision in national law did not provide for sufficient flexibility to be interpreted in conformity with the Directive.

The ECJ once again emphasized that Directive 2000/78 'merely gives expression to, but does not lay down, the principle of equal treatment in employment and occupation, and that the principle of non-discrimination on grounds of age is a general principle of European Union law in that it constitutes a specific application of the general principle of equal treatment'. It went on to state that it is for the national court to 'ensure the full effectiveness of that law, disapplying if need be any provision of national legislation contrary to that principle'.[59] Moreover, the Court argued that the full effectiveness of the principle of non-discrimination on grounds of age requires a national court that is 'faced with a national provision falling within the scope of European Union law which it considers to be incompatible with that principle, and which cannot be interpreted in conformity with that principle, [to] decline to apply that provision, without being either compelled to make or prevented from making a reference to the Court for a preliminary ruling before doing so'.[60]

[57] Case C-555/07 *Kücükdeveci* [2010] ECR I-nyr. On these two judgments, see Muir (2011).
[58] See the Opinion of A.G. Mazák in case C-411/05, *Palacios de la Villa* [2007] ECR I-8531.
[59] Case C-555/07 *Kücükdeveci*, paras 50–51; see also Thüsing and Horler (2010).
[60] Case C-555/07 *Kücükdeveci*, para. 53.

What the Court can be seen doing is to give horizontal direct effect to what is arguably a self-constructed general principle thereby effectively circumventing the limitation of the Court's own jurisprudence on the prohibition of horizontal direct effect of Directives (see already De Mol, 2010; Thüsing and Horler, 2010). The (potential) consequence of this approach is that national courts are obliged to disregard any national legislation that is contrary to provisions of an EU Directive to the extent that the latter gives expression to a general principle of Union law. This not only makes the stands of the ECJ on horizontal direct effects irrelevant and raises questions of legal certainty, but more generally also further widens the sphere of influence of Union law on systems of social security and other social and labour market policies.

In several judgments in the area of age discrimination in 2010 the ECJ mainly dealt with possible justifications of difference of treatment on the grounds of age based on national social policy objectives. In *Kücükdeveci*, the Court found that the national provision in question was not objectively and reasonably justified by legitimate aims of national employment and labour policy and was predominantly 'to afford employers greater flexibility in personnel management by alleviating the burden on them in respect of the dismissal of young workers, from whom it is reasonable to expect a greater degree of personal or occupational mobility'.[61] In the cases of *Colin Wolf* v *Stadt Frankfurt am Main*[62] and *Domnica Petersen* v *Berufungsausschuss für Zahnärzte für den Bezirk Westfalen-Lippe*,[63] the ECJ also had to review the compatibility of national legislation with Directive 2000/78. The Court found that the setting of a maximum age for recruitment to intermediate career posts in the fire service at 30 years could be justified by the legitimate objective of ensuring the operational capacity and proper functioning of the professional fire service,[64] and that setting a maximum age for practising as a panel dentist was not precluded by the provisions of Directive 2000/78 if the aim of such a measure is to share out employment opportunities between the generations in the profession of panel dentist.[65]

In the case *Gisela Rosenbladt* v *Oellerking Gebäudereinigungsges. mbH*, the ECJ had to address the question of whether Directive 2000/78 was compatible with national legislation that permits parties to a collective agreement and the parties to an individual employment contract to provide for the automatic termination of an employment relationship upon reaching a

[61] Case C-555/07, *Kücükdeveci*, para. 39.
[62] Case C-229/08, [2010] ECR I-nyr.
[63] Case C-341/08, [2010] ECR I-nyr.
[64] Case C-229/08.
[65] Case C-341/08.

specific fixed age.[66] The Court argued that the national legislation in question 'does not establish a regime of compulsory retirement but allows employers and employees to agree, by individual or collective agreements, on a means, other than resignation or dismissal, of ending employment relationships on the basis of the age of eligibility for a retirement pension'.[67] Moreover, the Court emphasized that 'the Member States and, where appropriate, the social partners at national level enjoy broad discretion in their choice, not only to pursue a particular aim in the field of social and employment policy, but also in the definition of measures capable of achieving it', further pointing out that 'the clause on the automatic termination of employment contracts at issue in the main proceedings is the result of an agreement negotiated between employees' and employers' representatives exercising their right to bargain collectively which is recognised as a fundamental right'.[68]

Interestingly, in the context of reviewing the proportionality of the arrangements the Court argued that the termination by operation of law of an employment contract need not have the effect of forcing the persons concerned out of the labour market, as the latter was 'not [prevented] from continuing to work beyond retirement age' and employees who have reached retirement age are not deprived 'of protection from discrimination on grounds of age where they wish to continue to work and seek a new job'.[69] Whether this judgment must be interpreted to allow employees that have reached the retirement age to reapply for their former position and be able to rely on the prohibition of age discrimination is subject to debate (Bauer and Diller, 2010).

Conclusions

The EU's regulatory activities in 2010 were dominated by the global financial and economic crisis and its fallout, particularly in the eurozone. The vast and largely unanticipated impact of the crisis both on the European financial system and on the economies of the Member States resulted in what may be at least in part characterized as frantic regulatory activities. The actual impact of the crisis on the policy stances of Member States and the Union institutions became clear when quasi-overnight Union regulatory activity could be discerned in certain policy areas that were previously well guarded by Member States and only subject to a limited degree of Union involvement. It was as if the Union suddenly discovered the usefulness of market regulation and

[66] Case C-45/09, [2010] ECR I-nyr.
[67] Case C-45/09, para. 39.
[68] Case C-45/09, para. 67.
[69] Case C-45/09, para. 75.

Member States recognized the limitations of national regulatory regimes in an internal market for financial services that was highly integrated into the global financial markets. In this regard, the crisis may have succeeded where years of critical academic contributions have failed.

The fact that the global financial and economic crisis soon became a crisis of the eurozone cannot only be attributed to the efforts by the Member States to rescue their respective financial systems from total collapse. Indeed, it is also a sign of a weak system of economic governance in Europe that allowed for unsustainable government financial positions to build up and failed to force Member States to take necessary structural reforms. At the point of a near-insolvency of a number of eurozone Member States, other Member States and the Union itself could be seen turning to measures of questionable legality. What is more, with the establishment of the ESM by mid-2013 at the latest, fears of an institutionalized 'transfer union' – a Union system that obliges economically strong Member States to financially support weak Member States on a structural basis – may have finally materialized.

The development in 2010 of the case law of the ECJ may seem modest. Yet it could also be argued that by following through the approach to integration by stealth, 2010 was marked as yet another year in which the ECJ has provided further building blocks to the expansion of European law. *Janko Rottman* v *Freistaat Bayern* and *Kücükdeveci* are cases in point.

References

Amtenbrink, F. (2008) 'Economic, Monetary and Social Policy'. In Kapteyn, P.J.G., McDonnell, A.M., Mortelmans, K. and Timmermans, C.W.A. (eds) *The Law of the European Union and the European Communities* (4th revised edition) (Alphen aan den Rijn: Kluwer Law International).

Barnard, C. (2010) *The Substantive Law of the EU: The Four Freedoms* (3rd edition) (Oxford: Oxford University Press).

Bauer, J.-H. and Diller, M. (2010) 'EuGH – Rosenbladt – rosiges oder dorniges Blatt für Altersgrenzen?' *Der Betrieb*, No. 49, pp. 2727–30.

Buckley, J. and Howarth, D. (2010) 'Internal Market: Gesture Politics? Explaining the EU's Response to the Financial Crisis'. *JCMS*, Vol. 48, s1, pp. 119–41.

Chiti, E. (2009) 'An Important Part of the EU's Institutional Machinery: Features, Problems and Perspectives of European Agencies'. *Common Market Law Review*, Vol. 46, pp. 1395–442.

Commission of the European Communities (2009) 'Communication from the Commission: European financial supervision'. *COM*(2009) 252 final.

Commission of the European Communities (2010) 'Report on Greek government deficit and debt statistics'. *COM*(2010) 1 final.

De Haan, J. and Amtenbrink, F. (2011) 'Credit Rating Agencies'. Working Paper 278 (Amsterdam: De Nederlandse Bank).

De Mol, M. (2010) 'Kücükdeveci: Mangold Revisited – Horizontal Direct Effect of a General Principle of EU Law'. *European Constitutional Law Review*, Vol. 6, pp. 293–308.

Featherstone, K. (2011) 'The JCMS Annual Lecture: The Greek Sovereign Debt Crisis and EMU: A Failing State in a Skewed Regime'. *JCMS*, Vol. 49, No. 2, pp. 193–217.

Geelhoed, L.A. (2003) 'Economisch, Monetair en Sociaal Beleid'. In Kapteyn, P.J.G., Geelhoed, L.A. and Timmermans, C.W.A. (eds) *Kapteyn VerLoren van Themaat. Inleiding tot het recht van de Europese Unie en van de Europese Gemeenschappen* (Deventer: Kluwer).

Gerken, L., Riebe, V., Roth, G.H., Stein, T. and Streinz, R. (2009) *'Mangold' als ausbrechender Rechtsakt* (München: Sellier).

Häde, U. (2009) 'Haushaltsdisziplin und Solidarität im Zeichen der Finanzkrise'. *Europäische Zeitschrift für Wirtschaftsrecht*, pp. 399–403.

Hailbronner, K. (2006) 'Hat der EuGH eine Normverwerfungskompetenz?' *Neue Zeitschrift für Arbeitsrecht*, pp. 811–16.

Herrmann, C. (2010) 'Griechische Tragödie – der währungsverfassungsrechtliche Rahmen für die Rettung, den Austritt oder den Ausschluss von überschuldeten Staaten aus der Eurogebied', *Europäische Zeitschrift für Wirtschaftsrecht*, pp. 413–18.

High-level Group on Financial Supervision in the EU (de Larosière Report) (2009) *Report*. Available at: «http://ec.europa.eu/internal_market/finances/docs/committees/supervision/communication_may2009/impact_assessment_fulltext_en.pdf».

Jeck, T. (2010) 'Euro-Rettungsschirm bricht EU-recht und deutsches Verfassungsrecht', cepStudie. Available at: «http://www.cep.eu/fileadmin/user_upload/Kurzanalysen/Euro-Rettungsschirm/CEP-Studie_Euro-Rettungsschirm.pdf».

Kochenov, D. (2010) 'Case C-135-/08, *Janko Rottmann v. Freistaat Bayern*, Judgment of the Court (Grand Chamber) of 2 March 2010, not yet reported'. *Common Market Law Review*, Vol. 47, pp. 1831–46.

Kube, H. and Reimer, E. (2010) 'Grenzen des Europäischen Stabilisierungsmechanismus'. *Neue Juristische Wochenschrift*, pp. 1911–16.

Lastra, R.M. (2003) 'The Governance Structure for Financial Supervision and Regulation in Europe'. *Columbia Journal of European Law*, Vol. 10, No. 1, pp. 49–68.

Louis, J.-V. (2010) 'Guest Editorial: The No-Bailout Clause and Rescue Packages'. *Common Market Law Review*, Vol. 47, pp. 971–86.

Moloney, N. (2010) 'EU Financial Market Regulation after the Global Financial Crisis: "More Europe" or more Risks?' *Common Market Law Review*, Vol. 47, pp. 1317–83.

Muir, E. (2011) 'Of Ages In – And Ages Of – EU Law'. *Common Market Law Review*, Vol. 48, pp. 39–62.

Nettesheim, M. (2011) 'Finanzkrise, Staatshilfen und "Bail-Out"-Verbot', *Europarecht*, Heft 4, n.y.p. Available at: «http://www.jura.uni-tuebingen.de/professoren_und_dozenten/nettesheim/aktuelles/finanzkrise-staatshilfen-und-201ebail-out201c-verbot».

Reich, N. (2007) ' "Mangold" und kein Ende – oder doch?' *Europäische Zeitschrift für Wirtschaftsrecht*, pp. 198–9.

Temming, F. (2008) 'Freie Rechtsschöpfung oder nicht: Der Streit um die EuGH-Entscheidung Mangold spitzt sich zu', *Neue Juristische Wochenschrift*, pp. 3404–6.

Thüsing, S. and Horler, S. (2010) 'Case C-555/07, *Seda Kücükdeveci v. Swedex*, Judgment of the Court (Grand Chamber) of 19 January 2010, not yet reported', *Common Market Law Review*, Vol. 47, pp. 1161–72.

JCMS 2011 Volume 49 Annual Review pp. 187–208

Relations with the Wider Europe

RICHARD G. WHITMAN
University of Kent
ANA E. JUNCOS
University of Bristol

Introduction

For the majority of the year, the European Union's neighbourhood exhibited a high degree of stability and stasis with a significant degree of continuity in the situation that prevailed in 2009 (Whitman and Juncos, 2010). This countered the expectation that the wider neighbourhood was to be the region in which the Lisbon Treaty's foreign policy innovations, and the drawing together of external relations and the common foreign and security policy, were anticipated to have impact. However, the High Representative's preoccupation with the creation of the External Action Service (EEAS) left no room for new policy initiatives or innovation.

The Union has now faced two years in which there has been a 'bedding down' of the Eastern Partnership and the Union for the Mediterranean, with neither exhibiting a substantive change in the Union's relationship with its neighbours. Rather, those neighbours largely exhibited familiar traits in their relationships with the Union, with no breakthroughs in relations with the most problematic neighbours or improvement of the neighbourhood's most intractable problems. The situation between Georgia and Russia over Abkhazia and South Ossetia remained in stalemate, the conflict between Hamas and Israel persisted and the government of Belarus resisted political reforms. By the end of 2010, the Union had not faced a replication of gas supply interruptions that had marked the preceding two winters. However, the hangover from the global financial and economic crisis meant that governments and political systems in the neighbourhood remained under severe pressure. This situation was exacerbated by rising global food prices and especially the southern neighbours struggling to hold down prices of subsidized basic foodstuffs. Advances in the Union's policy objectives, albeit modest, were to be found in its enlargement portfolio.

I. Enlargement

General Developments

The ratification of the Lisbon Treaty in December 2009 was expected to inject new life into the enlargement process, which had suffered badly in previous years from the uncertainties surrounding institutional reform and issues of absorption capacity. Speaking in November, Enlargement Commissioner Štefan Füle argued that:

> With the Lisbon Treaty in force, we removed the institutional bottlenecks in our decision-making, facilitating our ambition to remain a relevant global player. The second effect is that we can now combine forces with HR/VP Catherine Ashton in the enlargement area, while making full use of the entire CFSP [common foreign and security policy] and community toolbox to effectively address the key issues of the region. (European Union, 2010g)

However, the ratification of the Lisbon Treaty and the appointment of a new Commission and a new High Representative had little impact on the conduct of the enlargement policy during 2010. The enlargement policy continued to suffer from 'enlargement fatigue', a 'creeping nationalization' (Hillion, 2010) and credibility problems – all of which have undermined the power of conditionality.

Support for enlargement within the EU remained low in 2010. According to a recent Eurobarometer survey, a higher percentage of respondents within the EU is now against further enlargement (46 per cent) compared to those supporting enlargement (40 per cent) (Eurobarometer, 2010a, p. 234). As in previous surveys, respondents from new Member States remained more supportive of enlargement (64 per cent in favour) than those from the old EU-15 (34 per cent in favour) (Eurobarometer, 2010a, p. 235). Support for EU membership varied in the candidate countries. While Macedonian citizens were largely pro-EU membership (59 per cent considered EU membership a 'good thing'), support for membership continued to decline in Turkey where 48 per cent considered accession to the EU a 'good thing' as opposed to 36 per cent of respondents that believed it would be a 'bad thing'. Only a minority of respondents in Iceland (28 per cent) and Croatia (27 per cent) considered membership to be a positive thing (Eurobarometer, 2010b, p. 35).

In recent years, we have also witnessed a strengthening of Member States' control over the EU's enlargement policy as they sought to keep tighter control during the intergovernmental stages of the process, insisting on the use of benchmarks before the negotiation of chapters can be opened and the inclusion of new conditions in every step of the process. For example, in the case of Serbia, the Netherlands managed to include compliance with the International Criminal Tribunal for the former Yugoslavia (ICTY) in the October Council Conclusion (see below). The rising number of bilateral disputes holding up the enlargement process constitutes another indication of this 'nationalization' shift (Hillion, 2010). Such developments might help increase the credibility of enlargement from the viewpoint of the Member States that have long argued for the application of 'rigorous conditionality' (European Union, 2010g). However, from the perspective of the candidate countries, the enlargement policy is increasingly being perceived as a politicized process, where the 'rules of the game' change to suit the interests of the Member States.

Judging from the number of applications being considered by the Commission in 2010, it would seem that the process of enlargement remained in good health. Formal progress was recorded in the case of Croatia (which entered the final stages of accession negotiations); Iceland began accession negotiations in July; Montenegro was awarded candidate status; and Serbia's application was forwarded to the Commission for an opinion. Some progress was also achieved regarding bilateral issues, including the Croatian–Slovenian dispute; the negotiation of a new repayment agreement between Iceland and the Netherlands and the United Kingdom; and the prospect of a new round of negotiations between Serbia and Kosovo. Bosnia and Albania, which had failed to comply fully with the Commission's 'roadmap' in the previous year, joined the EU's visa-free regime in December. The Commission recommended in May 2010 that citizens of these two countries were allowed to enter the Schengen area without a visa. The European Parliament (EP) and the Council voted in favour of visa liberalization for Albania and Bosnia in the autumn. However, following concerns expressed by some Member States about a sharp increase in the number of asylum applications from the Balkans,[1] the Commission decided to establish a follow-up mechanism to monitor the situation (Commission, 2010b). Thus, Kosovo became the only country in the region without free visa access to the Schengen area

[1] *WAZ.EUobserver*, 21 October 2010.

and without a contractual relationship with the Union as it is not recognized by all the Member States.

Problems regarding the rule of law and public administration continued to plague the implementation of EU reforms in these countries – with the exception of Iceland. Freedom of expression also remained a concern. According to the *Press Freedom Index 2010*, Macedonia (ranked 68), Serbia (85), Kosovo (92) and Montenegro (104) fell compared to the previous year, despite freedom of the press being one political criterion monitored by the Commission as part of the accession process. The situation in Turkey was even more worrying, with the country being ranked 138, down from 122nd in 2009 (Reporters without Borders, 2010).

Bilateral issues also continued to hold up the accession process: the opening of accession negotiations with Macedonia was delayed by the name dispute with Greece; the Turkish-Cypriot conflict affected the membership prospects of Turkey; the rejection of the Icesave referendum in Iceland also complicated matters regarding that country's negotiations; and the Kosovo issue got in the way of regional co-operation on trade and energy matters. The effects of the economic crisis were still noticeable across the Western Balkans, where the crisis added pressure to already overburdened domestic budgets and high unemployment rates, and Iceland, which was heavily affected by the collapse of its banking system. Turkey seemed to have escaped from the worst of the effects of the economic crisis as its economy continued to grow in 2010.

Candidate Countries

Croatia

Croatia made considerable progress towards accession in 2010, entering the final stage of negotiations. The Commission's annual report on Croatia presented a very positive assessment regarding compliance with the Copenhagen criteria and the implementation of the *acquis communautaire*. As of December 2010, Croatia had opened 34 chapters, and 28 had been provisionally closed.[2] It is expected that Croatia will finalize negotiations in 2011 with a view to joining the EU in 2013–14. There were, however, a few issues of concern. First, there are outstanding issues regarding respect for fundamental rights, the protection of minorities and refugee return. Second, in the area of competition, Croatia has to adopt restructuring plans for its shipyards. Third, the Commission repeatedly stressed the need for an independent and efficient

[2] See «http://www.eu-pregovori.hr/files/Progress-in-EU-Croatia-accession-negotiations-M_101222.pdf».

judiciary and progress regarding the fight against organized crime and corruption. Regarding the latter issue, the new prime minister, Jadranka Kosor, stepped up the government's track record in the fight against corruption and throughout the year several high-profile cases were brought to justice, including those involving a deputy prime minister and a former minister. At the end of the year, the Croatian parliament also voted to lift the diplomatic immunity of former prime minister Ivo Sanader regarding charges of corruption during his term in office (2003–09). Sanader, who fled the country the same day as the parliament's vote, was arrested in Austria, where at the time of writing he is awaiting extradition to Croatia.[3] These developments suggest a willingness on the part of the Croatian government to fulfil EU demands regarding judicial matters. Thus, despite some indications that a monitoring mechanism such as the one established for Romania and Bulgaria was being considered for Croatia, Commissioner Štefan Füle (2010) stated that the progress in meeting benchmarks achieved so far had removed 'the need for the EU to consider a co-operation and verification mechanism after accession'.

Another obstacle that was removed from Croatia's path towards the EU was the bilateral border dispute with Slovenia. Although the dispute itself has yet to be resolved, the two countries agreed to submit the resolution of their dispute on the Bay of Piran to an international arbitration commission following an agreement reached in November 2009 and mediated by the Swedish Presidency. While Croatia ratified the agreement the same month, in Slovenia the opposition parties took the case to the Constitutional Court, which declared the agreement in accordance with the Constitution in March. Despite the ruling, the opposition successfully managed to organize a referendum on the Croat–Slovenian agreement held on 6 June 2010. The 'yes' vote won narrowly, allowing the Slovenian government to submit the dispute to the arbitration commission.

Some progress was achieved regarding regional co-operation with Serbia. While the year began with tensions among the two governments concerning a case at the International Court of Justice (ICJ) on Serbian genocide claims filed by Croatia in 1999, the election of Croatian President Ivo Josipović led to an improvement in the relations between the two countries. The Croatian president and his Serbian counterpart Boric Tadić met on several occasions to discuss an out-of-court settlement of the case (WEU, 2010, p. 10). An extradition agreement on co-operation in criminal matters was also signed between the two countries. Regarding co-operation with the ICTY and in particular the access to documents, the ICTY prosecutor complained in his November report that: 'None of the outstanding military documents were provided to the

[3] *BBC News*, 10 December 2010.

OTP [Office of the Prosecutor] and no information was given regarding their possible whereabouts during the reporting period'.[4]

Turkey

The pace of progress in Turkey's accession to the EU was very slow in 2010 because of the country's continued refusal to implement the Additional Protocol to the Association Agreement regarding access of Cypriot vessels and planes to Turkish ports and airports. As a consequence, more than half of the negotiating chapters have been blocked by Cyprus, France or the EU as a whole. During the second half of 2010, not a single chapter was opened for negotiation as the Belgian Presidency failed to open the one on competition – one of the few chapters that are still available for negotiation.[5]

Only a few signs of progress were reported in 2010. A reform of the Turkish constitution was adopted via referendum in September. The majority of the 26 amendments were supported by the EU as part of the process of political reform necessary to comply with the Copenhagen criteria. However, two of the amendments were criticized by the opposition as a strategy by the AKP government to increase their control over the judiciary.[6] The Commission also expressed the view that this reform should be followed by others in the areas of freedom of expression and freedom of religion. It also went on to say that 'a new civilian Constitution would provide a solid base for a sustained development of democracy in Turkey, in line with European standards and the EU accession criteria' (European Union, 2010f). Some progress was also reported in the area of migration. Turkey and Greece announced bilateral co-operation to deal with the high numbers of migrants crossing the Greek borders from Turkey; the EU also deployed armed patrols at the border to deal with the problem. At the end of the year, Turkey agreed to sign a readmission agreement with the EU. Turkey has also asked the EU to conclude a visa-free agreement, although to no avail.

With one of the few growing economies in the region and a renewed assertiveness in its neighbourhood, Turkey's role as a regional power has also become more significant in recent years. Throughout the year, Turkey continued to play an important role as a mediator between Syria and Israel and in the Middle East peace process. It also led the establishment of a new framework of co-operation with Syria, Jordan and Lebanon – a Quadripartite High Level Co-operation Council, with the view of establishing a zone of free movement of goods and persons among the countries. However, Turkey's role

[4] *WAZ.EUobserver*, 19 November 2010.
[5] *European Voice*, 9 December 2010. On the Belgian Presidency, see Drieskens in this volume.
[6] *BBC News*, 12 October 2010.

during the Flotilla affair, the crisis in Kyrgyzstan, its rapprochement to Iran and the disagreements with other Nato allies before the Nato summit in Lisbon raised concerns among EU Member States (Emerson, 2010). Hence, in its December Conclusions, the Council 'encourage[d] Turkey to develop its foreign policy as a complement to and in co-ordination with the EU, and to progressively align with EU policies and positions' (Council, 2010d).

Macedonia

Despite the Commission's recommendation to open accession negotiations with Macedonia in autumn 2009, progress in EU–Macedonia relations continued to be blocked by the unresolved name issue with Greece. Talks between Macedonia and Greece under United Nations sponsorship continued during 2010, but with no concrete results despite some indications of progress at the beginning of the year.[7] The economic crisis meant that the Greek government had to turn its attention to domestic issues. The Commission, also frustrated by the lack of progress, called on the parties to resolve the dispute on several occasions (European Union, 2010e; Commission, 2010c). Yet, in its December Conclusions, the Council reiterated the point that '[m]aintaining good neighbourly relations, including a negotiated and mutually accepted solution to the name issue, under the auspices of the UN, is essential' and that it was 'ready to return to the matter during the next Presidency' (Council, 2010d). Regarding compliance with EU criteria, the Commission noted satisfactory conformance with political criteria, but pointed to the need to continue with reform of the police, the judiciary and public administration, as well as the fight against organized crime and corruption. Concerns regarding freedom of expression were also raised by the Commission and the Council.

Iceland

Iceland made formal progress towards EU accession in 2010. In February, the Commission recommended to the Council opening accession negotiations with Iceland, and they officially opened on 27 July. While some in Iceland had argued for an accelerated negotiation process covering only key sensitive issues rather than all the negotiating chapters, prior to a referendum,[8] the EU has repeatedly argued that: 'Negotiations will be aimed at Iceland integrally adopting the EU acquis and ensuring its full implementation and enforcement' (Council, 2010d). This position also seeks to alleviate concerns about preferential treatment expressed by other candidate and potential candidate countries.

[7] *EUobserver*, 6 April 2010.
[8] *EUobserver*, 18 November 2010.

The enlargement package presented by the Commission in the autumn contained the first progress report on Iceland. The report confirmed the low degree of misfit between Iceland's political and economic institutions and EU requirements, and the good level of preparedness of the country since it had been a long-standing member of the European Economic Area (EEA) and the Schengen Agreement. However, the Commission's report also pointed out some weaknesses in Iceland's bid. Some problems that were mentioned in the Commission's Opinion in February were the close links between business and political interests, the financing of political parties, the need to adopt a new code of conduct for MPs and the need to ensure the independence of the judiciary. Progress was reported in these areas.

Another sticky issue was the Icesave dispute with the Netherlands and the United Kingdom, especially after President Ólafur Grímsson refused to sign a bill adopted by the Icelandic parliament to compensate British and Dutch account holders which forced a referendum on 6 March 2010. However, as the voters went to the polls, the Icelandic government was already renegotiating the terms of repayment with the British and Dutch governments, making the referendum pointless. Not surprisingly, an overwhelming majority of the voters rejected the deal.[9] At the end of 2010 the new bill had yet to be adopted by the parliament.

Tensions regarding fishing quotas also rose in the second half of the year after EU–Iceland talks broke up without agreement and Iceland decided to increase its mackerel catches unilaterally, prompting fears of a 'mackerel war'.

Another significant problem refers to the low levels of support for EU membership among the Icelandic public. A Eurobarometer Survey conducted in December 2010 found that only 30 per cent of respondents agreed that Iceland's future should be as part of the EU, while 54 per cent disagreed (Eurobarometer, 2011, p. 7). Not even a majority of Icelanders agreed that the euro would help their economy (40 per cent agreed, 46 per cent disagreed) (Eurobarometer, 2011, p. 8).

Potential Candidate Countries

Serbia and Kosovo

Serbia made some progress towards EU membership during the year. In particular, headway was made regarding regional reconciliation with Croatia (see above) and Bosnia. In March, the Serbian parliament adopted a resolution condemning the Srebrenica massacre of July 1995 and extending

[9] *The Guardian*, 8 March 2010.

'condolences and apologies to the families of the victims'. However, the debate in the parliament also showed how divisive the issue remained in the country. Moreover, the fact that another resolution condemning crimes committed against Serbs in the territory of the former Yugoslavia was adopted a couple of days later created some controversy.[10] Despite some efforts on the part of the Serbian government, co-operation with the ICTY was still problematic regarding the apprehension of the two remaining fugitives Ratko Mladić and Goran Hadžić (WEU Assembly, 2010, p. 15). This remains a key condition for progressing towards candidate status.[11]

At its meeting of 25 October, the Council decided to invite the Commission to submit its opinion on Serbia's application for EU membership. However, the Council Conclusions stressed that 'at each stage of Serbia's path towards EU accession, [. . .] further steps will be taken when the Council unanimously decides that full co-operation with the ICTY exists or continues to exist' (Council, 2010a). Reform of public administration, the judiciary (in particular, the procedure for the appointment of judges and prosecutors), the fight against organized crime and corruption, and the discrimination of minorities also remained problematic, according to the Commission (2010c).

As far as Serbia–Kosovo relations were concerned, Serbian refusal to accept the participation of Kosovo's representatives in regional initiatives hindered regional co-operation. The dispute also affected the functioning of EULEX in the areas north of the Ibar River, where parallel structures have been set up by the Serb majority (WEU Assembly, 2010, p. 17). The year 2010 was marked by the reactions to the ruling of the International Court of Justice (ICJ) on the independence of Kosovo. The Court ruled that Kosovo's declaration of independence did not violate either international law or United Nations Security Council Resolution 1244. After the ruling and with a view to helping its application for EU membership, Serbia became more pragmatic regarding the Kosovo issue, agreeing to co-sponsor with the EU a UN General Assembly Resolution. The Resolution '[w]elcome[d] the readiness of the EU to facilitate the process of dialogue between the parties. [. . .] The process of dialogue by itself would be a factor of peace, security and stability in the region' (UN General Assembly, 2010). While the Resolution did not imply the recognition of independence of Kosovo by Serbia or by those EU Member States that had yet to recognize Kosovo, it cleared the way for a new round of negotiations between Kosovo and Serbia, which is due to take place in 2011.

[10] *B92 News*, 30 March 2010.
[11] At time of going to press (May 2011), Mladić was captured.

Kosovo made some progress regarding the decentralization process and the establishment of functional institutions with the set-up of a Ministry for European Integration. However, as noted in the Commission's report and the Council Conclusions in December, many challenges remain in the areas of the rule of law, the fight against organized crime and corruption, public administration and minority rights. With the decision to grant visa-free access to Bosnia and Albania, Kosovo remains the only country in the region that does not have a visa-free agreement with the EU.

Early elections to Kosovo's parliament were held on 12 December, the first parliamentary elections since the declaration of independence, and were won by Hashim Thaçi's party, the Democratic Party of Kosovo (PDK). Despite some reports of electoral fraud, the Enlargement Commissioner Štefan Füle and High Representative Catherine Ashton congratulated Kosovo authorities for 'the calm and orderly manner in which the majority of the voting took place' (European Union, 2010h). Once again, the elections were marred by the boycott of the majority of the Serbian population in the north of Kosovo.

The year ended with the scandal over the involvement of Prime Minister Thaçi in human organs trafficking and drug smuggling during and after the Kosovo war. The allegations were made in a Council of Europe report presented by Dick Marty on 16 December.[12] The report caused turmoil within western circles as it suggested that several intelligence services and the Nato mission in Kosovo (KFOR) had long known about the alleged accusations. As the year came to an end, the pressure mounted for EULEX to open an investigation into the claims laid out in the report.

Bosnia and Herzegovina, Albania and Montenegro

Bosnia's political instability continued during 2010, especially prior to the 3 October general elections. Republika Srpska Prime Minister Miroslav Dodik kept on challenging the legitimacy of the Office of the High Representative (OHR) and the Bosnian state. In February, he managed to get a law on referendums adopted by the Republika Srpska Assembly, which would allow Republika Srpska to organize referendums on decisions by the High Representative and on independence.[13] In April, a new EU–United States initiative involving the visit of Spanish Foreign Minister Miguel Angel Moratinos and American Deputy Secretary of State James Steinberg failed to reach an agreement among the political parties (WEU Assembly, 2010, p. 13). This constituted a new setback to the EU's plans to replace the OHR with a

[12] *The Guardian*, 14 December 2010.
[13] *BBC News*, 11 February 2010.

reinforced EU Special Representative. In August, the mandate of Valentin Inzko, the double-hatted High Representative/EUSR, was extended for another year until August 2011.

The October elections saw the rise of the non-nationalist Social Democratic Party. Soon after the elections, it became clear that an agreement among the main political parties to form the new government at the state and entity level was going to be elusive. At the end of 2010, three months after the elections, no agreement had been reached. Worryingly, the divide between the Bosnian Serb and Bosnian Croat parties, on the one hand, and the Bosniak Party and the Social Democratic Party, on the other, seemed to become wider. Bosnian Croats, in particular, have become more vocal about their desire to establish a third entity, openly challenging the Dayton Agreement. This political instability has developed in the backdrop of a severe economic crisis which has required the introduction of cuts to social benefits (including cuts to income support for war veterans) and caused social unrest.

In its annual report about the country's progress, the Commission stressed the need for the country to align its constitution with the European Convention of Human Rights, to improve the functioning of its political institutions and to comply with the conditions set for the closure of the OHR (Commission, 2010c). In January 2010, EUFOR Althea's mandate was amended to include non-executive capacity-building and training tasks as part of the EU's contribution to security sector reform in the country. UN Security Council Resolution 1948 of 2010 extended the mandate of the operation until November 2011. Given the unstable political situation in the country, a final date for withdrawal has not been agreed by the Member States.

Albania's progress toward membership remained sluggish due to the political crisis affecting the country's political institutions, which deepened in 2010. The crisis started when the results of the 2009 general elections, won narrowly by Sali Berisha's Democratic Party of Albania, were challenged by the main contender, the Socialist Party led by Edi Rama, on grounds of electoral fraud. This was followed by a boycott of the parliament in the autumn. In fact, the opposition did not return to the legislature until mid-2010, and only after the mediation efforts of MEPs Joseph Daul and Martin Schulz, supported by the High Representative and the Enlargement Commissioner (European Union, 2010a). However, tensions among the government and the main opposition party remained throughout the year, having a negative impact on the reform process. This problem was identified as one of the key obstacles in the country's path towards EU integration and motivated the Commission's decision not to grant Albania the status of candidate country in its Opinion published in the autumn enlargement package. The Commission pointed to the need to 'ensure the proper functioning of Parliament on the basis of a constructive and sustained political dialogue among all political parties' as one of the key priorities; other priorities referred to the rule of law, public administration and minority rights, among others (Commission, 2010c, pp. 27–8). The Opinion stated that 'negotiations for accession to the European Union should be opened once the country has achieved the necessary degree of compliance with the membership criteria, and in particular the Copenhagen political criteria requiring the stability of institutions guaranteeing notably democracy and the rule of law' (Commission, 2010c, p. 27).

For its part, Montenegro was granted candidate status by the Council in December following a recommendation by the Commission. However, in order to open accession negotiations, the Commission recommended the fulfilment of some key priorities – particularly in the area of rule of law (Commission, 2010c, pp. 25–6). High levels of corruption and organized crime continue to be a concern (Commission, 2010c, p. 28). The government survived a no-confidence vote in April organized by the opposition which had accused the Democratic Party of Socialists government of failing to deal with these problems (WEU Assembly, 2010, p. 20). A few days after the Council's decision to grant candidate status, Montenegro's prime minister Milo Djukanović resigned, after almost 20 years serving the country either as president or prime minister. His successor, former deputy prime minister Igor Lukšić, announced that his main priority would be to 'implement measures for Montenegro to open accession talks with the European Union'.[14]

II. European Neighbourhood Policy

General Developments

The European Commission published its most recent assessment of the implementation of the European neighbourhood policy (ENP) in May 2010, replicating the processes conducted in 2006 and 2009 (Commission, 2010a). As with previous reports, the Commission offered an overall assessment of policy implementation and specific analysis by sectors and by countries. The Commission was candid in highlighting that corruption remains pervasive across much of the region and that democratic reforms have slowed and human rights standards have slipped. Furthermore, the EU – as a joint initiative of Ashton and Füle – launched a Strategic Review of the ENP in summer 2010 with a view to reporting on its findings in spring 2011.

[14] *BBC News*, 29 December 2010.

The Union for the Mediterranean

The two strands of the ENP continued to exhibit their distinctive characteristics in 2010. The Union for the Mediterranean (UfM) atrophied as a largely failed exercise in relaunching the Union's multilateral policy towards the Mediterranean basin. As with its predecessor, the Euro-Mediterranean Policy, the UfM has been stymied by a lack of progress in the Middle East peace process. This was clearly demonstrated in the decision to cancel the second summit of the UfM, which was due to be hosted by the Spanish Presidency of the EU in June 2010.[15] Although it was cancelled by the UfM's joint Egyptian–French Presidency, ostensibly to allow for unencumbered talks between Palestine and Israel, press reporting suggested that the real cause was an Arab threat to boycott the summit if Israel's foreign minister attended.

The operation of the UfM is largely encumbered by the consensus needed among its 48 members for projects to be agreed. Further, the lack of a secretariat for the UfM for over a year further held up agreements between the members. In contrast, the Eastern Partnership (EaP) continued to demonstrate a much greater degree of success with its structures and processes facilitating further development of the strands of its policy tailored to the EU's neighbours to the east.

Eastern Partnership

The EaP continued to follow the mode of operation outlined in the previous assessment of the EU's relationship with the wider Europe (see Whitman and Juncos, 2010). It replicates the ENP in having both bilateral and multilateral arrangements. Progress on the individual negotiation of the new-style Association agreements is noted country-by-country below.

The most visible element of the multilateral strand of the EaP was the annual meeting of Ministers of Foreign Affairs in December 2010 in Brussels. The meeting was chaired by High Representative Ashton 'joined by' Commissioner Füle, indicating that the EaP (alongside the ENP) remains a policy activity still divided between the Commission and the EEAS. At the meeting, the Commission presented an implementation report on the progress of the Partnership.

The organizing agenda for the multilateral strand of the EaP remains the four thematic platforms and their attendant work programmes covering the period 2009–11. The platforms, which are gatherings of senior officials, took place at least twice during 2010 and they reported to the annual Foreign Affairs Ministers meetings. The Flagship Initiatives established under the

[15] On the Spanish Presidency, see Heywood in this volume.

EaP (on integrated border management; the small and medium size enterprise facility; prevention and preparedness for natural and man-made disasters; regional energy markets and energy efficiency; the southern energy corridor; promoting good environmental governance) have been rather less noteworthy in their achievements and with funding resources being a hindrance to their success.

The civil society dimension of the EaP – the Eastern Partnership Civil Society Forum (CSF) – met for its second gathering on 18–19 November. The participating organizations from both EU and EaP states produced a set of recommendations that was presented to the Foreign Ministers meeting. However, it is still not clear the extent to which the CSF has made an impact on functioning on the EaP or the issues on the agenda of the participating states. The EU–Neighbourhood East Parliamentary Assembly (Euronest), which brings together the EP and the parliaments of Armenia, Azerbaijan, Belarus, Georgia, Moldova and Ukraine – did not meet in 2010 as there was a failure of agreement regarding the composition of the Belarusian representation. It is now anticipated that Euronest will meet for the first time in spring 2011.

Bilateral Relations

Belarus

Belarus remained outside the EaP in 2010 and relations with the EU underwent a downturn in late 2010. In October, the EU suspended the travel ban and other restrictions on President Aleksander Luksahenko and 35 other named members of the regime which were originally introduced after undemocratic elections in 2006. The hope was that these would facilitate an improvement in the standards of the presidential elections scheduled for December.

The failure to improve democratic standards in the 19 December elections triggered large-scale public protests in Minsk's Independence Square calling for the president's resignation and a rerunning of the election. The use of riot police against the protesters followed, with opposition candidates among those assaulted. Many demonstrators were detained, including Vladimir Neklyayev – a 64-year-old opposition candidate who was beaten unconscious and then abducted from his hospital bed by plain clothes officers. The Organization for Security and Co-operation in Europe (OSCE) election observer mission subsequently confirmed the failings of the electoral process. The EU's High Representative was initially criticized for what was seen as a tepid declaration on the election and the violence, but an unusual joint EU–US *communiqué* signed by Baroness Ashton and American Secretary of State Hillary Clinton, issued on 23 December, called for the release of all detained demonstrators and threatened unspecified action against Belarus for non-compliance. The year concluded with Member States divided on an appropriate response to the events in Belarus and with a concern in some quarters that punitive actions would drive the Belarusian regime even further into isolationism and further strengthening its relations with the Russian Federation to the EU's disadvantage.

Moldova

EU–Moldova relations continued to be stymied by the political situation in Moldova in 2010. However, its May 2010 ENP Progress Report was positive and compliance with the EU–Moldova Action Plan was noted. The opening of negotiations for an Association Agreement on 12 January 2010 made progress during the year, but as it follows the model of that for Ukraine, negotiations can be anticipated to last several years.

General elections in November were inconclusive and with no party enjoying an overall majority. The eventual outcome was a three-party coalition agreement reached in December, which allowed the Alliance for European Integration, committed to furthering relations with the EU, and for Prime Minister Vlad Filat, to remain in power. However, the governing alliance's parliamentary power still lacked the necessary three-fifths majority needed to appoint a replacement for President Vladimir Voronin, who resigned in September 2009, with the parliamentary Speaker continuing to conduct presidential duties.

EU–Moldova policies did, however, advance in two areas in 2010. First, a dialogue opened in June is the starting point for visa-free travel. Furthermore, the Member States reached agreement in October to ask the European Commission to draw up an Action Plan for visa-free travel for Moldova along the lines of the model agreed for Ukraine and detailed below. This is also in line with the Commission's preferred 'regional approach' to visa liberalization that envisages all EaP states developing a broadly similar relationship with the Union to a common timetable. Second, on 1 May, Moldova signed the treaty to join the Energy Community (Ukraine signed the accession protocol in September) which is open to states with direct physical links to the EU electricity and gas grids, thereby committing to accepting the EU energy market rules.

Ukraine

EU–Ukraine relations did not undergo the downturn that many commentators expected following the election of Viktor Yanukovych – an opponent of the

Orange Revolution – as president of Ukraine in February 2010. Yanukovych chose to make Brussels the location for his first overseas visit and outlined his intention to give priority to advancing the relationship with the EU. A key indicator of the relationship – the prolonged negotiations for an Association Agreement, which commenced in 2007 – continued throughout 2010. These were given impetus following a visit by Commissioner Füle to Kiev in April and the presentation of a 'to-do' list of 18 necessary reforms required to conclude the negotiations and covering political reforms, macro-financial stability, the business environment, the energy sector, the environment and civil aviation. Füle described this list as a 'political steering' instrument intended to guide the Ukrainian government in the priorities for reform and to facilitate the conclusion of the Association Agreement.[16]

A significant proportion of the negotiations have now been concluded and substantive areas of agreement reached as outlined in the fourth progress report on the negotiations produced in November (EEAS, 2010). A key element of complexity in the ongoing negotiations is the Deep and Comprehensive Free Trade Area (DCFTA) intended to be at the core of the agreement and for which the 14th round of negotiations were concluded in early December. Separately the EU agreed to supplement Ukraine's International Monetary Fund Standby Loan of July with a macro-financial assistance package of €610 million.

The EU–Ukraine summit in November 2010 was largely notable for the agreement on an Action Plan for visa-free liberalization for short-stay Ukrainian visitors to the EU (Council, 2010b). The Action Plan sets out in significant detail the the precise improvements needed in border control, migration and asylum policies, and the protection of travel documents to facilitate visa-free travel. The details of the Plan make clear that such travel is a longer-term objective, rather than one to be anticipated in the near future.

South Caucasus – Georgia, Armenia and Azerbaijan

The EU continued to struggle to have a discernible impact in the South Caucasus in 2010. Despite the creation of a common framework for three states through the EaP, each state's relationship with the EU is essentially conducted bilaterally. The EU's aspirations for a greater role in stimulating a greater degree of economic and political interdependence between the states of the South Caucasus are hostage to the resolution of the ongoing Armenia and Azerbaijan dispute over Nagorno-Karabakh and with the outcome of the 2008 Georgia–Russia war remaining in stalemate. With the EEAS in the

[16] EUObserver.com, 28 April 2011.

process of being established in 2010, the Union's key conflict management instruments in the region remained the EU Monitoring Mission (EUMM) and the EU Special Representatives.

The EU's attempt to treat the states as a grouping was indicated by the opening of negotiations for an Association Agreement with all three states in mid-July. However, as the Commission's own ENP monitoring reports on Action Plans indicate, the states continue to suffer from weak political systems and underperforming economies. However, it is noteworthy that the rise in world oil prices, and the consequent benefit to Azberbaijan, also indicates that the Union needs to pursue a policy in the region that takes into account the specific circumstances of each of the three states.

North Africa

The continuity and stability in the EU's relationship with North Africa in 2010 offered no indication as to the challenges to Union policy that were to emerge in early 2011. As noted above, the UfM was a largely insignificant vehicle for the conduct of relations and the predominant structure of the relationship was under the auspices of the Action Plans under the ENP and the European Neighbourhood and Partnership Instrument (ENPI). The first EU–Morocco summit in Granada, under the Spanish Presidency, on 7 March 2010 was the first summit the EU and a Mediterranean state held under the new arrangements for foreign policy representation introduced under the Lisbon Treaty. The occasion confirmed the status of Morocco as *primus inter pares* among the North African states. Tunisia's and Egypt's relationships with the EU fall into a second category and are conducted via the ENP Action Plans and the ENPI.

Libya remained outside the scope of the ENP and the UfM. Negotiations between the EU and Libya, on a Framework Agreement, which commenced in November 2008 (and intended to open the way for the first substantive agreement between the two parties), were not concluded in 2010. However, relations did move forward in a number of respects. During a visit to Tripoli between 4 and 5 October, Cecilia Malmström, European Commissioner for Home Affairs, and Štefan Füle signed an agreement on a migration co-operation border surveillance system, mobility-related issues, smuggling and trafficking in human beings, and dialogue on refugees and international protection. In 2010, the EU also agreed with the Libyan government to provide €60 million in financial support across 2011–13 for Libya's health sector, to support economic development (primarily for small and medium enterprises) and assist the Libyan administration in modernization. A further agreement was reached to open an EU Office in Tripoli.

Middle East

The humanitarian situation in Gaza remained a source of concern during 2010. On several occasions, the EU called on Israel to open the Gaza crossings to humanitarian aid, commercial goods and persons (see, for instance, European Union, 2010c). The attention of the world turned again to the Israeli-Gaza conflict when nine activists were killed during a raid by Israeli commandos on a flotilla carrying aid to the Gaza Strip. The attack brought worldwide condemnation. In a declaration, the EU 'condemn[ed] the use of violence that has produced a high number of victims among the members of the flotilla and demand[ed] an immediate, full and impartial inquiry into the events and the circumstances surrounding them' (European Union, 2010b). Following increasing international pressure, in June, Israel decided to ease the blockade of the Gaza Strip and to allow for more civilian goods to enter the territory.[17] However, the December Council Conclusions recognized that 'changes on the ground have been limited and insufficient so far' (Council, 2010c). In August, Israel and the Palestinian Authority agreed to resume direct talks – a move welcomed by Baroness Ashton (European Union, 2010d). The Israeli decision in September not to extend the moratorium of settlements constituted a new setback to the peace process and was severely criticized by the EU. According to the December Council Conclusions, the EU's 'views on settlements, including in East Jerusalem, are clear: they are illegal under international law and an obstacle to peace' (Council, 2010c).

Norway and Switzerland

Norway's high degree of economic integration into the single market and with the eurozone meant the EU's economic travails were of significant concern to the EU's Nordic non-member – and the other European Economic Area (EEA) states – in 2010. The EU's agreement on a new System of Financial Supervision with three supervisory authorities in the areas of banking, insurance and securities immediately had implications for all of the EEA Member States, who looked for clarification of the role of the supervisory authorities in the new European Systemic Risk Board (ESRB). The financial crisis also appeared to reduce levels of public support for possible future membership of the EU. This issue had been raised in the Norwegian press following Iceland's shift of stance on accession. However, the governing coalition led by Jens Stoltenberg of the Labour Party offered no suggestion that they would alter their collective position on ruling out accession during their term of office.

[17] *BBC News*, 17 June 2010.

Norway and the EU also reached two important agreements in 2010. In July 2010, there was the signing of the EEA financial mechanisms to provide financing of €1.789 million for the period 2009–14 for the EU's 12 most recent members plus Portugal, Greece and Spain. This was used to support projects in the fields of environmental protection and climate change, green industry innovation, health, research and scholarship, cultural heritage, decent work and civil society, and justice and home affairs. Second, there was the signing of the Agreement on further improving market access for fish in the period 2009–14.

EU–Switzerland relations exhibited a chill in 2010. Early 2010 saw EU Member States being drawn into the bilateral dispute between Switzerland and Libya over the arrest of a son of Muammar Gaddafi. Switzerland's membership of the Schengen Area had the consequence of temporarily extending the travel restrictions on Swiss nationals to EU Member States. In September, the Swiss Federal Council insisted that the bilateral, sectoral approach should remain the limit of relations between the two sides. This drew a riposte in December when the Union's foreign ministers made clear that the existing relationship based on 120 sector-by-sector agreements was 'unwieldy', 'inconsistent' and 'incoherent', and had 'clearly reached its limits'. The Swiss preference for another bespoke agreement – a 'Bilateral III' agreement – as against the EU's preference for a new comprehensive agreement was scheduled for bilateral discussions in early 2011.

Conclusions

The EU's policy towards its neighbourhood continues to demonstrate a high degree of policy stability through accession processes and with the ENP providing coherence in the strategic policies pursued by the EU. Although the current accession processes and accession partners present formidable challenges, there has not been the emergence of a competing vision for the neighbouring states that provides as compelling an incentive as EU membership. However, the region also exhibits a high degree of stasis in terms of the 'frozen' and unresolved conflicts within the neighbourhood – and the EU's current policy offerings have not proved significant in mitigating or resolving conflict. Further, the EU appears to be making a minimal or indeterminate contribution to democratization processes within its neighbourhood.

The extended start-up phase of the EEAS (see Dinan in this volume) meant that the Lisbon Treaty's foreign policy innovations made no appreciable impact on the neighbourhood in 2010. If this situation was to continue once these new foreign policy arrangements are operational, this would represent a failure of Lisbon to deliver on its objectives to draw together the main strands of the EU's foreign policy – dubbed 'external action' in the Treaty – and which are closely intermeshed in the policy responses needed by the Union in its neighbourhood.

Key Reading

A discussion of the dynamics of change and continuity in the EU's enlargement policy, focusing on the supply side of enlargement, can be found in İçener *et al.* (2010). For an assessment of the EU's Mediterranean policy, see articles in the special issue of *Mediterranean Politics*, Vol. 16, No. 1, edited by Federica Bicchi and Richard Gillespie. Musu (2010) provides a comprehensive analysis of the EU's involvement in the Middle East peace process. A number of works have explored the role of the EU in its eastern neighbourhood: see, for instance, Bosse and Korosteleva-Polglase (2009); Browning and Christou (2010); and Whitman and Wolff (2010).

References

Bosse, G. and Korosteleva-Polglase, E. (2009) 'Changing Belarus? The Limits of EU Governance in Eastern Europe and the Promise of Partnership'. *Co-operation and Conflict*, Vol. 44, No. 2, pp. 143–65.

Browning, C. and Christou, G. (2010) 'The Constitutive Power of the Outsiders: The European Neighbourhood Policy and the Eastern Dimension'. *Political Geography*, Vol. 29, pp. 109–18.

Commission of the European Communities (2010a) 'Communication from the Commission to the European Parliament and the Council: taking stock of the European Neighbourhood Policy'. *COM* (2010) 207, Brussels, 12 May.

Commission of the European Communities (2010b) 'EU visa liberalisation for Albania and Bosnia'. Press release, Brussels, 8 November.

Commission of the European Communities (2010c) 'Communication from the Commission to the European Parliament and the Council: enlargement strategy and main challenges, 2010–2011'. *COM* (2010) 660, Brussels, 9 November.

Council of the European Union (2010a) 'Council Conclusions', 3040th General Affairs Council meeting, Luxembourg, 25 October.

Council of the European Union (2010b) '14th EU–Ukraine Summit (Brussels, 22 November 2010)'. Joint Press Statement. Available at: «http://www.consilium.europa.eu/uedocs/cms_data/docs/pressdata/en/er/117912.pdf».

Council of the European Union (2010c) 'Council Conclusions on the Middle East Peace Process', 3058th Foreign Affairs Council meeting, Brussels, 13 December.

Council of the European Union (2010d) 'Council Conclusions on Enlargement/ Stabilisation and Association Process', 3060th General Affairs Council meeting, Brussels, 14 December.

Emerson, M. (2010) 'Turkey and Its Neighbourhood'. *CEPS European Neighbourhood Watch*, No. 61, June, pp. 1–2. Available at: «http://www.ceps.eu/newsletter/ceps-european-neighbourhood-watch-archive».

Eurobarometer (2010a) 'L'Opinion Publique dans l'Union Européenne'. Eurobarometre 73. Available at: «http://ec.europa.eu/public_opinion/archives/eb_arch_en.htm».

Eurobarometer (2010b) 'Public Opinion in the European Union'. Eurobarometer 74. Report. Available at: «http://ec.europa.eu/public_opinion/archives/eb_arch_en.htm».

Eurobarometer (2011) 'Iceland and the European Union. Summary'. Flash Eurobarometer, March. Available at: «http://ec.europa.eu/public_opinion/flash/fl_302_sum_en.pdf».

European External Action Service (EEAS) (2010) 'Fourth joint progress report: negotiations on the EU–Ukraine Association Agreement'. Available at: «http://eeas.europa.eu/ukraine/docs/joint_progress_report4_association_en.pdf».

European Union (2010a) 'Statement by High Representative Catherine Ashton and Commissioner Stefan Füle on Albania'. Brussels, 20 May.

European Union (2010b) 'EU declaration on the Israeli military operation against the Flotilla: Statement by EUHR Catherine Ashton'. Brussels, 31 May.

European Union (2010c) 'EU Foreign Affairs Council Conclusions on the Middle East peace process and Gaza'. Brussels, 27 July.

European Union (2010d) 'Statement by EUHR Ashton on resumption of direct talks between Israel and the Palestinians'. EEAS press release, Brussels, 20 August.

European Union (2010e) 'Statement by European Commission President Barroso following his meeting with fYROM President, Gjorge Ivanov'. Brussels, 9 September.

European Union (2010f) 'Statement by European Commissioner for Enlargement and ENP, Stefan Füle, on the result of the referendum in Turkey'. Press release, Brussels, 13 September.

European Union (2010g) 'EU Commissioner Füle on enlargement package', Press points on Enlargement Package. Brussels, 9 November.

European Union (2010h) 'Statement by EU HR Ashton and Commissioner Füle on elections in Kosovo'. Press release, Brussels, 13 December.

Füle, Š. (2010) Speech Given by the European Commissioner for Enlargement and Neighbourhood Policy European Commission at the Enlargement Package Press Conference. SPEECH/10/639, Brussels, 9 November.

Hillion, C. (2010) *The Creeping Nationalisation of the EU Enlargement Policy*. SIEPS Report 2010:6 (Stockholm: Swedish Institute for European Policy Studies).

İçener, E., Phinnemore, D. and Papadimitriou, D. (2010) 'Continuity and Change in the European Union's Approach to Enlargement: Turkey and Central and Eastern

Europe Compared'. *Southeast European and Black Sea Studies*, Vol. 10, No. 2, pp. 207–23.

Musu, C. (2010) *European Union Policy towards the Arab–Israeli Peace Process: The Quicksands of Politics* (Basingstoke: Palgrave Macmillan).

Reporters without Borders (2010) *Press Freedom Index 2010*. Available at: «http://en.rsf.org/press-freedom-index-2010,1034.html».

United Nations (UN) General Assembly (2010) 'Request for an Advisory Opinion of the International Court of Justice on Whether the Unilateral Declaration of Independence of Kosovo is in Accordance with International Law'. UN 64/298. Sixty-fourth General Assembly Plenary, 120th Meeting, 9 September.

Western European Union (WEU) Assembly (2010) 'The EU and the Western Balkans'. Document A/2066, Fifty-Eighth Session, 16 June.

Whitman, R. and Juncos, A. (2010) 'Relations with the Wider Europe', *JCMS*, Vol. 48, s1, pp. 183–204.

Whitman, R. and Wolff, S. (eds) (2010) *The European Neighbourhood Policy in Perspective: Context, Implementation and Impact* (Basingstoke: Palgrave Macmillan).

JCMS 2011 Volume 49 Annual Review pp. 209–230

Relations with the Rest of the World

DAVID ALLEN AND MICHAEL SMITH
Loughborough University

Introduction

We argued in our review of 2009 that a series of forces both within the European Union (EU) and in the world arena raised important questions about the EU's capacity to make its presence felt, and that these were questions for a 20-year rather than an annual perspective (Allen and Smith, 2010). We make no apology for returning to these issues in reviewing relations between the EU and the rest of the world in 2010 since it is clear that they became both more apparent and more pressing during the past year. The Union has effectively been subject to a dual process of transition. On the one hand, the implementation of the Lisbon Treaty has raised issues about the external representation of the Union, about the message it is to convey and about the instruments with which that message can be pursued (Joint Study, 2010). On the other hand, the process of global transformation has continued to intensify, and this in turn has created both new problems and new potential opportunities for a Union in transition. The question that inevitably arises is: did the EU in 2010 give evidence of its capacity to manage this dual process of transition and to develop a 'grand strategy' that might guide it in exploiting change for its own and the more general advantage (Biscop, 2009; De Vasconcelos, 2010; Howorth, 2010)? The sections that follow use this theme as their organizing device, and provide considerable but often contradictory evidence for an answer to the question.

I. General Themes

Foreign, Security and Defence Policy

Although the Lisbon Treaty was in force for all of 2010, there was a sense, by the end of the year, that its impact in external relations had yet to be felt. This was partly because the newly selected High Representative and Vice-President of the Commission (HR/VP), Catherine Ashton, was forced to devote a good part of the year to the establishment of the European External Action Service (EEAS). During this time she was heavily and often unfairly criticized by many within the EU for her lack of action, her lack of preparedness, her fondness for appointing British officials to her staff, her lack of linguistic fluency and her poor prioritization of relevant issues.[1] In truth her focus on events in the outside world was too often distracted by the ongoing turf wars between the Commission and the Council and the demands of the European Parliament (revelling in its new powers under the Lisbon Treaty) as she attempted to negotiate, first the basic structure of the EEAS, then the necessary changes to the EU's staff and financial regulations, and finally a budget for 2011 – all of which were necessary to bring the EEAS into being and all of which took up most of 2010.[2]

Part of the problem that Ashton faced arose from the fact that, whilst few substantive plans had been made for the introduction of the EEAS or for the implementation of the foreign policy powers granted to the HR/VP and the elected President of the European Council by the Lisbon Treaty, the EU institutions and the Member States had had plenty of time to consider their own positions on these matters and so they were more than well prepared for the turf wars that then followed. Ashton began 2010 with rival visions of the EEAS inherited from the European Parliament and from the 2009 Swedish Presidency with an expectation that the major legal decisions on its structure would be taken by the end of April 2010. As well as a group of high-level officials she was significantly assisted by the former Danish ambassador to the EU, Poul Skytte Christoffersen, who gave her robust advice as she sought compromises acceptable to all. However, the early tone was set by the President of the Commission who, acting quite lawfully, but most definitely against the spirit of the Lisbon Treaty reforms, unilaterally appointed in March a close aide and confidante, Joao Vale de Almeida, as the first EU ambassador to the United States (*EurActiv*, 2010). At this stage Ashton had not yet agreed who exactly would be joining the EEAS and how the relationship between herself, the EEAS and the former Commission delegations

[1] *The Guardian*, 2 December 2010.
[2] See Joint Report (2010, pp. 147–52) for a detailed account of this process, and Dinan in this volume.

would evolve, but later in the year she quickly moved to make her own appointments, after consultation with the Commission, to a number of the newly renamed EU Delegations.

Just as the President of the Commission was keen to make his pitch for a major role in the emerging system, so too was the Spanish Presidency, which acted as if the provisions in the Lisbon Treaty designed to hand over the foreign policy responsibilities of the Council Presidency to the HR/VP did not exist.[3] Spain's determination to act as if nothing had changed on the foreign policy front was in the end challenged by President Obama, who rejected an invitation by the Spanish to attend an EU–US summit in Madrid, preferring to wait until December when, under the new Lisbon procedures, he eventually met with Presidents Van Rompuy and Barroso with no formal role for the EU Council Presidency, which by then had passed to Belgium.

By the end of the year the EEAS formal structures and some senior appointments were in place and the service was set to begin work as a 'functionally autonomous body' under the leadership of Ashton effectively from 1 January 2011. By this time also, the foreign policy roles of both the HR/VP and the President of the Council had become clearer (see Dinan in this volume for the full details), with Van Rompuy seeking mainly to mediate within the European Council rather than stop the traffic around the world and with Ashton consolidating her power base within the Council/EEAS structures to the neglect of her position in the Commission possibly as a result of President Barroso's apparent need for foreign policy prominence.

Viewed from outside the EU, the shared representational roles of Presidents Van Rompuy and Barroso at the expense of the Council Presidency, especially at the numerous bilateral summits probably made more of an impression in 2010 than did Ashton. Even when she was in attendance, she shunned the international limelight that her predecessor, Javier Solana, had so enthusiastically embraced. This was partly because of her formidable EEAS agenda and partly because it was quite clear that, whilst she was effectively now acting as the EU's foreign minister, she was ultimately serving the collective interests of the EU Member States and their 'President' Van Rompuy.

Despite the distractions listed above and despite being generally acknowledged that the HR/VP has been given an impossible job that can only be made workable in the long term by providing her with a variety of deputies for her many roles, Ashton nevertheless did occasionally manage to escape the Brussels infighting. In her first full year in office she established an apparently close and effective relationship with American Secretary of State Hillary

[3] On the Spanish Presidency, see Heywood in this volume.

Clinton, took a bolder stance than her predecessor in her strong political support of the Palestinians and her willingness to criticize Israel[4] – a willingness which received heavyweight support inside the EU[5] – and she did play a significant role in the negotiations over the recognition of Kosovo. Whilst Ashton was criticized in France for not attending a meeting of EU defence ministers in Mallorca she was in fact in Ukraine attending the inauguration of the newly elected President,[6] and in the summer she successfully presided over the process that led to the EU announcing a significantly enhanced package of sanctions against Iran that further strengthened those agreed by the UN in its bid to bring Iran back to the negotiating table over its nuclear programme.[7]

Ashton was also handicapped by the unhelpful behaviour of the EU's major Member States – all of whom face serious internal financial problems which make them inclined to be difficult over the funding for the EEAS,[8] reluctant to co-operate in the necessary agreements to commit their own diplomatic staff to the EEAS, reluctant to take on any further CSDP missions as they seek to cut further their already depleted defence budgets and generally more reluctant than before to work together on foreign affairs. Britain, France and Germany in particular were partly responsible, by their own neglect of the need to round up the necessary votes, for the EU's failure in September to secure the right for either Ashton or Van Rompuy to speak at the UN.[9] If ever there was a good example of the EU's continuing inability to co-ordinate its external actions with those of its Member States or make effective use of its many external 'levers' it was this one, for at the UN it was the EU, proud to be the world's largest provider of development aid, whose representatives were denied the right to speak on development matters by the negative votes of the African, Caribbean and Pacific countries who most benefit from EU development aid (Emerson and Wouters, 2010).

In a similar vein the inability of the EU to present a coherent collective stance towards Turkish membership (with the United Kingdom in direct conflict with both France and Germany) has made it almost impossible for Ashton to work with Turkey on foreign policy matters with the result that Turkey has emerged as a serious regional actor in its own right with the power to exert influence in both the Balkans and the Middle East where the EU has fundamental foreign policy concerns. It is easy to blame the HR/VP for her

[4] *The Guardian*, 26 August 2010.
[5] *The Guardian*, 11 December 2010; *Financial Times*, 10 December 2010.
[6] *Financial Times*, 10/11 July 2010.
[7] *The Guardian*, 14 July 2010.
[8] *Financial Times*, 6 September 2010.
[9] *Financial Times*, 20 September 2010.

neglect of such issues, but without the willing co-operation of the EU's most important Member States any such initiative would be meaningless.

The example of Turkey leads us to the problems that exist in the EU's 'strategic' bilateral relationships with the major powers. Ashton has established that the United States, China, Russia, Brazil, India, South Africa, Canada, Japan and Mexico are already 'strategic partners' of the EU and that Egypt, Israel, Indonesia, Pakistan, Ukraine and South Korea may join the list in the future. In September, Van Rompuy called a meeting of the European Council specifically to consider strategic partnerships and in particular the management of the bilateral summits that go with them.[10] Despite the diversion of a very public row about French treatment of the Roma between President Sarkozy and President Barroso, some progress was made and in the Presidency Conclusions it was noted that there was a need for 'improved synergies between the EU and the national levels, for enhanced co-ordination between institutional actors, the better integration of all relevant instruments and policies and for summit meetings with third countries to be used more effectively' (European Council, 2010a). An annex (1) to the Presidency Conclusions then listed six key points concerning changes to the internal preparations for summits that were required to improve the EU's performance. Apart from the obvious need for the EU institutions and the Member States to work more effectively together, by Member States not adopting their own contradictory unilateral actions and demanding EU collective positions towards Russia or China, for instance, that are firmer than their own individual position (Garton Ash, 2010), there were some very specific recommendations about the need for EU bilateral summits with strategic partners to be better prepared and co-ordinated with those involving individual EU Member States; about the need to focus on just two or three core issues; and about the need to clearly identify EU interests and possible leverage to achieve them. Ashton was tasked with progressing these suggestions for improving EU summitry and reporting back to the European Council in December.

Vogel[11] argues that in the three weeks that followed the September Council the EU held summits with South Africa and China and within the wider EU–Asia grouping with no evidence that any lessons had been learned, although maybe it was a little early to rush to judgement. At its October meeting, the European Council did note that there had been discussions about the key political messages that Van Rompuy and Barroso would promote at the forthcoming summits with the United States, Russia, Ukraine, India and

[10] *European Voice*, 14 October 2010.
[11] *European Voice*, 14 October 2010.

the African Union (European Council, 2010b), and in December Mrs Ashton presented her first progress report on strategic partnerships (Ashton, 2010; European Council, 2010c) which covered summits in general and then separate reports on progress in three strategic relationships (Russia, China and the United States). All three partner-specific papers are slightly tougher and more realistic than previous efforts and all focus on the need for fewer priorities, greater coherence and more results from bilateral summits. There is also an emphasis on the need for a better linking of foreign and security policies with sectoral policies such as trade, energy, climate and migration, and the need for common messages to be prepared by the EEAS for the use of the EU Member States – the 'desired outcome' being 'not the proverbial "single voice" but instead one message, 27 voices' (Ashton, 2010).

On the evidence of 2010 there is still much work to be done in improving the EU's development of strategic partnerships, but this will in 2011 provide an objective test of Van Rompuy's ability to mediate between the EU Member States to facilitate consistent and coherent collective positions as well as his ability to gain effective support from Ashton and the EEAS to enhance his own representational performance at summits. If the EU Member States allow him some freedom of manoeuvre and stick to agreed common positions and if he can reach similar agreements with Barroso as now govern their joint performance at G20 meetings, then this could be an area where the EU might be able to act more effectively in 2011 as a result of the Lisbon Treaty changes.

In 2010 there were 13 ongoing CSDP missions with the Support for Security Sector Reform mission in Guinea-Bissau coming to an end in September and the EU Somalia Training Mission, which is designed to strengthen the Somalia security forces and thus to hopefully stabilize the country, began work in Uganda in May. It should, however, perhaps be noted that the EU did decide to send an additional armed European force on a mission in 2010, but it was to Greece and it concerned a rapid border intervention team drawn from border guards across the EU who were dispatched to assist Greece in patrolling its border with Turkey to prevent the influx of illegal immigrants.[12]

When Ashton finally got to chair a meeting of EU Defence Ministers[13] it did not prove possible to agree on a successor for the European Defence Agency (EDA) Chief Executive Alexander Weis, who left his post in October, because of Italian objections to Madame Claude-France Arnould,[14] but early in the new year Arnould's appointment was announced by Ashton. There were further signs of Member State tensions at the Defence Council when a paper on the EU's future security policy was submitted by Sweden and

[12] *The Guardian*, 26 October 2010.
[13] *European Voice*, 2 December 2010.
[14] *European Voice*, 25 November 2010.

Germany – a move seen by many as a message to France and the United Kingdom that they did not have exclusive rights over the definition of EU security. What was not addressed but what will most certainly exercise Ashton in 2011, however, is how the EU's established military collaboration is going to 'survive austerity' (Valasek, 2011).

In 2010 the EU continued to use its Instrument for Stability to launch a number of conflict prevention interventions and a total of 27 fast track crisis response programmes (Commission, 2011, p. 93). Finally, in March 2010 it was decided to end the Western European Union (WEU) by July 2011 because the Lisbon Treaty contains a solidarity clause similar to the WEU mutual defence clause.

The Common Commercial Policy

During 2010, the EU acquired both a new Trade Commissioner – the Belgian, Karel de Gucht – and a new trade strategy. The new Commissioner was confronted by a commercial policy context in which the intensification of linkages between elements of the global financial crisis, and the uncertainty of responses to the crisis by major actors, made it difficult to insulate trade policy from politics more generally, both within and outside the Union. In addition, EU foreign economic policy acquired new dimensions and new forms of management process: the tensions and potential crises surrounding the euro in the face of national economic crises in Greece, Ireland and Portugal posed new challenges for the EU's role in global economic management through the G20 and other channels, whilst the implementation of the Lisbon Treaty meant that for the first time it was possible to add investment policy to the portfolio of external policy concerns.

Unsurprisingly, the year saw a number of reviews and restatements of elements in the EU's external commercial relations. The review of trade policy resulted in late 2010 in a revised version of the EU's existing 'Global Europe' strategy, with its emphasis on competitiveness and on an assertive use of both 'trade defence' instruments and mechanisms of trade promotion (Commission, 2010a). Alongside it went the beginnings of a review of the EU's Generalised System of Preferences, which was to lead to formal proposals in early 2011. The trade policy review was also placed firmly within the context of the EU's emerging '2020' strategy for economic growth and competitiveness in general (Commission, 2010a, pp. 95–6). The review proposed a new and more assertive trade policy posture, but it was pointed out by some that this carried a number of risks and dangers.[15]

[15] *European Voice*, 10 December 2010.

Some of these risks and dangers were directly linked to the persistence and intensification of the global financial crisis, which had led to a significant fall in global trade, described by WTO Director General Pascal Lamy as the largest since the end of World War II.[16] Attempts at multilateral management of the crisis and its effects were hampered not only by divergence in domestic policies, but also underlying differences in approaches to management in general. These threw into question the activities of groups such as the G7, G8 and G20, and created potentially damaging linkages between apparently disparate areas of policy. In October, the Commission called for the removal of 330 trade barriers established during the financial crisis, explicitly linking this call to the need to respect G20 decisions (Commission, 2011, p. 97).

At the level of more specific trade policy measures, the year saw a number of challenges for the Union. In particular, the World Trade Organization (WTO) strongly criticized the Union's mechanisms for determining the level of anti-dumping duties.[17] The WTO also found against the EU in a complaint about the ways in which it had interpreted the 1996 information technology agreement in applying duties to innovative technologies.[18] More positively, the banana dispute with a number of Central American countries and the United States was implemented following the agreement initialled at the end of 2009; the EU came to an agreement with Russia on its entry into the WTO; the Union took an active role in negotiations designed to deal with counterfeit goods in international trade; and there was continuing progress in the extension and revision of customs co-operation agreements with major partners.[19] One factor that had to be taken into account in any negotiation of significant international agreements was the new assertiveness of the European Parliament, which had been endowed with new powers of approval (and rejection) in the Lisbon Treaty (Dinan, 2010).

Development Co-operation Policy and Humanitarian Aid

As the plans for the EEAS evolved during 2010, concern was expressed in many quarters about their impact on the EU's development aid programmes. There were fears that, rather than providing for the more effective co-ordination of EU development policy with other major EU sectoral policies, the Lisbon arrangements could lead to an even more fragmented approach with increased rivalry and turf wars (Engel, 2011).

[16] *The Guardian*, 25 February 2010.
[17] *Financial Times*, 11 August 2010.
[18] *Financial Times*, 17 August 2010.
[19] *European Voice*, 4 March 2010; *Financial Times*, 25 November 2010; *European Voice*, 9 September 2010; Commission (2011, p. 97).

The arrangements that had been agreed by the end of 2010 affected development policy in the following way. Following the principle of 'single geographic desks', the EEAS has absorbed all the staff on country desks from the two previous Commission Directorate Generals (DGs) dealing with Development (covering the African, Caribbean and Pacific (ACP) countries) and External Relations covering aid to Asia and Latin America and the Neighbourhood). In the Commission the Development Commissioner will take charge of a new DG (EuropeAid, Development and Co-operation) which will contain the remaining officials from DG Development and those from the EuropeAid Co-operation Office. Whilst the EEAS will control the Foreign Policy Instruments Service and will help prepare Council aid allocations and strategies for individual recipients, overall responsibility for development aid will remain in the hands of the Development Commissioner who will liaise with Ashton via the Commission's newly established Group of Commissioners on external relations.[20] These arrangements can lead to either a better co-ordination of the various EU policies that are relevant to development co-operation or to enhanced turf wars. Many fear that the Council-dominated foreign policy considerations will overwhelm pure 'development' considerations despite the efforts of the European Parliament to preserve the Commission's authority in this area but, as with so many aspects of the Lisbon Treaty institutional innovations, it is just too soon to tell.

The Joint ACP–EU Council was held in Burkina Faso in June, at which the revised Cotonou Agreement was signed.[21] This is the second revision of the agreement since it was first signed in 2000 and it takes into account the growing importance of regional integration, particularly amongst the African recipients of ACP aid, with the African Union becoming a full partner in the EU–ACP relationship as well as the EU's determination to push ahead with the controversial Economic Partnerships Agreements (EPAs) which group the ACP recipients into seven such partnerships (five in Africa, and one each for the Caribbean and the Pacific) which are unpopular because they are designed eventually to lead towards an opening up of ACP markets to EU exporters. The revised agreement also seeks to deal with the co-ordination of security and development issues, the question of sustainable development with a particular emphasis on food security, fisheries and HIV-AIDS, the relationship between climate change and development, trade following the expiry of preferences in 2007, and a widening of the participants in the EU–ACP process to include not just governments and international organizations, but also national parliaments, local authorities, civil society and the private sector.

[20] See Dinan in this volume.

[21] Second revision of the Cotonou Agreement is available at: «http://ec.europa.eu/development/icenter/repository/second_revision_cotonou_agreement_20100311.pdf».

In November the Commission published its Green Paper (Commission, 2010b) on the future of development policy in which the Development Commissioner, Andris Piebalgs, states a clear preference for updating the 2005 European Consensus on Development (Commission, 2006) with a refocusing of EU development policy on employment and sustainable growth involving, for instance, risk sharing with the private sector to develop infrastructure. The Green Paper was generally well received, although some noted with concern that the document refers throughout to EU rather than Commission development policy, suggesting that the focus of policy-making in the future might still swing back towards the EEAS and the Member States with negative consequences for the overall EU aid effort.

The EU is the largest global donor of development aid and humanitarian aid. Despite Ashton's failure to rush immediately to Haiti after the earthquake, the EU managed to deliver €120 million in assistance, and later Ashton, representing both the EU and its Member States, was able to offer over €1 billion at the New York pledging conference. Some €131 million was sent to Darfur and €20 million to the Horn of Africa for drought relief, and the EU also funded relief efforts in the Kenyan refugee camps that housed many of those escaping the conflict and breakdown of government in Somalia.

II. Regional Themes

Russia

For the EU, 2010 seemed like a good year to try to recalibrate its relationship with Russia to match the policy 'reset' that President Obama had initiated in the America–Russia relationship and to take advantage of a noticeably better atmosphere (Polikanov, 2010). However, by the end of 2010, in the first of her reviews of the EU's strategic partnerships, Ashton (2010) argued that the relationship with Russia continued to consist essentially of untapped potential (see also Barysch, 2011). Both sides had clear but conflicting views about what they wanted from each other, and both sides, weakened by the impact of the global financial crisis and facing difficult domestic situations, had sound reasons to try to develop the relationship positively. From the EU, Russia sought above all else to progress its WTO membership and extract from the EU specific financial, trade, visa and technological resources and concessions to advance its much-needed 'modernization' programme. For its part, the EU saw the opportunity to push for a stronger focus on the rule of law within Russia; to integrate Russia more fully into the essentially 'western' system of global economic and financial regulation; to persuade Russia to both sign up and adhere to measures designed to guarantee security of EU energy supply;

and to get Russia to work more co-operatively with the EU to resolve the frozen conflicts in the shared neighbourhood, particularly in Transdniester.

There were two EU–Russia summits in 2010 held in Rostov and Brussels. Both were more harmonious than in previous years. In Rostov agreement was reached on a 'partnership for Russia's modernization' and in Brussels agreement was reached on the trade concessions needed to bring Russia into the WTO, probably in 2011. However, despite this progress a new Partnership and Co-operation agreement (PCA) continues to be elusive because even when relations are calm, EU and Russian ambitions for the relationship do not match – Russia wants technocratic support and investment, the EU wants to see progress towards government and judicial reform, although it has become noticeably softer on a number of human rights issues.

Energy of course remains an important issue with a row between Russia and Belarus[22] replacing the more traditional Russia–Ukraine[23] spat, both of which tend to lead to a break in the flow of Russian gas to the EU. After Russia refused to ratify the Energy Charter Treaty the EU had hoped that binding energy supply guarantees could be built into the new PCA, but that still remains some way off. For its part, Russia has complicated its relationship with the EU by its pursuit of a customs union with Belarus and Kazakhstan because the EU is not prepared to extend trade concessions that it might concede to Russia to its new (or rather old!) partners.

There is nevertheless potential for further improvements in the EU–Russia relationship. Ashton's report to the December European Council (Ashton, 2010) has some low-key but useful suggestions for improving the partnership process with fewer but more focused meetings and relying in future on a clearer identification of core EU interests and objectives by the EEAS. The real process problem, however, from the EU perspective is the continued reluctance of the EU Member States to toe the collective EU line in their own bilateral dealings with Russia. This problem will not be solved by a more effective EEAS, but it might be eased somewhat if Van Rompuy could bring pressure to bear within the European Council on the EU Member States by discretely, and only within the walls of the European Council, naming and shaming those Member States who continue to undermine the EU's collective stance.

Africa

In Africa the EU finds itself dealing with a group of states that remain very poor and fragile, but whose situation was not significantly worsened by the

[22] *The Guardian*, 23 and 24 June 2010.

[23] Although this did threaten to raise its head again in September. See *Financial Times*, 23 September 2010.

global financial crisis because they are still not that well integrated into the global economic system and because, up to now at least, EU aid keeps flowing. One reason why this is the case is perhaps a consequence of the competition for influence that the EU faces from China in Africa. The Chinese do not seem interested in adding strings or conditions to their economic assistance and this must also make the EU think twice about its own ambition to more effectively apply conditionality to its development aid and to replace direct EU aid with loans and leveraged private capital. This new situation was reflected in the manoeuvrings that surrounded the UN development meeting in September and it may well be that a number of African states felt able to deny Van Rompuy and Ashton speaking rights because they were confident that the flow of EU aid would be maintained and could, if threatened, be replaced by Chinese assistance.

The third EU–Africa summit was held in Tripoli in November and controversially Ashton left most of the preparations to the Development Commissioner and his newly established DG (see above). It was significant that neither Ashton nor the Trade Commissioner attended the summit and that the question of the controversial Economic Partnership Agreements were not on the agenda, suggesting perhaps that, for the HR/VP, the EU–AU framework is essentially for development matters leaving her to focus on individual African states that present foreign and security policy problems such as Sudan, Ivory Coast or Somalia. Whilst this could be seen as a sensible division of labour, it could also be viewed as an early failure of the new foreign policy system which was meant to bring the various strands of EU external activity together in a co-ordinated and coherent whole. It is unlikely that an increasingly influential China will choose to manage its African relations in this way. One commentator suggested that leaving EU–Africa policy in the hands of the Development Commissioner was a bit like handing over EU–Russia relations to the EU Energy Commissioner.[24]

The EU undertook a number of election observation missions in Africa in support of democracy promotion and respect for human rights. Over 800 observers from all the Member States worked in Burundi, Ethiopia, Guinea, Ivory Coast, Niger, Rwanda, Sudan, Tanzania and Togo, led by chief observers drawn from the European Parliament (Commission, 2011, p. 93). Towards the end of the year, the EU imposed a travel ban on the Ivory Coast's President Laurent Gbagbo who refused to give up power following the electoral victory of his rival Alasane Outtara, whose right to rule has been recognised by the UN, the United States, the African Union and France.[25]

[24] *European Voice*, 4 November 2010.
[25] *The Guardian*, 21 December 2010.

The travel ban itself is not that significant, but the further involvement of the EU and some of its Member States in Ivory Coast, Somalia and particularly in North Africa in 2011 is now clear and is presenting the EU's new joined-up foreign policy machine with some interesting challenges.

Asia

The continuing rise of Asia on the EU's international agenda poses a number of policy problems for the Union, and has intersected with the broader questions posed by the changing constellation of global power. The EU has responded to this challenge with a variety of bilateral, inter-regional and multilateral strategies, but this in its turn has created new problems of management and consistency in the context of 'complex inter-regionalism' (Hardacre, 2009). During 2010, the full range of possibilities and problems was on view in EU relations with the region. At the broadest level, the Asia–Europe Meeting (ASEM) provided evidence of the changing conception of 'Asia' in EU policy – it now encompasses 46 members and a number of observer organizations, and during 2010 Russia, Australia and New Zealand were added to the list. The eighth ASEM was held in October, and the EU also met with other groups in the inter-regional context, including the Association of Southeast Asian Nations (ASEAN). At the same time, bilateral summits were held with key regional partners, including Pakistan,[26] China and India, whilst there were key encounters with India and China especially in the context of global multilateral negotiations such as those on climate change (Bonn and Cancún), on trade (the continuing but still uncompleted Doha Round of the WTO) and in the new multilateral arena provided by the G20.

The EU's dominant concern in respect of Asia (but also at the global level) remains the rise of China. Whilst this could be seen as a major challenge of a purely 'external' nature, the picture is considerably more complex. China can be seen as a 'problem' because of its dominance in EU external trade (and specifically because of its enormous trade surplus with the Union), and because of its apparent protectionism pursued through regulatory and monetary policies as well as through straightforward trade policy measures, it is also true that for countries such as Germany, the Chinese market is a major source of economic recovery and growth.[27] Not surprisingly, there is often a division between those EU Member States that benefit – or think they might benefit – from cordial relations with China and those that see things through

[26] *European Voice*, 3 June 2010. Interestingly, the summit considered an upgraded 'partnership for peace and development' in which the strategic issues would be considered by Van Rompuy as President of the European Council, and regular meetings at foreign minister level would involve Ashton as High Representative for Foreign Policy and External Relations.
[27] *Financial Times*, 9 July 2010.

the lens of protectionism and retaliation. At the same time, China itself has pursued a policy largely dominated by its confrontation with the United States in the so-called 'G2', and this in turn has created spillover effects (and potentially, new policy opportunities) for EU policy-making in such areas as currency management and defence-industrial trade (Grant, 2010). Alongside these general issues of policy management, the EU has to deal with specific trade disputes – and with the increasing tendency of China to use its membership of the WTO as a means of addressing its problems with the EU. Thus during 2010, the Chinese mounted a complaint through the WTO about continuing EU anti-dumping actions on footwear,[28] and the EU in its turn imposed provisional anti-dumping duties on cargo scanners imported from China (the latter assuming added significance because it focuses on a 'high-tech' product and not on the types of products traditionally seen as problematic in EU–China relations).[29]

Although China is a continuing concern for the EU, in 2010 South Asia was if anything more prominent on the agenda of EU–Asia relations. First, there was a confrontation with Sri Lanka in the aftermath of the civil war about the ways in which Colombo should be punished for apparent human rights infringements. The Union threatened to withdraw the privileges accorded to Sri Lanka under the 'GSP+' scheme, which rewards countries for human rights progress among other things; this in turn evoked an angry response from the Sri Lankan government, but the provisions were nonetheless suspended in the middle of the year.[30]

By the autumn, the primary focus of EU policies in South Asia was Pakistan, where the disastrous floods led to urgent needs for assistance. The Union provided immediate emergency aid, delivered through civilian strategic airlift under the aegis of the EU Military Committee (Commission, 2011, p. 104), but then entered into a complex debate about whether further aid should be delivered through financial assistance or trade measures. As the debate went on, trade measures came to dominate, but inevitably any waivers of duties on imports from Pakistan would require approval from the WTO, in which a number of Pakistan's neighbours expressed their reservations in light of the economic damage this might cause them. As the *Financial Times* noted, this demonstrated the complexities attending EU decisions even where all Member States agree on the aims and the methodologies; not only are the internal divisions and institutional niceties a barrier to swift action, so also are international commitments and obligations.[31]

[28] *Financial Times*, 5 February 2010.
[29] *European Voice*, 6 May 2010.
[30] *European Voice*, 11 February 2010 and 1 July 2010.
[31] *Financial Times*, 16 September 2010; *European Voice*, 7 October 2010.

In the case of India, there were no immediate crises to address, just the continuing divergence of views which does nothing to ease agreement on such issues as climate change; but it was notable that agreement was reached on counter-terrorist measures during 2010 – an agreement in which Europol was a full contracting party (Commission, 2011, p. 89) – and that the agenda of EU–India summit discussions had notably broadened to reflect the increasing breadth and depth of the 'strategic partnership'.

Trade relations between the EU and a number of Asian countries were a notable focus during 2010. In particular, the negotiation of free trade agreements has become a significant element in EU strategy towards a number of its Southeast and East Asian partners. The most advanced of these is the agreement between the Union and South Korea (see below). It is clear that the EU–South Korea agreement will form a template for further agreements with members of ASEAN in particular. By the end of the year, negotiations had been opened with Singapore (in March) and Malaysia (in October) and were projected with other members, partly as the result of failure to make progress with an inter-regional agreement.

The EU remained concerned during 2010 with what might broadly be described as political change – or lack of it – in Asia. In South and Southeast Asia, the longest-standing concern has been with Burma (Myanmar), and the EU as was to be expected registered its concern with the process of elections that took place there during the year. After the elections, the Burmese junta allowed the release of Aung San Suu Kyi, whose safety has been a long-standing preoccupation for the Union, and this was greeted with cautious optimism (not to mention some debate about just what the EU could and should do in such an event).[32] In Central Asia, which has become steadily more prominent in EU foreign policy debates, the key issue during the year was that of Kyrgyzstan, where the incumbent leadership was ousted, but was unclear what the EU could do other than to express concern for the safeguarding of human rights.

Latin America

As with Asia, EU–Latin American relations occur on bilateral, inter-regional and other levels. During 2010, the key bilateral events were summits with two of the EU's 'strategic partners' – Brazil and Mexico – and the main focus of those talks was trade. Trade was actually a central theme of EU–Latin American relations at all levels since the EU has sought to establish free trade agreements either with individual countries in Latin America or with some of

[32] *European Voice*, 10 June 2010, 11 November 2010 and 18 November 2010.

the several sub-regional groupings. During 2010, a free trade agreement was initialled with Peru and Colombia, and Ecuador set in motion the process for adding itself to this. At the same time, a free trade agreement was also initialled with a group of six Central American countries (Costa Rica, El Salvador, Guatemala, Honduras, Nicaragua and Panama).[33] Finally, negotiations were restarted with the Mercosur group (Brazil, Argentina, Uruguay and Paraguay), although almost as soon as they were started, they ran up against the problem of agricultural trade that has blighted them over more than a decade.[34] Interestingly, all of these bilateral and inter-regional negotiations were crystallised alongside the EU–Latin America summit held in Madrid during May 2010, which evidently provided a context within which a variety of linked issues could be addressed more effectively. The summit also launched the Latin American Investment Facility and the EU–LAC Foundation, providing further evidence of the deepening of the institutional relationship between the two regions (Commission, 2011, pp. 89, 108).

The United States, Japan and Other Industrialised Countries

During 2010, the Union continued to face challenges in its key 'strategic partnership' – that with the United States. Perceptions of an EU–US 'special relationship' are fundamental to the idea that the EU is or can be a 'pole' in an emerging multipolar – or an actor in an 'inter-polar' – world, or can contribute significantly to the development of transatlantic co-operation on issues of global governance (Hamilton and Burwell, 2009; Smith, 2011). The Spanish Presidency, installed in January 2010, certainly shared this view, but was doomed to frustration in its efforts to manage the EU–US agenda. Most obviously, the Spaniards failed in their attempts to organise an EU–US summit during their Presidency; the White House made it known that they would not engage on the top level with the EU if there was no substantial agenda to be dealt with.[35] The summit was eventually held on the margins of the Nato ministerial meeting in Lisbon – a two-hour meeting between Obama, Barroso and Van Rompuy, which focused on three broad issues: growth and jobs, climate change and development, and security (Council, 2010a). This was hardly the grand reinvigoration of the EU–US partnership that had been demanded not only by a number of EU leaders but also by a number of American commentators. In this context, it was also suggested that American leaders remained uncertain about 'who speaks for Europe?', reflecting an age-old problem that was given a new twist by the Lisbon

[33] *European Voice*, 12 May 2010 and 20 May 2010.
[34] *European Voice*, 12 May 2010.
[35] *Financial Times*, 2 February 2010.

Treaty.[36] Opinions differed on whether the very public snub over the summit was therapeutic for the EU, but clearly it represented a key challenge for the new EU Ambassador to Washington, João Vale de Almeida (see above) who showed himself to be a persistent advocate of the EU's interests in Washington.

This background – of EU eagerness to be taken seriously, and Washington's apparent inclination to take the Union for granted – was given added poignancy by the development of transatlantic relations in political and security affairs during the year. In February, Robert Gates, the American Secretary of Defence, mounted a public attack on the weakness of Europeans in the face of security challenges by noting the 'pacification' of European countries and of the Europeans collectively,[37] and this atmosphere persisted through the year as the Americans tried to get solid European support for their renewed 'surge' in Afghanistan.[38] More positively, the EU stood alongside the United States in pursuing stronger UN sanctions against Iran in relation to its nuclear aspirations, and even when new sanctions were adopted (with at least the tacit support of China and Russia) by the UN Security Council, of installing new measures that actually went further than the formal requirements.[39] This strengthened position incidentally involved a sidelining of proposals put forward by Brazil and Turkey – two more of the EU's strategic partners – for exchanges of fissile material that would have given Iran a new type of relationship with its neighbours.[40] When talks with Iran restarted in late 2010, Ashton was given a co-ordinating role on behalf of the international community, but the talks themselves made little progress.

A significant trend in previous years had been the increasingly assertive role of the European Parliament in debating and expressing its position on EU–US relations, and the Lisbon Treaty's conferral of new powers on the EP in respect of international agreements created new potential frictions in this area. The first major test of the Parliament's position came early in 2010, when the so-called 'SWIFT' agreement (dealing with the provision of information to the United States in relation to bank transfers, and named after the organization that administers such transfers) came up for approval. The threat of rejection by the Parliament became a reality in February 2010, despite attempts to impose the agreement for a trial period, and there followed a process of renegotiation, in which issues of privacy were at the centre of the

[36] *The Guardian*, 3 February 2010.
[37] *The Guardian*, 24 February 2010.
[38] *The Guardian*, 16 November 2010.
[39] *Financial Times*, 10 June 2010; *The Guardian*, 24 July 2010.
[40] *The Guardian*, 18 May 2010 and 19 May 2010; *Financial Times*, 9 June 2010.

EP's concerns, before a revised agreement was grudgingly passed in the summer.[41] Not surprisingly, this process was greeted by some with concern and others as a manifestation of a new 'democratization' of EU external policy-making.[42] It is clear that this was seen by the Parliament as not only a substantive issue, but also as an opportunity to exercise and test the boundaries of its new powers. During the year, there was also discussion of new EU measures dealing with the use of passenger data – another matter that had been sensitive in previous years and in which the EP had a strong interest. Significantly, the Commission was anxious to propose new legislation both in this area and in that covered by the SWIFT agreement that would mirror the American measures in this area and would thus avert accusations of one-sidedness and dependency.[43]

Tensions between the EU and the American approaches were also evident in the management of the transatlantic political economy during 2010. At the most general level, there continued to be differences of approach on the best ways to respond to the financial crisis. As noted earlier and in last year's Annual Review (Allen and Smith, 2010), the various stimulus measures adopted by the United States (and to a degree within the EU by Britain) were at odds with the approach supported by a majority of EU Member States, and with the need to deal with urgent financial crises in a number of the smaller EU economies. This disparity made itself felt in several international forums, especially the G20, where there was a distinct lack of co-ordination at the transatlantic level and where tensions developed over such issues as bank regulation and further stimulus measures.[44] This was the largest stage on which EU–US frictions could be discerned, but it was accompanied by continuing lack of consensus on issues ranging from climate change to the Airbus–Boeing dispute. One key feature of these areas of dispute – and a portentous one in the context of potential future issues – was a growing awareness that if the EU and the United States could not agree, then the initiative might be lost in global terms. This was at least a factor in the ability of the EU and the United States to sign up to new climate change measures after the Cancún summit in later 2010, and it was an explicit fear of EU aerospace manufacturers confronted with ambiguous findings from WTO investigations of subsidies to Airbus and to Boeing. Late in the year, European Aeronautic Defence and Space Company (EADS) leaders openly urged Boeing to come to terms and argued that if they did not, then the Chinese and

[41] *European Voice*, 1 July 2010.
[42] *European Voice*, 18 February 2010.
[43] *European Voice*, 15 April 2010 and 6 May 2010.
[44] *European Voice*, 24 June 2010 and 29 July 2010.

others would take advantage of the window of opportunity this would open.[45] Despite these continuing areas of friction, the EU and the United States did come to a 'second phase' agreement on 'open skies' during the year, but with some key questions still unanswered, especially on the American restrictions on foreign ownership of airlines.[46]

The uncertainties of EU–US relations tended to dominate the transatlantic partnership as in previous years, but there were also significant developments in EU–Canada relations to report. These centred on the negotiations aimed at concluding a comprehensive economic and free trade agreement (CETA), and threw up some intriguing questions not only about 'who speaks for Europe?' but also 'who speaks for Canada?' The negotiations involve (directly or indirectly) not only the 27 EU Member States, but also the ten Canadian provinces, and have generated or focused a number of tensions, for example, over animal welfare (seal hunting), environmental issues (the use of tar sands for generation of oil and gas), labour mobility and government procurement as well as the inevitable agricultural problems.[47] Progress continued to be made, but with difficulty owing to the complexity and multi-level nature of the process.

The EU's other major traditional 'strategic partner' is Japan, and although there were no significant disputes to report during the year, there was a new commitment to intensify the partnership in general; the EU–Japan summit in April established a High Level Group to produce proposals on this front (Council, 2010b). As noted earlier, the free trade agreement between the Union and South Korea had been adopted by the Council in 2009 but (after the Lisbon Treaty) also required approval by the European Parliament. Continued resistance from Italy especially in the Council reflected concern over the provisions for trade in automobiles, and led to the postponement of the implementation of the agreement until mid-2011.[48] In the Parliament, concern focused on the extent to which private groupings and non-governmental organizations could initiate complaints under the agreement, and also on the need to ratify a 'safeguard clause', which led to delays in the approval process.[49] Perhaps significantly, the free trade agreement was not the only agreement signed with South Korea during the year; a second agreement covering political and security dialogue was signed in Brussels during early May (Commission, 2011, p. 96).

[45] *European Voice*, 8 July 2010.
[46] *European Voice*, 17 June 2010.
[47] *European Voice*, 15 April 2010, 27 May 2010 and 8 July 2010.
[48] *European Voice*, 9 September 2010.
[49] *European Voice*, 21 October 2010.

Conclusions

As noted in the Introduction, the EU in 2010 was subject to a continuing 'double transition' in its relations with the wider world. The evidence we have reviewed suggests that whilst both elements of the transition – internal and external – had seen significant movement during the year, much inevitably remained open. In 'internal' terms, the fact that the EEAS would only enter into full operation at the beginning of 2011 promised a further intensification of the debates about representation, communication and negotiation that we have identified, but now in the practical world rather than the sometimes abstract terms of 2010. In 'external' terms, a wide range of issues that had been addressed in a rather tentative manner during 2010 remained on the agenda, and the very dynamism of the broader global arena meant that new challenges were not just possible, but also probable, in 2011. The move from transition to stress-testing of the EU's new arrangements was unlikely to be long delayed.

Key Readings

As in previous years, Commission (2011) provides a good general (if increasingly selective) overview. The Joint Study (2010) by three Brussels think tanks provides, in its section on 'External Action: A Work in Progress', a concise and well-focused review of the implications of Lisbon, as does the report, *Upgrading the EU's Role as Global Actor*, by the same group (Emerson *et al.*, 2011) which deals specifically with the post-Lisbon restructuring of European diplomacy. The weekly *European Voice* remains a very useful source.

References

Allen, D. and Smith, M. (2010) 'Relations with the Rest of the World'. *JCMS*, Vol. 48, s1, pp. 205–23.

Ashton, C. (2010) 'Strategic Partners: Progress Report to the European Council', 16–17 December. Available at: «http://www.europolitique.info/pdf/gratuit_fr/285183-fr.pdf».

Barysch, K. (2011) *The EU and Russia: All Smiles and No Action?* Policy Brief (London: Centre for European Reform).

Biscop, S. (ed.) (2009) *The Value of Power, the Power of Values: A Call for an EU Grand Strategy* (Brussels: Egmont Institute).

Commission of the European Communities (2006) 'Joint Statement by the Council, the European Parliament and the European Commission on the European Consensus on Development'. *Official Journal*, 2006/C 46/01, 24 February.

Commission of the European Communities (2010a) 'Trade, growth and world affairs: trade policy as a core component of the EU's 2020 strategy'. *COM*(2010)612, November.

Commission of the European Communities (2010b) 'EU development policy in support of inclusive growth and sustainable development: increasing the impact of EU development policy'. *COM*(2010) 629 final, 10 November.

Commission of the European Communities (2011) *General Report on the Activities of the European Union 2010* (Brussels: European Commission).

Council of the European Union (2010a) *EU–US Summit Lisbon, 20 November 2010: Joint Statement*. Available at «http://www.consilium.europa.eu/press».

Council of the European Union (2010b) *Joint Statement Following the EU–Japan Summit*. Available at: «http://www.consilium.europa.eu/press».

De Vasconcelos, A. (ed.) (2010) *A Strategy for EU Foreign Policy* (Paris: EU Institute for Security Studies).

Dinan, D. (2010) 'Institutions and Governance: A New Treaty, a Newly Elected Parliament and a New Commission'. *JCMS*, Vol. 48, s1, pp. 95–118.

Emerson, M. and Wouters, J. (2010) 'The EU's Diplomatic Debacle at the UN: And Now What?' *European Voice*, 23 September, p. 13.

Emerson, M. *et al.* (2011) *Upgrading the EU's Role as a Global Actor: Institutions, Law and the Restructuring of European Diplomacy* (Leuven: Centre for European Policy Studies/Egmont Institute/European Policy Centre/Leuven Centre for Global Governance Studies, University of Leuven).

Engel, P. (2011) 'On Development Policy, the EU's External Action Service is Looking Vulnerable'. *Europe's World Community Posts*, 10 March. Available at: «http://www.europesworld.org/NewEnglish/Home_old/PartnerPosts/tabid/671/PostID/2318/language/en-US/Default.aspx».

EurActiv (2010) 'Barroso Sparks Row over EU Overseas Appointments'. *EurActiv*. Available at: «http://www.euractiv.com/en/future-eu/barroso-sparks-row-over-eu-overseas-appointments-news-276317».

European Council (2010a) 'Conclusions', European Council, 16 September. EUCO 21/1/10 REV 1, CO EUR 16, CONCL 3.

European Council (2010b) 'Conclusions', European Council, 28–29 October. EUCO 25/1/10 REV 1, CO EUR 18, CONCL 4.

European Council (2010c) 'Conclusions', European Council, 16–17 December. EUCO 30/1/10 REV 1, CO EUR 21, CONCL 5.

Garton Ash, T. (2010) 'The View from Beijing Tells You Why We Need a European Foreign Policy'. *The Guardian*, 11 November.

Grant, C. (2010) 'The US–China "Reset": An Opportunity for the EU'. Bulletin 73 (London: Centre for European Reform).

Hamilton, D. and Burwell, F. (2009) *Shoulder to Shoulder: Forging a Strategic US–EU Partnership* (Washington, DC: Atlantic Council of the United States, jointly with seven other institutes).

Hardacre, A. (2009) *The Rise and Fall of Inter-regionalism in EU External Relations* (Dordrecht: Republic of Letters).

Howorth, J. (2010) 'The EU as a Global Actor: Grand Strategy for a Global Grand Bargain?' *JCMS*, Vol. 48, No. 3, pp. 455–74.

Joint Study (2010) *The Treaty of Lisbon: A Second Look at the Institutional Innovations*. Centre for European Policy Studies/Egmont Institute/European Policy Centre.

Polikanov, D. (2010) 'Russia–EU Relations Getting Warmer, but Still Not Cordial'. *Europe's World*, Spring, pp. 165–6.

Smith, M. (2011) 'The European Union, the USA and Global Governance'. In Wünderlich, J.-U. and Bailey, D. (eds) *The European Union and Global Governance: A Handbook* (London: Routledge).

Valasek, T. (2011) *Surviving Austerity: The Case for a New Approach to EU Military Collaboration* (London: Centre for European Reform).

JCMS 2011 Volume 49 Annual Review pp. 231–249

The EU Economy: The Eurozone in 2010*

DERMOT HODSON
Birkbeck College, University of London

Introduction

Last year's *JCMS* Annual Review saw Greece in dire fiscal straits after the true scale of government borrowing in the years leading up to the global financial crisis came to light (Hodson, 2010). By the beginning of 2010, it had become clear that the Greek government would be unable to weather this fiscal storm without outside help from Brussels or further afield. It took several long months of protracted negotiation, however, before eurozone heads of state or government reluctantly agreed in May 2010 on a €110 billion package of loans for Athens co-financed by the European Union (EU) and the International Monetary Fund (IMF).[1]

This decision was, to paraphrase Winston Churchill, not so much the beginning of the end for the eurozone's sovereign debt crisis as the end of the beginning. Fears that other eurozone members might share Greece's fate saw the EU and IMF set aside up to €720 billion in loans and credit guarantees, with the former pledging €60 billion of this sum via a newly created European financial stabilization mechanism and €440 billion through a new European financial stability facility. Ireland became the first country to tap these funds in November 2010, securing €67.5 billion in

* Thanks to my students at Birkbeck for their thoughts on key developments in the eurozone in 2010, and to Nat Copsey and Tim Haughton for helpful comments on an earlier draft.

[1] The EU contributed around two-thirds to this package, with the rest coming from the IMF.

external assistance after the costs of recapitalizing the country's banks spiralled out of control.[2]

It is against the backdrop of these turbulent events that this article explores key developments in the eurozone in 2010. Section I summarizes the economic outlook in 2010, noting the eurozone's emergence from recession as well as cross-country differences in economic performance. Section II discusses tensions in the euro system over the phasing out of crisis management measures. Section III explores the EU's evolving approach to financial supervision, with the European Central Bank (ECB) assuming responsibility for, but not complete control over, a new European Systemic Risk Board in 2010. Section IV focuses on the Stability and Growth Pact's still surprising resilience in spite of the eurozone's fiscal woes. Section V takes stock of plans to overhaul eurozone governance launched by the Commission and the Van Rompuy Taskforce. Section VI looks at the eurozone's role in international financial institutions and forums over the course of the year.

I. The Economic Situation in 2010

Gross domestic product (GDP) grew by 1.7 per cent in real terms in 2010 as the eurozone continued its recovery from recession (see Table 1). A resurgent international environment was a key driver in this regard, with the world economy growing by 4.5 per cent in 2010, having contracted by 0.7 per cent in 2009.[3] The result for the eurozone was increased international demand for its goods and services, with total exports from Member States sharing the single currency to the rest of the world rising by 10.7 per cent in 2010, having fallen by double digits in 2009. The eurozone also experienced a modest increase in domestic demand thanks to higher consumer expenditure and the continued effects of fiscal stimulus packages in several countries.

The growth performance of individual eurozone members in 2010 was mixed, but uniformly better than in 2009.[4] Germany led the pack with a real GDP growth rate of 3.7 per cent, its strongest showing since 1991. This remarkable recovery was due not only to the surge in demand for German exports, which grew by 14.7 per cent in 2010, but also an intensification of domestic demand amid rising consumer expenditure and investment. That

[2] Under this agreement, Ireland received €22.5 billion and €17.7 billion from the European financial stabilization mechanism and European financial stability facility, respectively, €22.5 billion from the IMF and a total of €4.8 in bilateral loans from Denmark, Sweden and the United Kingdom. The Irish government also contributed €17.5 billion from the country's pension reserve fund.

[3] The data referred to in this section are based on Commission (2010a)

[4] Estonia, which became the 17th country to join the eurozone in January 2011, is included in this grouping.

Table 1: Real GDP Growth (% Annual Change) – Eurozone (2006–11)

	2006	*2007*	*2008*	*2009*	*2010*[e]	*2011*[f]
Belgium	2.7	2.9	1.0	–2.8	2.0	1.8
Germany	3.4	2.7	1.0	–4.7	3.7	2.2
Estonia	10.6	6.9	–5.1	–13.9	2.4	4.4
Ireland	5.3	5.6	–3.5	–7.6	–0.2	0.9
Greece	4.5	4.3	1.3	–2.3	–4.2	–3.0
Spain	4.0	3.6	0.9	–3.7	–0.2	0.7
France	2.2	2.4	0.2	–2.6	1.6	1.6
Italy	2.0	1.5	–1.3	–5.0	1.1	1.1
Cyprus	4.1	5.1	3.6	–1.7	0.5	1.5
Luxembourg	5.0	6.6	1.4	–3.7	3.2	2.8
Malta	3.6	3.7	2.6	–2.1	3.1	2.0
Netherlands	3.4	3.9	1.9	–3.9	1.7	1.5
Austria	3.6	3.7	2.2	–3.9	2.0	1.7
Portugal	1.4	2.4	0.0	–2.6	1.3	–1.0
Slovenia	5.9	6.9	3.7	–8.1	1.1	1.9
Slovakia	8.5	10.5	5.8	–4.8	4.1	3.0
Finland	4.4	5.3	0.9	–8.0	2.9	2.9
Eurozone	3.0	2.9	0.4	–4.1	1.7	1.5

Source: Commission (2010a, p. 184, table 1).
Note: Estimates are denoted by *e* and forecasts by *f*.

Greece found itself in last place with a real GDP growth rate of –4.2 per cent is unsurprising, with attempts to raise government revenue and rein in public expenditure taking their toll on domestic demand.

The eurozone's unemployment rate increased to 10.1 per cent in 2010 and is expected to remain close to double digits over the forecast horizon (see Table 2). National labour markets have responded in quite different ways to the global financial crisis, as evidenced by the gap between unemployment rates in Spain (20.1 per cent) and Austria (4.4 per cent). Nickell (2011) attributes such differences to three principal factors. First, countries facing a contraction in low productivity industries have experienced a comparatively steep reduction in employment relative to GDP; the devastation of Spain's construction sector following the end of the country's housing bubble provided a case in point. Second, countries with lax employment protection legislation, which is true of a significant share of the Spanish labour market, have experienced a sharp rise in layoffs as economic conditions have slowed. Third, several eurozone members, and Austria is among them, have made use of public subsidies to reduce the number of hours worked per worker rather than the overall number of workers employed. Though these subsidies helped firms to survive the recession with fewer layoffs than would otherwise have

Table 2: Unemployment (% of the Civilian Labour Force) – Eurozone (2006–11)

	2006	*2007*	*2008*	*2009*	*2010*[e]	*2011*[f]
Belgium	8.3	7.5	7.0	7.9	8.6	8.8
Germany	9.8	8.4	7.3	7.5	7.3	6.7
Estonia	5.9	4.7	5.5	13.8	17.5	15.1
Ireland	4.5	4.6	6.3	11.9	13.7	13.5
Greece	8.9	8.3	7.7	9.5	12.5	15.0
Spain	8.5	8.3	11.3	18.0	20.1	20.2
France	9.2	8.4	7.8	9.5	9.6	9.5
Italy	6.8	6.1	6.7	7.8	8.4	8.3
Cyprus	4.6	4.0	3.6	5.3	6.8	6.6
Luxembourg	4.6	4.2	4.9	5.1	5.5	5.6
Malta	7.1	6.4	5.9	7.0	6.6	6.6
Netherlands	4.4	3.6	3.1	3.7	4.5	4.4
Austria	4.8	4.4	3.8	4.8	4.4	4.2
Portugal	7.8	8.1	7.7	9.6	10.5	11.1
Slovenia	6.0	4.9	4.4	5.9	7.2	7.2
Slovakia	13.4	11.1	9.5	12.0	14.5	14.2
Finland	7.7	6.9	6.4	8.2	8.3	7.8
Eurozone	8.4	7.5	7.5	9.5	10.1	10.0

Source: Commission (2010a, p. 195, table 23).
Note: Estimates are denoted by *e* and forecasts by *f*.

been the case, Nickell (2011) warns that they may have propped up inefficient industries and discouraged workers from moving to more productive activities.

Worries over deflation in the eurozone subsided in 2010, with the harmonized index of consumer prices rising by 1.5 per cent as compared to 0.3 per cent 12 months earlier. The ECB's low interest rates may have added to inflationary pressures, although the impact of conventional monetary policies has been rendered uncertain by the global financial crisis. Other potential drivers of eurozone inflation include rising energy and commodity prices linked to the recovery in the world economy (Table 3). A notable outlier in the eurozone is Ireland, which saw consumer prices fall by 1.5 per cent in 2010. High unemployment and falling wages, particularly in the public sector, seem to have had an impact here, with some commentators pointing to the competitive advantages for Ireland of falling unit labour costs as well as the dangers of a debt-deflation trap (Wolf, 2010).

The eurozone's budget deficit remained constant at 6.3 per cent in 2010, but this figure masked divergent trends between eurozone members (see Table 4). Countries with comparatively sound budgetary positions – Austria, Germany, Finland, Luxembourg, Malta, the Netherlands, Slovakia and France – saw their

Table 3: Inflation Rates (% Change on Preceding Year) – Eurozone (2006–11)

	2006	*2007*	*2008*	*2009*	*2010*[e]	*2011*[f]
Belgium	2.3	1.8	4.5	0.0	2.3	1.9
Germany	1.8	2.3	2.8	0.2	1.1	1.8
Estonia	4.4	6.7	10.6	0.2	2.7	3.6
Ireland	2.7	2.9	3.1	−1.7	−1.5	0.4
Greece	3.3	3.0	4.2	1.3	4.6	2.2
Spain	3.6	2.8	4.1	−0.2	1.7	1.5
France	1.9	1.6	3.2	0.1	1.7	1.6
Italy	2.2	2.0	3.5	0.8	1.6	1.8
Cyprus	2.2	2.2	4.4	0.2	2.8	3.3
Luxembourg	3.0	2.7	4.1	0.0	2.8	2.1
Malta	2.6	0.7	4.7	1.8	1.9	2.0
Netherlands	1.7	1.6	2.2	1.0	1.0	1.5
Austria	1.7	2.2	3.2	0.4	1.7	2.1
Portugal	3.0	2.4	2.7	−0.9	1.4	2.3
Slovenia	2.5	3.8	5.5	0.9	2.1	2.0
Slovakia	4.3	1.9	3.9	0.9	0.7	3.2
Finland	1.3	1.6	3.9	1.6	1.6	2.1
Eurozone	2.2	2.1	3.3	0.3	1.5	1.8

Source: Commission (2010a, p. 191, table 16).
Note: Estimates are denoted by *e* and forecasts by *f*.

budget deficits increase by between 0.2 and 1.1 percentage points. In the case of Germany, this increase was more than a percentage point lower than had been foreseen in 2009, reflecting the windfall gains from higher than expected growth. Member States with comparatively high budget deficits, in contrast, upped the pace of fiscal consolidation in an effort to win the confidence of financial markets. The pace of consolidation was particularly dramatic in Greece, which cut nearly six percentage points off its budget deficit in 2010 as a result of swingeing expenditure cuts and emergency revenue-raising measures. Ireland also undertook painful consolidation measures in 2010, but saw its budget deficit skyrocket to 32.3 per cent of GDP following one-off capital injections into the Anglo Irish Bank, among other financial institutions.

II. Monetary Policy in 2010

The financial crisis has pushed the ECB well beyond its comfort zone. Having been reluctant to cut interest rates in the early stages of the crisis – the Governing Council actually voted to increase interest rates in June 2008 at a time when other central banks were cutting the cost of credit – the ECB had little choice but to initiate a series of interest rate cuts in October 2008 amid

Table 4: Net Lending (+) or Net Borrowing (–) General Government Balance (% of GDP) – Eurozone (2006–11)

	2006	*2007*	*2008*	*2009*	*2010*[e]	*2011*[f]
Belgium	0.2	–0.3	–1.3	–6.0	–4.8	–4.6
Germany	–1.6	0.3	0.1	–3.0	–3.7	–2.7
Estonia	2.4	2.5	–2.8	–1.7	–1.0	–1.9
Ireland	2.9	0.0	–7.3	–14.4	–32.3	-10.3
Greece	–5.7	–6.4	–9.4	–15.4	–9.6	–7.4
Spain	2.0	1.9	–4.2	–11.1	–9.3	–6.4
France	–2.3	–2.7	–3.3	–7.5	–7.7	–6.3
Italy	–3.4	–1.5	–2.7	–5.3	–5.0	–4.3
Cyprus	–1.2	3.4	0.9	–6.0	–5.9	–5.7
Luxembourg	1.4	3.7	3.0	–0.7	–1.8	–1.3
Malta	–2.7	–2.3	–4.8	–3.8	–4.2	–3.0
Netherlands	0.5	0.2	0.6	–5.4	–5.8	–3.9
Austria	–1.5	–0.4	–0.5	–3.5	–4.3	–3.6
Portugal	–4.1	–2.8	–2.9	–9.3	–7.3	–4.9
Slovenia	–1.3	0.0	–1.8	–5.8	–5.8	–5.3
Slovakia	–3.2	–1.8	–2.1	–7.9	–8.2	–5.3
Finland	4.0	5.2	4.2	–2.5	–3.1	–1.6
Eurozone	–1.4	–0.6	–2.0	–6.3	–6.3	–4.6

Source: Commission (2010a, p. 202, table 37).
Note: Estimates are denoted by *e* and forecasts by *f*.

the economic and financial turmoil that followed the collapse of Lehman Brothers. This course of action took the interest rate on the ECB's main refinancing operation to an unprecedented low of 1.0 per cent in May 2009, where it remained throughout 2010.

These concerns over inflation gave way to deflationary risks in 2009 and provided the ECB with the cover it needed to cut interest rates; the Treaty, it should be recalled, permits the Bank to support general economic objectives only insofar as they do not prejudice the pursuit of price stability (Article 127 TFEU). This line of reasoning remained valid over the course of 2010, but its plausibility was slowly stretched as year-on-year changes in the consumer price index came close to the ECB's target of 2.0 per cent. Having insisted in his final press conference of 2010 that inflationary expectations were firmly anchored (Trichet, 2010a), the ECB President changed tack in his next appearance, acknowledging the existence of short-term inflationary pressures because of rising energy costs and thus paving the way for interest rate increases in 2011 (Trichet, 2011a).

The Bank has been more decisive about pursuing unconventional policy responses to the financial crisis, with the decision in October 2008 to extend the list of eligible assets used in the euro system's credit operations one of many examples (ECB, 2008), but it has been at pains to avoid the prolongation of such measures (Trichet, 2010b). In retrospect, the ECB's decision in December 2009 to announce the phasing out of unconventional policies (see Trichet, 2009) added fuel to the fire of concerns over the risk of sovereign default in Greece and elsewhere and, in any case, turned out to be well wide of the mark. Having initially planned to restore its original collateral framework by the end of 2010, the Bank reluctantly decided in May 2010 to accept Greek government bonds in credit operations irrespective of the country's sovereign credit rating (ECB, 2010a). Likewise, having originally envisaged an end to its modest programme of bond purchases by June 2010, the ECB launched an altogether more ambitious scheme in May 2010 in the form of the Securities Markets Programme (ECB, 2010b).

The ECB's covered bond scheme, as discussed in last year's review (Hodson, 2010), involved the purchase of a particular class of private debt security – namely corporate bonds backed by mortgages or public sector loans – with a view to providing direct support to banks, which in turn provide the bulk of financing to eurozone corporations. The Securities Markets Programme, in contrast, allows the ECB to engage in the purchase of public as well as private debt securities, thus providing a valuable line of support to those Member States struggling to sell government bonds because of fears over a sovereign default. As of March 2011, the Bank had spent around €77.4 billion through its Securities Markets Programme, which was already well in excess of the completed covered bond scheme (ECB, 2011).

Tensions within the euro system over unconventional policy responses to the financial crisis were plain to see in relation to the Securities Markets Programme. Though Jean-Claude Trichet insisted in October 2010 that the programme enjoyed the support of an overwhelming majority of ECB Governing Council members (Trichet, 2010c), this statement served only to underline strains in the Bank's consensual style of policy-making. Press reports indicated that only Axel Weber had opposed the Securities Markets Programme (Münchau, 2010), but this did not deter the President of the Bundesbank from arguing in October that such measures blurred the responsibilities between monetary and fiscal policies and calling for them to be phased out without delay (Weber, 2010).

III. Financial Supervision in 2010

Plans to overhaul the EU's system of financial supervision in the light of the financial crisis, inspired by the de Larosière Report of February 2009 and discussed in detail in last year's review (Buckley and Howarth, 2010; Hodson, 2010), led to the launch in December 2010 of the European Systemic Risk Board. This new body is responsible for safeguarding financial stability in the EU or, as the statutes adopted by the European Parliament and Council of Ministers in November 2010 confusingly put it, 'the macro-prudential oversight of the financial system within the Union in order to contribute to the prevention or mitigation of systemic risks to financial stability in the Union that arise from developments within the financial system and taking into account macroeconomic developments, so as to avoid periods of widespread financial distress' (Council Regulation (EC) No 1092/2010, OJ L 331/1 of 24 November 2010).

If this opaque mandate has the potential to create confusion over the precise role of the European Systemic Risk Board, then so too do its governance structures. Though Jean-Claude Trichet was elected as chair, the ECB's authority over the new body is constrained by a number of factors. First, the Board has two vice-chairs, with the first currently occupied by the Governor of the Bank of England and the second to be filled by the chair of the new Joint Committee of European Supervisory Authorities.[5] Second, the statutes of the European Systemic Risk Board leave open the question of how the chair will be appointed in the future, with the Parliament and Council of Ministers agreeing to come back to this issue before December 2013. Finally, and most significantly, the European Systemic Risk Board's principal decision-making organ, the so-called 'Governing Council', has no less than 37 voting members, with up to 28 non-voting participants invited to join proceedings.[6] As an instance of decision-making by committee (Blinder, 2007), these arrangements take some beating, with Buiter (2009) among those who have warned of a diffusion of responsibility at the heart of EU financial supervision.

Whether the European Systemic Risk Board has effective instruments of financial supervision remains to be seen. Whereas the de Larosière Report insisted on the need for macro-prudential risk warnings to which the follow-up should be mandatory, the European Systemic Risk Board is empowered only to issue a non-binding public recommendation in the event

[5] The authorities in question, the European Banking Authority, European Insurance and Occupational Pensions Authority and the European Securities and Markets Authority, officially came into being on 1 January 2011.

[6] The voting members of the European Systemic Risk Board are: the President and the Vice-President of the ECB; the national central bank governors of the 27 EU Member States; the heads of the European Banking Authority, the European Insurance and Occupational Pensions Authority and the European Securities and Markets Authority; and the chair and the two vice-chairs of the Advisory Scientific Committee and the chair of the Advisory Technical Committee. Non-voting members include representatives of each national supervisory authority and the chair of the Economic and Financial Committee.

that its warnings have gone unheeded. Speaking about these provisions in February 2011, Jean-Claude Trichet argued that the European Systemic Risk Board would rely to a significant extent on its 'intellectual, professional and moral authority' (Trichet, 2011b). In this respect, the EU's new arrangements for financial supervision look set to carry on the experiment in new governance that, for better or worse, has come to define European economic governance (Hodson, 2011).

The European Systemic Risk Board's statutes emphasize the impartiality of its activities. In practice, impartiality seems to have much the same meaning as independence, with members of the Board both required to act in the interests of the EU as a whole and prohibited from seeking or taking instructions from Member States, EU institutions or any other public or private body in the exercise of their responsibilities. The European Systemic Risk Board is, furthermore, subject to few checks and balances, being required only to keep the European Parliament abreast of its activities and to examine specific issues at the invitation of the Parliament, the Council or the Commission. Buiter (2009) is sceptical about such arrangements, arguing that supervisors should not be afforded the same degree of independence as central banks because supervision is inherently more politicized than monetary policy.

IV. The Stability and Growth Pact in 2010

A key finding of last year's review was that EMU's fiscal rules had displayed a surprising degree of resilience during the global financial crisis. Though an unprecedented 13 eurozone members found themselves in a state of excessive deficit in 2009, EU policy-makers continued to enforce the Stability and Growth Pact while Member States, for the most part, took the required steps to restore compliance. A similar conclusion, it would seem, holds true for 2010, with Finland and Cyprus joining the list of eurozone members facing excessive deficit procedures, but all countries concerned deemed to have taken effective action with a view to restoring compliance with the EU's fiscal rules.

The Article 126(7) recommendation issued to Finland in July 2010 was a largely symbolic affair, with EU finance ministers accepting that the budget deficit for 2011 would in all likelihood be below 3 per cent of GDP (Council, 2010a). That the Stability and Growth Pact's 'exceptionality clauses' were not invoked in this case – the official reason given was that Finland's estimated budget deficit for 2010 (at 4.1 per cent, according to the Spring Forecast for 2009) appeared to be temporary but not sufficiently close to the 3.0 per cent of GDP threshold – confirmed, once again, that the loopholes in EMU's fiscal rules are not as wide as some critics have suggested (Feldstein, 2005).

Cyprus was given greater leeway by Ecofin (the Economic and Financial Affairs Council) in the form of a three-year, rather than the standard two-year, deadline to correct its excessive deficit in an Article 126(7) recommendation issued in June 2010 (Council, 2010b). This decision was in keeping with the revised Stability and Growth Pact and consistent with the treatment of other eurozone members in 2009, even if the 'special circumstances' used to justify Cyprus' extension, which included the severity of the recession and the effect of stimulus measures implemented in the context of the European Economic Recovery Programme, seemed a little generic.

All eurozone members against which excessive deficit procedures were opened in 2009 were adjudged to have taken effective action in response to Ecofin recommendations. Of this group, Germany, the Netherlands, Malta and Austria made the most progress, with the expectation in mid-2010 being that these countries were on track to eliminate their excessive deficits by 2012. Belgium, France, Italy, Portugal, Slovakia, Spain and Slovenia face the prospects of excessive deficits for the foreseeable future, but these Member States were still judged to have taken adequate action in a review conducted by the Commission in June 2010 (Commission, 2010b). Financial markets appeared less sanguine about some of these cases, however, as suggested by Standard and Poor's decision to downgrade the sovereign credit ratings of Portugal and Spain in April 2010.

That Greece and Ireland found themselves on the brink of sovereign default in 2010 was without doubt a major blow for the Stability and Growth Pact. Not only did this show the limits of EU fiscal co-ordination prior to the financial crisis, with Greece, in particular, finding itself in an unsustainable budgetary position in spite of repeated warnings during EMU's first decade, it also showed that the Stability and Growth Pact was an unsuitable mechanism of crisis management, with financial markets ultimately unconvinced by the efforts of the Commission and the Council of Ministers to get government borrowing under control in these Member States (Table 4). Most serious of all, the financial rescue of Greece and Ireland opened the door of eurozone governance to the IMF, with officials from the Fund rather than the Commission taking the lead on some of the more technical aspects of the financial rescue packages (Hodson, 2011).

That the Stability and Growth Pact was bruised by these developments but not buried is suggested by EU policy-makers' decision to press ahead with the excessive deficit procedures against both countries. Having issued an Article 126(9) recommendation in February 2010 to Greece, Ecofin agreed in May 2010 to issue a revised version of this recommendation, taking account of the worsening economic and financial outlook (Council, 2010c). This amended Article 126(9) recommendation was by turns more pragmatic and more prescriptive, increasing Greece's deadline for correcting its excessive deficit from 2012 to 2014 while being even more explicit about the policy actions expected of the country. Two further revisions to this Article 126(9) recommendation were issued in September and December 2010 to coincide with the first and second reviews of the EU–IMF financial rescue package (Council, 2010d, 2010e). The frequency of such revisions is unprecedented in the history of the Stability and Growth Pact but, if nothing else, it confirms that the excessive deficit procedure against Greece is ongoing.

The case of Ireland was procedurally somewhat different since Irish authorities found themselves turning to the EU and IMF for support in November 2010 at an earlier stage in the excessive deficit procedure. Indeed, as late as July 2010, Ecofin's official line was that Irish authorities had taken effective action in response to a revised Article 126(7) recommendation issued in December 2009 and that, consequently, no further disciplinary action under the excessive deficit procedure was foreseen (Council, 2010f). Surprisingly, this judgement seems to have been largely unaffected by the sovereign debt crisis of November 2010, with Ecofin concluding one month later that Ireland's predicament was due to unexpected adverse economic events rather than a lack of fiscal consolidation on the part of Irish authorities. In view of this assessment, EU finance ministers decided to issue yet another revised Article 126(7) recommendation, extending Ireland's deadline for correcting its excessive deficit from 2014 to 2015 but containing only scant information about the detailed policy conditions attached to the EU–IMF financial support package (Council, 2010g). Procedurally, this lack of prescription was due to the fact that only recommendations issued under Article 126(9) can recommend specific measures for debt reduction. Politically, it may have reflected EU policy-makers' reluctance to pile further peer pressure on the Irish government given the backlash against Brussels that followed the Article 121(4) recommendation against this country in February 2001.

V. The Future of Eurozone Governance

The Stability and Growth Pact may have muddled through in 2010, but the fact remains that it failed to forestall the EU's sovereign debt crisis, leaving the single currency to face serious questions about its long-term sustainability. In view of this fact, EU leaders' invitation to the President of the European Council, Herman Van Rompuy, in March 2010 to lead a taskforce to consider 'all options to reinforce the legal framework' surrounding EU economic governance was not unexpected (Council, 2010h).

In the end, the Commission stole much of the Van Rompuy Taskforce's thunder by coming forward with a package of six legislative proposals in September 2010 – a matter of weeks before the latter was due to publish its final report.[7] The headline message of these proposals was that eurozone governance required a more rigorous set of fiscal rules backed by stronger enforcement mechanisms as well as measures to tackle the problem of global imbalances.

On the first of these points, the Commission called for a new principle of prudent fiscal policy-making, which would require Member States to keep annual government expenditure growth below the medium-term growth rate of GDP and a numerical benchmark that would be used to gauge whether government debt in excess of 60 per cent of GDP is diminishing at a sufficient pace. From a political economy perspective, the prudence principle can be seen as an attempt to focus EU fiscal surveillance on inputs into the budget process over which national governments exercise a comparatively high degree of discretion. The numerical benchmark, meanwhile, seeks to redress the excessive deficit procedure's perceived benign neglect of debt levels once prospective eurozone members are deemed to have met the convergence criteria.

On the subject of enforcement mechanisms, the Commission suggested a shift from peer pressure to pecuniary sanctions in what can only be considered a volte-face from the reforms to the Stability and Growth Pact in March 2005. Specifically, the EU executive recommended that Member States should face the possibility of fines for breaching the prudence principle and as soon as they are deemed to be in a state of excessive deficit. The Commission also proposed a new principle of reverse voting, meaning that a recommendation by the EU executive to implement sanctions under the Stability and Growth Pact would be carried unless a qualified majority of Member States votes against it in the Council. This would make it considerably more difficult for an EU finance minister to overturn Commission recommendations under Article 126 TFEU, as was witnessed in relation to France and Germany in November 2003, thus greatly increasing the EU executive's agenda-setting powers in relation to EU fiscal surveillance.

Looking beyond the fiscal sphere, the Commission also called for the creation of an excessive imbalance procedure to prevent and, if necessary, correct macroeconomic developments that adversely affect 'the proper functioning of the economy of a Member State or of economic and monetary

[7] Details of the Commission's proposals are available at: «http://ec.europa.eu/economy_finance/articles/eu_economic_situation/2010-09-eu_economic_governance_proposals_en.htm».

union, or of the Union as whole'. Imbalances would be monitored via a scoreboard of macroeconomic and macro-financial indicators established by the Commission in co-operation with the Council. In the event that imbalances are deemed to be excessive, the Commission would recommend that the Council issue recommendations to the Member States concerned under Article 121(2) TFEU and, if corrective action is considered necessary, Article 121(4) TFEU. Persistent offenders would face the possibility of an extra sanction, with the Commission empowered to recommend a yearly fine worth 0.1 per cent of GDP, with reverse voting applying once again.

Though it received less attention than the Commission's plans for the Stability and Growth Pact, the excessive imbalance procedure is of the utmost importance for debates about the European political economy. The economic rationale for the procedure seems to be fairly robust since cross-country differences in economic growth and inflation rates have plagued the single currency since its launch in 1999. Politically, the feasibility of employing pecuniary sanctions against errant Member States is open to question given the sometimes nebulous link between current account developments and public policy. This is particularly true in relation to wage setting, with the role of governments in collective bargaining arrangements varying considerably across Member States.

The Van Rompuy report, which was published in October 2010, endorsed the basic thrust of the Commission's proposals while seeking to qualify the conditions under which financial penalties and reverse voting would apply. In the end, the report hit the headlines not for these modifications, but for its acceptance of the need to establish a credible crisis resolution mechanism for the eurozone in the medium term. The report was vague on what form this framework should take, beyond emphasizing the need to overcome problems of moral hazard among policy-makers and the private sector by offering *ex ante* financial guarantees to stricken Member States. It also accepted that such a mechanism 'may imply a need for Treaty changes, depending on its specific features' (Taskforce to the European Council, 2010, p. 12).

Franco–German fingerprints were clearly discernible on these plans. A matter of days before the Van Rompuy report was published, Nicolas Sarkozy and Angela Merkel issued a joint declaration at a summit in Deauville calling for the creation of a permanent crisis resolution mechanism by means of a limited change to the Lisbon Treaty by mid-2013. Precisely what Sarkozy saw in the Deauville declaration is hard to discern – the concession that sanctions under the pact should be 'more automatic' rather than fully automatic is one possibility – but the benefits for Merkel were clear. Having survived a preliminary challenge before the German Constitutional Court in May 2010 concerning the EU's emergency aid for Greece, the chancellor was forthright in her view that a change to the Treaty was essential to ensure that a framework for preventing future financial crises was 'legally unchallengeable' (Peel, 2010).

Though other EU leaders pushed back on some aspects of the Deauville declaration – the idea of punishing persistent offenders against the Stability and Growth Pact by suspending their voting rights in Ecofin, for example, seems to have been quietly shelved – plans for a treaty change were adopted with surprisingly little fuss. In December 2010, the European Council agreed to seek a change to Article 136 TFEU, which would allow eurozone members to create a stability mechanism to safeguard the stability of the eurozone as a whole before the European financial stability facility expires in July 2013.[8] The consensus in late 2010 seemed to be that such changes could be completed without the need for a referendum in any Member State. This assumption was surely premature given that national judiciaries and legislatures, not to mention the public at large, are only beginning to come to terms with a modification to EMU's constitution that is far from trivial.

VI. The Eurozone as a Global Actor

Another key finding of last year's review was that the eurozone had shown influence on the international stage in spite, and in some cases because, of its fragmented system of external representation. This was especially true in the Group of Twenty (G20), with EU Member States working together to set the agenda for the landmark leaders' summits in London and Pittsburgh and to put up a fairly unified front at these gatherings. A key question for 2010 is whether this capacity for collective action diminished as the global economy returned to a more even keel.

As regards the first of these questions, the EU continued to put in a fairly strong showing at G20 leaders' summits in 2010. The first of these summits, which took place in Toronto in June 2010, was a fairly mundane affair compared to the meetings in London and Pittsburgh, offering few bold initiatives and failing to reach agreement on a global bank levy in spite of several months of lobbying by officials from France, Germany, the United Kingdom and the United States. In spite of these shortcomings, the collective influence of EU Member States was discernible in the summit communiqué, with the commitment by advanced economies to at least halve deficits by 2013 and stabilize or reduce government debt-to-GDP ratios by 2016 a case in point (G20, 2010). Though the credibility of this commitment should not be overstated, it still

[8] EU leaders also agreed to take forward the Commission's proposals on eurozone governance with a view to completing the necessary legislative changes by mid-2011.

counted as a win for the EU, with Jean-Claude Trichet among those who had pushed for movement on fiscal issues at Toronto in spite of the Obama administration's apparent reluctance to do so (Peel and Wiesmann, 2010).

EU efforts at collective diplomacy were also in evidence at the G20 leaders' summit in Seoul in November 2010. On a procedural level, the Presidents of the Commission and the European Council, who jointly occupy the EU's seat at the G20, took the unusual step of issuing a joint letter to EU heads of state or government on preparations for the Seoul summit, which served as a basis for a discussion over dinner at the European Council in October 2010 (Van Rompuy and Barroso, 2010a). The results of this discussion fed into a second joint letter from the two men to other G20 leaders, setting out EU priorities for the summit itself (Van Rompuy and Barroso, 2010b). On a substantive level, the EU and its Member States walked a fine line in Seoul between championing action to prevent a so-called 'currency war' and avoiding binding commitments in relation to the problem of global imbalances. On the first of these issues, pointed criticism from German finance minister Wolfgang Schäuble (2010) among others about the impact of quantitative easing by the Federal Reserve on the external value of the dollar produced little discernible effect. On the second of these issues, the G20's failure to agree binding targets on tackling global imbalances will not have disappointed those who feared measures that might have undermined the competitiveness of the EU in general and Germany in particular.

If the EU is gradually finding its feet in international forums such as the G20, this does not mean that other aspiring global actors are not doing the same. One sign of the growing global reach of rising powers in 2010 was the reform to IMF quotas agreed by the Fund's Board of Governors (Tweedie *et al.*, 2010). Under this reform, emerging market and developing countries will see their quota shares, which are a key determinant of voting power in the IMF, increase by more than 6 per cent, with China becoming the third largest economy represented in the Fund, and Brazil, India and Russia entering the top ten. The BRICs' gain, in this instance, was the EU's loss, with France, Germany and the United Kingdom seeing their quotas decline relative to that of China and the total number of seats occupied by European countries on the Executive Board set to decline by two.

Conclusions

Hindsight may bring 20:20 vision but recent events can remain a blur for some time. With this warning in mind, this article has sought to identify what was significant in 2010 for scholars of EMU. This was, above all, the year in which the fiscal consequences of the global financial crisis were brought home to the eurozone, with Greece and Ireland forced to seek financial assistance from the EU and the IMF after markets lost faith in the ability of these countries to get government borrowing under control. This was also the year, however, in which the eurozone emerged from a steep recession and the threat of deflation passed, with Germany, putting in its best growth performance for nearly two decades.

In the monetary sphere, this combination of crisis and recovery created a particular headache for the ECB in 2010. On one level, the ECB was keen to phase out the unprecedented policy measures taken at the height of the financial crisis, particularly as inflation approached its target towards the end of the year. Frankfurt's room for manoeuvre was curtailed, however, by the sovereign debt crisis, with the extension of the Bank's bond purchase programme creating serious tensions in the ECB Governing Council.

In the financial sphere, the EU's new-look approach to prudential supervision came into effect with the launch of a new European Systemic Risk Board, with ECB President Jean-Claude Trichet at the helm. Key questions for this fledgling body are whether it has the clarity of purpose and the necessary tools at its disposal to safeguard financial stability in the EU. A more normative concern is whether the European Systemic Risk Board can be held to account given its Byzantine governance structure and deficit of democratic checks and balances.

In the fiscal sphere, the Stability and Growth Pact found itself in the eye of the eurozone's sovereign debt storm. On the enforcement side, EU policymakers continued to prosecute Member States posting budget deficits in excess of 3 per cent of GDP so as to reassure financial markets about the sustainability of Member States' public finances. On the compliance side, eurozone members have been content to play along with this approach, with one group seemingly on track to correct their excessive deficits over the forecast horizon and the rest taking adequate action in the eyes of the Commission and Ecofin. In spite of its resilience, the Stability and Growth Pact's credibility has been sorely affected by the eurozone's sovereign debt crisis, prompting a wave of reform proposals in 2010 for overhauling EMU's fiscal rules and other aspects of eurozone governance.

In the sphere of external relations, EU Member States pursued a fairly coherent line at the G20 leaders' summits in Toronto and Seoul in 2010, even if the spirit of co-operation in this new forum shows signs of dissipating. The EU may finally be learning to speak with one voice on the world stage, but it faces stiff competition from rising powers, as evidenced by the reform of IMF quota shares, which saw China among others gain a greater say at the expense of representatives from EU Member States.

References

Blinder, A. (2007) 'Monetary Policy by Committee: Why and How?' *European Journal of Political Economy*, Vol. 23, No. 1, pp. 106–23.

Buckley, J. and Howarth, D. (2010) 'Gesture Politics? Explaining the EU's Response to the Financial Crisis'. *JCMS*, Vol. 48, s1, pp. 119–41.

Buiter, W. (2009) 'The Proposed European Systemic Risk Board is Overweight Central Bankers'. *Financial Times*, 28 October.

Commission of the European Communities (2010a) *European Economic Forecast, Autumn 2010*. European Economy 7/10 (Brussels: European Commission).

Commission of the European Communities (2010b) 'Assessment of the action taken by Belgium, the Czech Republic, Germany, Ireland, Spain, France, Italy, the Netherlands, Austria, Portugal, Slovenia and Slovakia in response to the Council Recommendations of 2 December 2009 with a view to bringing an end to the situation of excessive government deficit'. *COM* (2010) 329.

Council of the European Union (2010a) 'Council recommendation to Finland with a view to bringing an end to the situation of an excessive government deficit'. 11305/10, 6 July.

Council of the European Union (2010b) 'Council recommendation to Cyprus with a view to bringing an end to the situation of an excessive government deficit'. 11296/10, 6 July.

Council of the European Union (2010c) 'Council decision addressed to Greece with a view to reinforcing and deepening fiscal surveillance and giving notice to Greece to take measures for the deficit reduction judged necessary to remedy the situation of excessive deficit'. 2010/320/EU, 10 May.

Council of the European Union (2010d) 'Council decision addressed to Greece with a view to reinforcing and deepening fiscal surveillance and giving notice to Greece to take measures for the deficit reduction judged necessary to remedy the situation of excessive deficit'. 2010/486/EU, 7 September.

Council of the European Union (2010e) 'Council decision addressed to Greece with a view to reinforcing and deepening fiscal surveillance and giving notice to Greece to take measures for the deficit reduction judged necessary to remedy the situation of excessive deficit'. 17754/10, 17 December.

Council of the European Union (2010f) '3027th Council meeting: economic and financial affairs'. 12076/10, 13 July.

Council of the European Union (2010g) 'Council recommendation with a view to bringing to an end the situation of an excessive deficit in Ireland'. 17210/10, 7 December.

Council of the European Union (2010h) *Statement of the Heads of State or Government of the Euro Area, 25 March* (Brussels: Council of Ministers of the European Union).

Council of the European Union (2010i) 'Conclusions'. Nr: EUCO 30/1/10 REV 1, 17 December.

European Central Bank (ECB) (2008) 'Technical Specifications for the Temporary Expansion of the Collateral Framework'. Press Release, 17 October.

European Central Bank (ECB) (2010a) 'ECB Announces Change in Eligibility of Debt Instruments Issued or Guaranteed by the Greek Government'. Press Release, 3 May.

European Central Bank (ECB) (2010b) *Monthly Bulletin* 05/2010.

European Central Bank (ECB) (2011) 'Consolidated Financial Statement of the Eurosystem as at 18 March 2011'. Press Release, 22 March.

Feldstein, M. (2005) 'The Euro and the Stability and Growth Pact'. Working Paper W11249 (Cambridge, MA: National Bureau for Economic Research).

G20 (2010) 'The G20 Toronto Summit Declaration', Toronto, 27 June.

Hodson, D. (2010) 'The EU Economy: The Euro Area in 2009'. *JCMS*, Vol. 48, s1, pp. 225–42.

Hodson, D. (2011) *Governing the Euro Area in Good Times and Bad* (Oxford: Oxford University Press).

Münchau, W. (2010) 'Frankfurt's Shroud of Secrecy should be Shed'. *Financial Times*, 6 June.

Nickell, S. (2011) 'The European Unemployment Challenge'. In Marsden, D. (ed.) *Employment in the Lean Years: Policy and Prospects for the Next Decade* (Oxford: Oxford University Press).

Peel, Q. (2010) 'Merkel Insists on EU Treaty Change'. *Financial Times*, 27 October.

Peel, Q. and Wiesmann, G. (2010) 'Berlin Warns of Risks from Debt Ahead of G20 Meeting'. *Financial Times*, 21 June.

Schäuble, W. (2010) 'The US has Lived on Borrowed Money for Too Long'. *Spiegel Online International*, 11 August.

Taskforce to the European Council (2010) *Strengthening Economic Governance in the EU* (Brussels: European Council).

Trichet, J.-C. (2009) 'Introductory Statement to the Press Conference', European Central Bank, Frankfurt, 13 January.

Trichet, J.-C. (2010a) *'Introductory Statement to the Press Conference*', European Central Bank, Frankfurt, 2 December.

Trichet, J.-C. (2010b) 'State of the Union: The Financial Crisis and the ECB's Response 2007–09'. *JCMS*, Vol. 48, s1, pp. 7–20.

Trichet, J.-C. (2010c) 'Interview with *La Stampa* Conducted by Stefano Lepri', European Central Bank, Frankfurt, 14 October.

Trichet, J.-C. (2011a) 'Introductory Statement to the Press Conference', European Central Bank, Frankfurt, 13 January.

Trichet, J.-C. (2011b) 'The Conditions for Efficient Global and Regional Macro-supervision: Key Success Factors in International Co-operation'. Keynote address at the Eurofi G20 High Level Seminar, Paris, 17 February.

Tweedie, A., Hagan, S. and Moghadam, R. (2010) *IMF Quota and Governance Reform: Elements of an Agreement* (Washington, DC: International Monetary Fund).

Van Rompuy, H. and Barroso, J.M.B. (2010a) 'Joint letter of President Van Rompuy and President Barroso on the G20 Summit in Seoul'. PCE 250/10, Brussels, 29 October.

Van Rompuy, H. and Barroso, J.M.B. (2010b) 'Joint letter of President Van Rompuy and President Barroso to the G20 Leaders'. Brussels, 5 November.

Weber, A. (2010) 'Monetary Policy after the Crisis: A European Perspective'. Keynote speech at the Shadow Open Market Committee Symposium, New York City, 12 October.

Wolf, M. (2010) 'The Eurozone's Next Decade will be Tough'. *Financial Times*, 5 January.

JCMS 2011 Volume 49 Annual Review pp. 251–273

Developments in the Economies of Member States Outside the Eurozone

RICHARD CONNOLLY
University of Birmingham

Introduction

As 2009 ended, the global economy began to recover from the deepest recession in the post-war period. This recovery continued into 2010, with strong growth in many of the world's major emerging economies – especially China and India – along with a firm rebound in the two largest advanced economies, the United States and Japan. This recovery was aided by the continuation of a historically unique, accommodative monetary policy in all of the world's important economies. Outside some European economies afflicted by sovereign debt risks, most countries also continued to pursue expansionary fiscal policies. These factors caused international trade to grow at 12.3 per cent, wiping out the catastrophic fall of 11.3 per cent in 2009 (OECD, 2010). Asset and commodity prices grew at a healthy pace, with much of the losses of the Great Recession all but made up by the end of 2010. This generated higher levels of inflation, which in 2009 had threatened to turn negative, leading to a slight increase to 1.8 per cent, easing earlier concerns that the world might enter a deflationary spiral of the sort that characterized the Great Depression. Globally, unemployment also began to fall slightly, albeit at a much slower rate than in previous periods of recovery from severe recession. Indeed, this reflected the general pattern of the global recovery: slow, steady, but also uncertain. And the issue of most importance to the long-term prospects for the global economy – the persistent and large current account imbalances that were arguably the ultimate cause of the Great Recession – remained unsolved (Wolf, 2009).

Within Europe, the patterns of recovery reflected those at the global level. Following a savage 4.6 per cent contraction in output in 2010, gross domestic product (GDP) increased by 2.3 per cent across the European Union (EU) as a whole. This pace of recovery was slow compared to previous recoveries, and a number of significant risks remained, including: heightened fears of the solvencies of a number of sovereigns across the region; concerns over the health of the European banking system which is extremely exposed to sovereign default risks; and evidence of persistently subdued domestic demand, especially in the private sector. The recovery – for those economies that experienced it – was largely based on either external demand – manifested in the rapid rebound in international trade, and stimulated by strong domestic demand in major emerging economies; or by the actions of public authorities, with the maintenance of large fiscal deficits, alongside loose monetary policies, helping to compensate for anaemic private sector activity, illustrated by a slow rebound in the rate of investment. Output slowed in the second half of 2010 as demand from emerging economies began to decelerate and domestic stocks were rebuilt. Furthermore, not only was the recovery sluggish, but the average growth rate of 2.3 per cent obscured considerable heterogeneity. While growth exceeded 3 per cent in Germany, Poland, Slovakia and Sweden, negative growth was observed in Greece, Ireland, Latvia, Romania and Spain.

This article assesses how the broader trends in the wider global and European economies outlined above affected the performance of the ten EU economies outside the eurozone in 2010.[1] In particular, it will examine the sources of recovery and attempts to explain the heterogeneous nature of the recovery. Overall, it will be argued that the strength of recovery was determined by how much each of the economies was (a) able to benefit from the acceleration in international trade that boosted demand for European exports; and (b) constrained by balance sheet weaknesses – both public and private – that held back growth in domestic demand. Where an economy was positioned with regard to these two variables explained the majority of variation in the rate of recovery. Section I gives an overview of key economic performance indicators. Section II explores the determinants of the heterogeneity of the recovery. Section III summarizes key developments in each of the ten European economies outside the eurozone. The final section provides a brief summary and suggests key issues for the year ahead.

[1] Because the EU gave final approval for Estonia's entry into the eurozone in July 2010, Estonia is not included in the review of 2010. It did not formally enter the eurozone until 1 January 2011. Estonia is included in Hodson's contribution to this volume, which reviews developments in the eurozone.

I. Economic Performance Outside the Eurozone: Main Economic Indicators

Economic Growth

A brief perusal of Table 1 reveals the heterogeneity of the recovery across the countries outside the eurozone. Sweden and Poland registered the fastest rates of growth, with both economies growing significantly faster than the EU and eurozone average. Respectable rates of growth – that is, at or above the EU and eurozone average – were observed in the Czech Republic, Denmark and the United Kingdom, although in all cases, the recovery in 2010 still left them at aggregate income levels far below that of 2007 – the last year before the Great Recession ravaged the global economy. However, the pace of the recovery across the remaining economies of the eurozone was well below the EU average, and in the cases of Bulgaria, Latvia and Romania, 2010 saw a continuation of negative growth. The fact that many of the countries with the lowest levels of per capita income in the EU were either recovering at a sluggish rate, or experiencing outright recession was of particular concern: conditional convergence suggested that poorer countries should grow faster than richer ones, but this was not the case across much of the non-eurozone in 2010. Comparing the actual growth rates in 2010 with the forecasts made by the Commission in the previous year is also instructive as it shows the influence of factors that were not forecast in 2009. Despite being in or close to recession, Latvia and Lithuania both performed considerably better than

Table 1: Real GDP Growth (% Annual Change) – Non-Eurozone (2006–10)

	2006	*2007*	*2008*	*2009*	*2010*^{e}	*Difference between forecast and estimate for 2010*
Bulgaria	6.3	6.2	6.0	–4.9	–0.1	–2.6
Czech Republic	6.8	6.1	2.5	–4.1	2.4	–0.2
Denmark	3.3	1.6	–1.2	–5.2	2.3	1.9
Latvia	12.2	10.0	–4.6	–18.0	–0.4	8.4
Lithuania	7.8	9.8	2.8	–14.7	0.4	3.1
Hungary	4.0	1.0	0.6	–6.7	1.1	–3.7
Poland	6.2	6.8	5.0	1.7	3.5	1.2
Romania	7.9	6.3	6.2	–7.1	–1.9	–7.2
Sweden	4.2	2.6	–0.2	–5.1	4.8	1.9
United Kingdom	2.9	2.6	0.6	–5.0	1.8	3.6
Eurozone	3.0	2.8	0.6	–4.1	1.7	0.0
EU average	3.2	3.0	0.5	–4.2	1.8	0.0

Source: Commission (2010, p. 184, table 1).
Note: Estimates are denoted by *e*.

expected in the autumn of 2010, as did the United Kingdom. However, Bulgaria, Hungary and Romania all registered much slower growth than forecast last year.

Employment

The unemployment rate is an indicator that lags developments in overall output. Consequently, while many economies experienced positive output growth, unemployment continued to rise in all the economies covered here, with the exception of Sweden where it remained stable (Table 2). The worst levels of unemployment were observed in the two Baltic economies, Latvia and Lithuania, where it approached 20 per cent – levels not seen since the 'transition depression' of the 1990s and three times higher than that experienced during the pre-crisis boom. However, while the level of unemployment in these three countries was comparatively bad, all other economies of the non-eurozone enjoyed unemployment rates that were lower than both the eurozone average and the overall EU average. Notwithstanding this relatively strong performance, the fact that unemployment was higher than forecast in autumn 2010 for eight out of the ten economies reveals that the problem was far from under control. While a combination of flexible labour markets, increased discretionary public sector spending in some cases and vibrant external demand all helped to stop unemployment from rising even further, a

Table 2: Unemployment (% of the Civilian Labour Force) – Non-Eurozone (2006–10)

	2006	*2007*	*2008*	*2009*	*2010*[e]	*Difference between forecast and estimate for 2010*
Bulgaria	9.0	6.9	5.6	6.8	9.8	2.8
Czech Republic	7.2	5.3	4.4	6.7	7.3	0.4
Denmark	3.9	3.8	3.3	6.0	6.9	2.4
Latvia	6.8	6.0	7.5	17.1	19.3	2.4
Lithuania	5.6	4.3	5.8	13.7	17.8	3.3
Hungary	7.5	7.4	7.8	10.0	11.1	0.6
Poland	13.9	9.6	7.1	8.2	9.5	1.1
Romania	7.3	6.4	5.8	6.9	7.5	−1.5
Sweden	7.0	6.1	6.2	8.3	8.3	−0.2
United Kingdom	5.4	5.3	5.6	7.6	7.8	0.0
Eurozone	8.3	7.5	7.5	9.5	10.1	0.6
EU average	8.2	7.2	7.0	8.9	9.6	–

Source: Commission (2010, p. 195, table 23).
Note: Estimates are denoted by *e*.

more vigorous and broad-based recovery was required if permanent losses to potential output were not to occur.

Inflation

The sharp decline in inflation caused by the collapse in output over the course of late 2008 and early 2009 was, in most cases, reversed over 2010 (Table 3). As commodity prices rose apace throughout 2010, pressure on prices worldwide for net commodity importers increased. As a result, despite severely subdued domestic demand across many economies of the non-eurozone, the general trajectory for prices was upwards, largely due to negative terms of trade developments. Only in the two Baltic economies that experienced recessions that were among the worst in the world did inflation continue to fall, with Latvia experiencing outright price deflation in 2010. Changes in nominal exchange rates were also important in determining prices in the economies outside the eurozone. Inflation tended to be higher in those countries that had experienced depreciation in nominal exchange rates, especially Romania. By contrast, where exchange rates appreciated, as in the Czech Republic and Sweden, inflationary pressures were more subdued. The long-term threat of persistent inflation appeared unclear. On the one hand, monetary policy across the globe continued to be historically loose, fuelling growth in asset prices and commodities. This, of course, was the aim of policy-makers, who in 2009 feared the onset of deflation. On the other hand, wage inflation showed little evidence of matching overall price inflation, thus dampening

Table 3: Inflation Rate[a] (% Change on Preceding Year) – Non-Eurozone (2006–10)

	2006	*2007*	*2008*	*2009*	*2010[e]*	*Difference between forecast and estimate for 2010*
Bulgaria	7.4	7.6	12.0	2.5	2.9	0.6
Czech Republic	2.1	3.0	6.3	0.6	1.2	–0.3
Denmark	1.9	1.7	3.6	1.1	2.2	0.7
Latvia	6.6	10.1	15.3	3.3	−1.3	2.4
Lithuania	3.8	5.8	11.1	4.2	1.2	1.9
Hungary	4.0	7.9	6.0	4.0	4.7	0.7
Poland	1.3	2.6	4.2	4.0	2.6	0.7
Romania	6.6	4.9	7.9	5.6	6.1	2.6
Sweden	1.5	1.7	3.3	1.9	1.8	0.1
United Kingdom	2.3	2.3	3.6	2.2	3.2	1.8
Eurozone	2.2	2.1	3.3	0.3	1.5	0.4
EU average	2.3	2.4	3.7	1.0	2.0	–

Source: Commission (2010, p. 191, table 16).
Note: Estimates are denoted by *e*. [a] Harmonized index of consumer prices.

fears of a 'cost-push' inflationary spiral. Furthermore, the spike in commodity prices that followed political instability across the Middle East and North Africa threatened to break the commodity bull cycle.

Private Sector Financial Balances

The private sector financial balance measures the extent to which the private sector – both household and corporate (financial and non-financial) – is either a net acquirer of financial assets (if it is in surplus), or a net borrower. In the pre-crisis period, many of the economies in the non-eurozone ran persistent and often large private sector financial deficits. This fuelled the boom that preceded the recession. However, as the Great Recession struck, private sector agents cut back spending causing financial balances to shift towards surplus in most cases (Figure 1). As households and financial sector organizations repaid debt amid tightening credit conditions, firms also cut investment expenditure (see Table 4). In 2009, this contraction in private sector spending contributed towards the severe recessions that were observed across the region (Connolly, 2010). It was hoped that this private sector retrenchment would soften in 2010 if domestic demand were to support the recovery. However, private sector financial balances continued to shift towards surplus in all but two cases. The private sectors in Bulgaria and Romania, in particular, accelerated at the pace at which saving exceeded expenditure, holding

Figure 1: Change in Private Sector Financial Balance,[a] 2009–10 (% of GDP) – Non-Eurozone

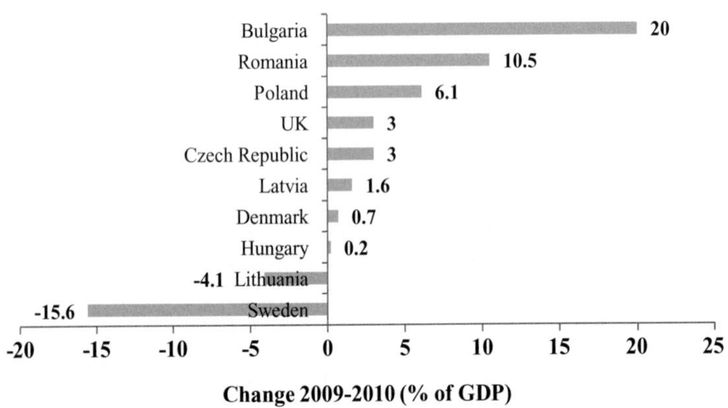

Source: Commission (2010); author's calculations.
Notes: Estimates are denoted by *e*. [a]The Private Sector Financial Balance is the difference between private income and private spending. It can be written as: Private Sector Financial Balance = Government Balance + Current Account Balance.

Table 4: Total Investment, 2006–10 (% Annual Change) – Non-Eurozone

	2006	*2007*	*2008*	*2009*	*2010^e^*	*Difference between forecast and estimate for 2010*
Bulgaria	13.1	11.8	21.9	−29.0	−9.8	−1.1
Czech Republic	6.0	10.8	−1.5	−7.9	−1.8	−2.1
Denmark	14.3	0.4	−3.3	−14.3	−3.8	0.3
Latvia	16.4	7.5	−13.6	−37.3	−24.8	−12.8
Lithuania	19.4	23.0	−5.2	−40.0	−8.5	−1.2
Hungary	−3.2	1.7	2.9	−8.0	−1.9	−2.9
Poland	14.9	17.6	9.6	−1.1	0.1	−1.8
Romania	19.9	30.3	15.6	−25.3	−9.9	−11.0
Sweden	9.2	8.9	1.7	−16.0	5.9	7.4
United Kingdom	6.4	7.8	−5.0	−15.1	2.8	6.6
Eurozone	5.4	4.7	−0.8	−11.4	−0.8	1.1
EU average	6.1	5.8	−0.8	−12.1	−0.6	–

Source: Commission (2010, p. 188, table 9).
Note: Estimates are denoted by *e*.

back the prospects of a broad-based and robust recovery. This deficiency in domestic demand can be observed elsewhere; even in Poland – the only country to avoid recession in 2009, and where 2010 output growth was healthy – growth was held back by the reluctance of the corporate sector to expand investment projects. The most obvious exception is Sweden, where vigorous private sector consumption drove its strong output performance in 2010. In all cases where private sector retrenchment continued, growth was generated by either net export growth or through public sector spending, with private sector demand muted.

Public Finances

The state of public finances and the issue of sovereign debt were particularly important issues in the eurozone during 2010.[2] The non-eurozone was no different in this respect, with increasing emphasis placed on cutting government expenditure in order to prevent a repetition of events witnessed in Greece, Ireland and Portugal. However, because of the private sector retrenchment described above, the role of the public sector in supporting domestic demand became even more important; without public intervention, private sector weakness may have restrained the recovery even further. Consequently, it was perhaps unsurprising that governments tended to take time to reduce fiscal deficits, particularly as the recession and subsequent anaemic

[2] On the eurozone, see Hodson's contribution to this volume.

Table 5: Net Lending (+) or Net Borrowing (–), General Government Balance (% of GDP) – Non-Eurozone (2006–10)

	2006	*2007*	*2008*	*2009*	*2010*[e]	*Difference between forecast and estimate for 2010*
Bulgaria	3.0	0.1	1.8	–4.7	–3.8	–2.6
Czech Republic	–2.6	–0.7	–2.1	–5.8	–5.2	0.3
Denmark	5.2	4.5	3.4	–2.7	–5.1	–0.3
Latvia	–0.5	–0.3	–4.1	–10.2	–7.7	4.6
Lithuania	–0.4	–1.0	–3.2	–9.2	–8.4	0.8
Hungary	–9.3	–5.0	–3.8	–4.4	–3.8	0.4
Poland	–3.6	–1.9	–3.6	–7.2	–7.9	–0.4
Romania	–2.2	–2.5	–5.5	–8.6	–7.3	–0.5
Sweden	2.5	3.8	2.5	–0.9	–0.9	2.4
United Kingdom	–2.7	–2.7	–5.0	–11.4	–10.5	2.4
Eurozone	–1.3	–0.6	–2.0	–6.3	–6.3	0.6
EU average	–1.5	–0.9	–2.3	–6.8	–6.8	–

Source: Commission (2010, p. 204, table 42).
Note: Estimates are denoted by *e*.

private sector recovery tended to diminish the tax base. As Table 5 illustrates, fiscal balances across the non-eurozone, on the whole, exhibited larger deficits than the EU and eurozone average. Sweden – a regional anomaly in the sense that domestic demand was exceptionally buoyant – was the only economy where the government balance was within the limits imposed by the Growth and Stability Pact. The difference between the actual and forecast levels of government borrowing revealed the extent to which the heterogeneity of the recovery was mirrored by the degree to which governments were able to reduce deficits from 2009 levels. In the Czech Republic and Sweden the unexpected strength of the recovery helped reduce the deficit through increased GDP – the denominator in the fiscal equation. In Hungary, Latvia, Lithuania and the United Kingdom, fiscal balances improved not so much because of stronger than anticipated growth, but because of concerted government efforts at deficit reduction.

Increased flows of government borrowing resulted in stocks of government debt building up across nearly all countries of the non-eurozone throughout 2010, with Sweden being the only economy where fiscal deficits were reduced (Table 6). Such developments were entirely consistent with the historical experience of countries emerging from financial crises (Reinhart and Rogoff, 2009). Although overall levels of government debt were lower than both the EU and eurozone average in all cases, the fact that private debt levels were higher in the non-eurozone meant that sovereign default risk was

Table 6: Gross General Government Debt (% of GDP) – Non-Eurozone (2006–10)

	2006	*2007*	*2008*	*2009*	*2010^e*	*Difference between forecast and estimate for 2010*
Bulgaria	22.7	18.2	14.1	14.7	18.2	2.0
Czech Republic	29.4	29.0	30.0	35.3	40.0	–0.6
Denmark	31.3	26.8	33.5	41.5	44.9	9.6
Latvia	10.7	9.0	19.5	36.7	45.7	–2.9
Lithuania	18.0	16.9	15.6	29.5	37.4	–3.3
Hungary	65.6	65.9	72.9	78.4	78.5	–1.3
Poland	47.7	45.0	47.2	50.9	55.5	–1.5
Romania	12.4	12.6	13.6	23.9	30.4	3.0
Sweden	45.9	40.5	38.0	41.9	39.9	–3.7
United Kingdom	43.2	44.2	52.0	68.2	77.8	–2.5
Eurozone	68.3	66.0	61.5	79.1	84.1	0.1
EU average	61.5	58.8	61.8	74.0	79.1	–

Source: Commission (2010, p. 204, table 42).
Note: Estimates are denoted by *e*.

not necessarily any less likely. This was because public balance sheets were exposed to the contingent liabilities of the private sector, leading to a worsening of the overall consolidated balance sheets of these economies (see Roubini and Setser, 2004). It was for precisely this reason that some governments felt compelled to reduce borrowing at perhaps excessively fast rates: Hungary, Latvia, Lithuania and the United Kingdom all had comparatively high levels of private sector debt, and saw fiscal retrenchment as the most likely route to keeping private debt off the public balance sheet. For those economies where fiscal rectitude was seen as most urgent – Hungary and the United Kingdom – actual government debt levels were better than those forecast in autumn 2009. The most unexpected increase came in Denmark, where an expansionary fiscal policy contributed to a higher stock of government debt in 2010.

Competitiveness

With the exception of Sweden, the tendencies described above – private sector weakness and rising government debt – were a continuation of the patterns described in the previous year's review (see Connolly, 2010). This caused the issue of competitiveness to remain particularly important: if excessive private and public sector debt burdens were dampening domestic demand, then any hope of achieving the sort of economic growth required to reduce debt to GDP ratios would have to be based on strong export growth. As such, the need to achieve cost competitiveness captured the attention of many

Table 7: Real Effective Exchange Rate (% Change on Preceding Year) – Non-Eurozone (2006–10)

	2006	*2007*	*2008*	*2009*	*2010*[e]	*Difference between forecast and estimate for 2010*
Bulgaria	3.0	11.0	12.5	7.8	−1.0	−3.5
Czech Republic	5.6	3.4	13.5	−4.5	3.0	0.4
Denmark	1.1	3.8	5.2	3.0	−3.4	−3.8
Latvia	13.2	23.0	19.1	−7.0	−10.5	−1.7
Lithuania	7.8	3.0	5.1	4.1	−7.2	−4.5
Hungary	−4.8	9.0	1.2	−10.9	−0.1	−4.9
Poland	1.1	3.8	12.8	−19.9	8.1	5.8
Romania	6.8	19.4	8.0	−1.2	1.7	−3.6
Sweden	−1.6	3.2	−3.3	−7.8	6.6	3.7
United Kingdom	2.3	2.8	−14.0	−9.0	2.0	3.8
Eurozone	−0.5	1.6	3.4	3.9	−7.1	−7.1
EU average	1.0	6.0	1.6	−3.4	−7.3	–

Source: Commission (2010, p. 203, table 17).
Note: Estimates are denoted by *e*.

policy-makers.[3] This was deemed to be of particular importance in those countries that exhibited large increases in the Real Effective Exchange Rate (REER) in the pre-crisis boom, especially Bulgaria, Latvia and Romania (Table 7). In these three cases, the REER depreciated in Bulgaria and Latvia, but appreciated slightly in Romania. Strong export growth across the region also caused the nominal exchange rate to appreciate in the Czech Republic, Poland and Sweden, going some way to reversing some of the cost competitiveness achieved during 2009. However, as the next section argues, the relationship between increased cost competitiveness and export performance in recent years is far from clear, at least within the EU. If increased competitiveness was not supported by overall productivity increases, and failed to generate an improvement in export performance, the reduction in labour costs may have only served to reduce domestic demand further.

II. Explaining Patterns of Performance in the Economies of the EU

The significant variation in the extent of recovery across the non-eurozone economies was largely explained by two factors. First, rates of recovery were

[3] This is not to suggest that improving cost competitiveness is necessarily the best means of achieving higher growth. The strong and positive long-run relationship between productivity and income suggests that long-term growth is best achieved through productivity increases – not relative wage and exchange rate depreciation.

determined by the degree to which countries were able to benefit from the swift recovery in international trade that began in the second half of 2009 and continued into 2010. Second, the pace of the recovery was also a function of the degree to which economic growth was held back by considerably subdued domestic demand. As Figure 2 shows, net exports tended to play a more important role in driving growth across the economies of the EU than domestic demand. However, in the countries that were ostensibly the best performers in terms of the contribution of net exports towards GDP growth, the improved performance was largely explained by an even greater slowdown in imports, as illustrated by a corresponding contraction in domestic demand. As such, there are two important questions that can help explain the heterogeneity of the recovery. First, what caused some economies to increase their rate of export growth? This question is addressed in the first part of this section. The second part explores the issue of why domestic demand was so subdued in so many cases. To try to answer these questions, cross-country regressions

Figure 2: Net Export and Domestic Demand Growth in 2010 (% Annual Growth) – European Union

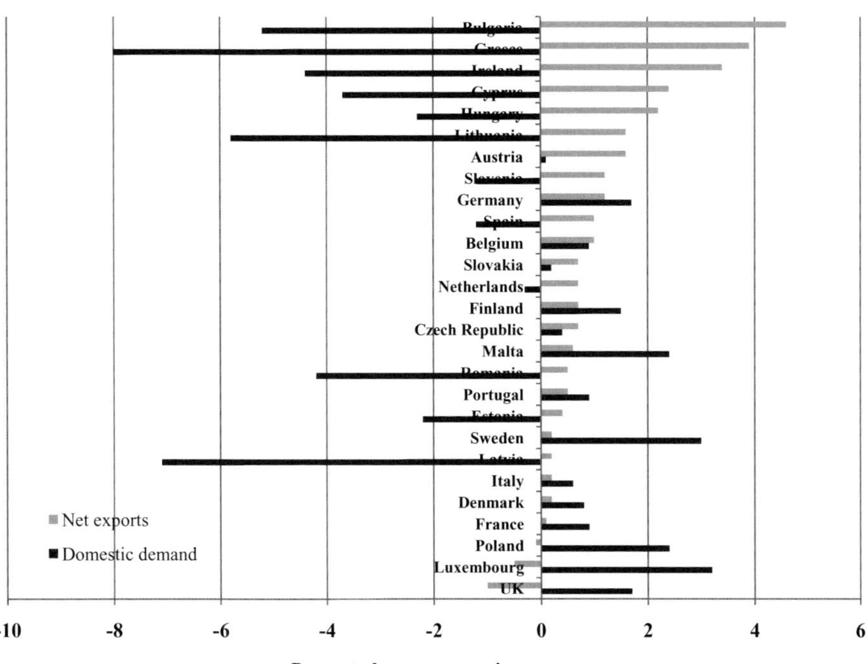

Source: Commission (2010).

using data from all 27 countries of the EU are used to identify those factors that can help explain the variation in export performance and levels of domestic demand observed across the non-eurozone.

Why were Some Economies Able to Benefit from the Recovery in International Trade?

The economies that experienced the most export growth in 2010 were able to benefit from the recovery in international trade. But there was much variation in the extent to which individual countries were able to benefit from this rebound. In order to identify the sources of this variation, on a sample that includes all the economies of the EU, real export growth in 2010 was regressed on several hypothesized determinants. The first variable measures the sophistication of a country's export basket.[4] This is to test the hypothesis that more sophisticated export structures were associated with a more rapid recovery in export growth. A second variable measures a country's openness to trade to test the view that greater trade orientation might facilitate a quicker response to the recovery in external trading conditions. The third and fourth measures – REER change in 2009 and 2010 – are included to explore whether changes in a country's cost competitiveness were associated with improved export performance. Two years are included because it is plausible that there may be a lag of a year before the effects of changes in competitiveness are revealed in export performance.

The results of the regression are contained in Table 8. A number of observations can be made on the results from this simple exercise. First, the structure of a country's export basket appears to be unrelated to export performance in 2010, with ExpY exhibiting a negative association with export growth that is statistically insignificant. Second, trade openness is positively related to export performance and highly significant. This suggests that it was those countries that were already open to trade that were most likely to benefit from the recovery in international trade in 2010. A corollary of this is that countries, such as Greece, that were not comparatively export-oriented, were unable to switch quickly to an export-oriented growth model. Finally, changes in competitiveness do not appear to have exerted any influence on export

[4] The ExpY measure of export sophistication is also used to measure the relative sophistication of a country's export basket. This index measures the productivity level associated with a country's export specialization pattern. ExpY is calculated in two steps. First, using 4-digit SITC.4 product classification (which yields more than 1,000 different products), the weighted average of the incomes of the countries exporting each traded product are calculated, where the weights are the RCA of each country in that product (normalized so that the weights sum up to 1). This gives the income level of that product, which is termed 'ProdY'. Following this, ExpY is then calculated as the weighted average of the ProdY for each country, where the weights are the share of each commodity in that country's total exports. This method is taken from Hausmann *et al.* (2006).

Table 8: OLS Regression of Real Export Growth on Hypothesized Determinants

	Annual export growth, 2010
Constant	11.5 (0.113)
Export sophistication (Exp Y), 2007	–0.00004 (0.312)
Trade openness, 2007	0.053* (0.007)
Real effective appreciation, 2009	–0.055 (0.680)
Real effective appreciation, 2010	0.111 (0.598)
Observations	27
R^2	0.259

Sources: Export growth and REER data from Commission (2010); Export sophistication (ExpY) from United Nations Comtrade (2010), World Bank (2010) and author's own calculations.
Notes: p-values in parentheses. * $p < 0.01$.

growth at all. REER changes in 2009 are negatively associated with export growth, indicating that increased competitiveness was associated with stronger export growth, but this relationship was statistically insignificant. Similarly, REER changes in 2010 were also statistically insignificant, although the direction of the association was *positive*, with losses in competitiveness associated with improved export performance. Overall, this analysis reveals that those countries that were already export-oriented before the onset of the Great Recession were able to benefit more from the improvement in external trading conditions. Other hypotheses, such as the importance of increased cost competitiveness, were not important, indicating that the persistent calls for cost-cutting may have been misplaced and counterproductive, causing a suppressed domestic demand but with no evidence of improved export performance yet to be seen. Thus, policy-makers might have been better served by emphasizing policies that encourage investment in tradable sectors than in simple cost-cutting exercises.

Why was Domestic Demand so Subdued across Europe?

Subdued growth in domestic demand was also a salient feature of the European recovery from the Great Recession, in both the eurozone and non-eurozone. Indeed, domestic demand grew by over 2 per cent in only two cases out of 27 countries in 2010. Historically speaking, this was an exceptionally slow rate of recovery, especially in light of the severity of the output collapse in late 2008/early 2009. To try to explain why demand was so muted in 2010, growth in domestic demand is regressed on six variables. First, the change in the private credit-to-GDP ratio in the pre-crisis period (2003–07) is included to capture the size of the pre-crisis borrowing expansion. Where this was greatest, private sector agents (both corporate and household) might have been expected to have been weighed down by large debt burdens. Second, the size of the stock of central government debt in 2010 is included to test the hypothesis that large amounts of government debt discourage private sector activity because of the prospect of having to pay higher taxes in the future to reduce the public sector's balance sheet. Thus, larger stocks of public debt would be expected to be negatively associated with domestic demand growth. Third, the government's fiscal balance for 2010 is included to test whether flows of government borrowing exerted any noticeable effect on domestic demand growth. Fourth, some governments undertook significant fiscal tightening over 2010 – something that might have been expected to have influenced domestic demand growth. This is measured by the difference between the 2009 and 2010 fiscal balances. Fifth, the change in the level of unemployment between 2009 and 2010 is included because it might have been expected that falling unemployment might be associated with faster domestic demand growth, and vice versa. Finally, while REER changes were not associated with export performance, it might be hypothesized that changes in exchange rates and relative unit labour costs might also have affected domestic demand. After all, if wages were falling, it might be expected that domestic demand would be adversely affected. For this reason, REER changes in 2010 are included within the model.

The regression output contained in Table 9 reveals a number of significant findings. First, the size of the pre-crisis credit boom appeared to be unrelated to post-crisis domestic demand growth, with the data revealing a statistically

Table 9: OLS Regression of Domestic Demand Growth on Hypothesized Determinants

	Annual growth in domestic demand (excluding stocks), 2010
Constant	4.686*** (0.001)
Change in private credit-to-GDP, 2003–07	–0.016 (0.618)
Stock of central government debt, % of GDP, 2010	–0.008 (0.671)
Central government fiscal balance, % of GDP, 2010	0.312* (0.085)
Change in fiscal balance, % of GDP, 2009–10	–0.223 (0.307)
Change in level of unemployment, % of civilian labour force, 2009–10	–1.187** (0.023)
Real effective exchange rate, 2010	0.296** (0.020)
Observations	26
R^2	0.755

Sources: Private sector credit data from World Bank (2010); all other variables from Commission (2010).
Notes: p-values in parentheses; Luxembourg the missing observation due to data unavailability on REER.
*** $p < 0.01$; ** $p < 0.05$; * $p < 0.1$.

weak and insignificant association between the two variables. The size of central government stocks also appeared to be of little importance in explaining changes in domestic demand; although the direction of the association was expected (that is, negatively associated with domestic demand growth), it was statistically insignificant. Third, efforts at fiscal tightening did not appear to have any relationship with changes in domestic demand. While the sign of the coefficient indicates that fiscal tightening depressed domestic demand, this relationship was again statistically insignificant. The three other variables were, however, significant. Of these, the significance was weakest for the central government balance in 2010, where smaller deficits were associated with higher rates of domestic demand growth. The two variables that exhibited the strongest levels of significance were the change in unemployment, and the change in the REER. In terms of changes in the level of unemployment, there was an extremely strong and negative relationship between unemployment growth and domestic demand growth. This seems plausible enough as higher unemployment would be expected to hold back domestic demand growth. Finally, changes in the REER were positively associated with growth in domestic demand, with greater appreciation – whether through the nominal exchange rate in countries with floating exchange rates, or through rising labour costs – linked to higher demand growth. On its own, this suggests that the effect of cost-cutting on domestic growth was negative, particularly as domestic demand typically constituted up to 60–85 per cent of GDP in the countries under examination here. Taken together with the findings from the regression results in Table 8, these findings indicate that REER depreciation neither helped stimulate export growth, nor did it help stimulate domestic demand; instead, REER depreciation appeared to serve only to suppress economic activity in 2010.

To sum up, it is evident from the first regression analysis carried out here that export growth in 2010 was related to one factor: whether a country was open and trade-oriented prior to the onset of the Great Recession. If they were, they tended to benefit more from the improvement in external trading conditions. Other hypotheses, such as the importance of increased cost competitiveness, were not important. Explaining variation in domestic demand growth was more complicated. Changes in the REER and unemployment were the two most important factors in explaining why domestic demand growth varied across the region. If the REER depreciated, and if unemployment rose, domestic demand growth tended to be much lower. Perhaps surprisingly, government efforts in undertaking fiscal tightening were not important; neither was the extent of the pre-crisis credit boom. In the following section, the importance of the variables that were identified as important in the cross-country analysis is explored at the individual country level.

III. Economic Developments in the Non-Eurozone

Bulgaria

Compared to many of its neighbours, the recession in Bulgaria began quite late, with the contraction in output continuing into the first quarter of 2010. Estimates differ, but GDP was estimated to have been flat over 2010. This relatively poor performance was driven by exceptionally depressed domestic demand, with gross fixed capital formation falling by 11.8 per cent in 2010, private consumption declining by 3.6 per cent, and – due to efforts to reduce public expenditure at a fast pace – public consumption contracting by 2.4 per cent. Unemployment increased from 6.8 per cent in 2009 to 9.8 per cent in 2010, with many labour intensive sectors, such as construction, particularly badly affected. In line with the rise in unemployment, real labour costs fell by 1 per cent over the year. Thus, according to the preceding analysis, Bulgaria had all the elements required for a slump in domestic demand. In addition, Bulgaria had experienced a higher than average pre-crisis expansion in private credit – an expansion that was in the process of unwinding over 2010. As a result, private sector balance sheet adjustments were also important factors in restraining domestic demand growth. Fortunately, strong export growth – and imports that barely grew at all – helped net exports make the largest contribution to GDP growth during the year, perhaps causing Bulgaria to avoid another year of recession. At 135 per cent of GDP, the sum of Bulgaria's imports and exports made it a small, export-oriented economy, enabling it to benefit from the upturn in international trade that began midway through 2009.

Czech Republic

The Czech Republic experienced growth in both domestic demand and net exports, although the latter was more important in contributing to a 2.4 per cent rise in GDP over 2010. As an open economy (trade openness of 142 per cent of GDP in 2007) that was tightly integrated into international production networks (IPNs) that were focused on machinery exports, the Czech Republic was boosted by robust growth in Germany and Slovakia. This strong export performance was achieved despite a 3 per cent appreciation in the REER, generated more by a rise in the nominal exchange rate than in unit labour costs, which stayed roughly stable. This strong performance in exports was supported by a relatively positive rebound in domestic demand, driven primarily by private consumption, which grew by 1.3 per cent after a –0.2 per cent fall in 2009. Although gross fixed capital formation fell by –1.8 per cent, this decline was much shallower than in many other countries. This helped real unit labour costs grow at a modest rate (0.2 per cent), with unemployment also rising at only a gentle pace, from 6.7 to 7.3 per cent. This enabled the government to reduce its deficit slowly and ahead of previous forecasts – from –5.8 per cent to –5.2 per cent of GDP – without too much fear of tipping the economy back into recession. Unlike many of its neighbours, the balance sheets of private sector agents in the Czech Republic were relatively strong, reducing the prospect of the sort of debt-induced collapse in consumption that was present in some other cases.

Denmark

As with the Czech Republic, both domestic demand and net exports made positive contributions to GDP growth in 2010, with growth estimated to reach around 2.3 per cent. While Denmark is a relatively small and open economy, and in the context of rising demand from its two main trading partners – Germany and Sweden – export growth of a comparatively modest 6.4 per cent was recorded. This is especially curious given that Denmark experienced the third largest REER depreciation (–3.4 per cent) in the non-eurozone, although this was not as fast a depreciation as the eurozone average. Moreover, this failure of REER depreciation to generate faster export growth is consistent with the preceding regression analysis. As a result of this steady but unspectacular growth in exports, the main driver of growth in Denmark was domestic demand, caused primarily by growth in both private and public consumption. Because Denmark entered the recession in strong fiscal shape, the government was able to enact a number of expansionary policies over 2009 and 2010 that helped prop up domestic demand. Thus, while gross fixed capital formation continued to decline (–3.8 per cent), consumer confidence rose as income taxes were cut, resulting in an increase in household real disposable incomes.

Latvia

Latvia experienced one of the most severe recessions in the world during 2009, and this recession continued into 2010, although the overall decline of an estimated –0.4 per cent concealed three straight quarters of output expansion, technically ending the recession in Q3 of 2010. This performance, while still not the sharp rebound needed to help recover the severe output losses caused by the recession, was much better than forecast in late 2009. While it has been argued that this better than expected performance was caused by the considerable REER depreciation observed over 2010, the extent of export growth was a relatively modest 8.6 per cent, with Latvia ranking 19th out of the 27 economies from the EU. Indeed, given Latvia's small, open economy (trade openness of 105 per cent), Latvia would have been expected to have benefited from any improvement in external trading conditions. Consequently, net exports made only a meagre, if positive, contribution to growth. Of more importance to the performance of the Latvian economy was the continued weakness in domestic demand. Private and public consumption continued to decline, with gross fixed capital formation falling by an enormous 24.8 per cent – even more impressive in the context of a 37.3 per cent drop in 2009. Only the strong and positive influence of inventory restocking helped mitigate the collapse in domestic demand, perhaps because of the indirect spillover from the resumption of export growth. The overall picture of deflationary tendencies in Latvia that saw unemployment rise and wages fall, combined with the existence of still-high levels of private debt, pointed to the need for a more impressive growth in exports in future if strong and sustained output growth were to resume.

Lithuania

Like Latvia, Lithuania is only just beginning to suffer from an exceptionally deep recession. After registering a collapse in output of 14.9 per cent in 2009, the Lithuanian economy grew by a modest 0.4 per cent in 2010. This was also much better than forecast the previous year. As in Latvia, this relative change in fortunes has been attributed to the positive effects of REER depreciation, which registered as a fall of 7.2 per cent in 2010, following unit cost stagnation in 2009. This relationship appears stronger in the Lithuanian case; after all, export growth was 11 per cent in 2010, placing Lithuania ninth out of 27 EU economies. However, given its small size (trade openness of 118 per cent), Lithuania would have also been expected to benefit from increased international trade, especially in its main export markets – Germany and Russia. As such, it was unclear whether REER depreciation significantly helped Lithuania perform any better than would have been expected. Indeed, the positive effects of REER depreciation are even less evident when placed against domestic demand performance, which continued to decline at a rapid rate: private consumption fell by 5.9 per cent, and public consumption fell by 1.3 per cent. Combined with a sharp increase in the level of unemployment, from 13.7 per cent in 2009 to 17.8 per cent in 2010, this compression of domestic consumption looked to be a permanent feature of the Lithuanian economy, especially as it also exhibited quite severe private sector balance sheet weaknesses.

Hungary

The Hungarian economy experienced a modest rebound from the severe recession of 2009, registering overall GDP growth of an estimated 1.1 per cent in 2010. Domestic consumption remained especially subdued, with private consumption falling by 3.2 per cent, and public consumption declining by –0.9 per cent as the tough fiscal demands imposed by the joint EU–IMF financial support package continued to bite. Indeed, Hungary was a relative anomaly in the non-eurozone because of its large stock of government debt (78.5 per cent of GDP in 2010). This debt – in part a legacy of the socialist period, and in part a result of fiscal incontinence during the pre-crisis period – marked Hungary out as a potential victim whenever sovereign debt fears flared, as they did on several occasions during 2010. This was exacerbated by a high and growing level of unemployment, as well as weak private sector balance sheets. As another small, open economy (trade openness of 141 per cent), exports grew by 13.5 per cent in 2010, helped by booming demand in Germany. It was this strong export performance that enabled Hungary to avoid recession, with Hungary's fortunes looking as though they would be determined almost entirely by external events.

Poland

The Polish economy, which was the only EU economy to avoid recession in 2009, continued to grow, with growth increasing in pace to 3.5 per cent in 2010. This was driven by positive developments in both export growth (9.8 per cent) and domestic demand (4.8 per cent). However, while exports grew at a healthy pace, imports also picked up on the back of nominal exchange rate appreciation and strong domestic demand. The contribution of net exports was, as a result, slightly negative. The strong growth in domestic demand was based on consumption growth, both public (3.5 per cent) and private (2.8 per cent). However, signs of shaky corporate confidence in the Polish economy were evident in the failure of gross fixed capital formation to grow. While unemployment continued to rise, the overall picture of the labour market in Poland was relatively positive, with employment continuing to grow. The only real worry was how Poland would achieve fiscal consolidation after using the strong public balance sheet to enact a significant stimulus package during 2009 and 2010. Despite the strong GDP growth registered during 2010, the deficit increased to –7.9 per cent of GDP. Thus, managing public finances appeared to represent the key challenge in the medium term.

Romania

The Romanian economy continued to suffer from a prolonged slump in economic activity throughout the year. After experiencing an unprecedented boom during the years preceding the Great Recession, the Romanian economy contracted by 7.1 per cent in 2009, and a further 1.9 per cent in

2010. This persistently poor performance could be explained by the severity of the collapse in domestic demand, caused in large part by the unwinding of unsustainable balance sheet weaknesses built up during the pre-crisis period in both the public and the private sector. The international community (the EU, IMF, World Bank and the European Bank for Reconstruction and Development) was heavily involved in helping Romania implement an adjustment programme that would alleviate the pressure on the public finances. While this helped Romania avoid a full-blown balance of payments crisis, and helped reduce public expenditure from the unsustainable levels of the pre-crisis period, the effect on domestic demand was negative. Thus, public consumption fell by 3.9 per cent, and private consumption declined by 1.6 per cent. Gross fixed capital formation fell by a considerable 9.9 per cent. Private sector debt stocks, fuelled in the pre-crisis period by external capital flows, also constrained consumption. Fortunately, exports grew at 16.9 per cent – the second highest rate of growth in the EU. With imports growing much more slowly due to depressed domestic demand, the current account deficit continued to narrow from the pre-crisis levels of around nearly 14 per cent of GDP to around 5.5 per cent.

Sweden

The Swedish economy experienced a brisk rebound in 2010, growing at 4.8 per cent, following the decline of 5.1 per cent in 2009. This recovery was driven primarily by strong growth in private consumption (3.4 per cent). This increase in private sector sentiment was helped by the discretionary fiscal measures enacted in 2009 and 2010 that saw the Swedish fiscal balance swing from surplus to deficit. Low levels of public debt facilitated such an expansion, and the improved economic performance of 2010 caused the deficit to stay at a relatively modest 0.9 per cent of GDP. The importance of monetary policy should also not be underestimated, with low interest rates helping reduce pressure on indebted households and effecting an overall increase in household disposable income over the year. Gross fixed capital formation, which had either contracted or grown at a slow rate in the rest of the non-eurozone, grew at a brisk 5.9 per cent, lending corporate support to household sector demand. Export performance was also strong, growing at nearly 11 per cent, and, despite faster strong import growth generated by the expansion of domestic demand, net exports were able to make a positive contribution to GDP growth. While the outlook was comparatively rosy, a number of potential weaknesses remained that were not addressed during the recession, not least the high level of household indebtedness (*c.*160 per cent of disposable income) that was inextricably linked to the Swedish housing market, which saw prices resume growth throughout 2010. While the debt dynamics appeared relatively benign in an environment of low interest rates and only mild levels of unemployment, the risks associated with any increase in interest rates was substantial.

United Kingdom

The recovery in the British economy was, despite exceptionally loose monetary policy, slow to begin and volatile in nature. After slow growth of 0.4 per cent in the first quarter of 2010, growth in the second (1.2 per cent) and third (0.8 per cent) quarters was much faster, causing optimism to rise about the prospects for the recovery. However, a sharp contraction in the fourth quarter (estimated at 0.5 per cent) – only partially explained by adverse weather conditions – raised questions about the sustainability of any recovery, particularly in light of the plans for fiscal consolidation proposed by the Conservative–Liberal Democrat coalition government that was formed after the May general election. Private consumption grew at only 1.1 per cent and gross fixed capital formation, which collapsed in 2009 when it fell by 15.1 per cent, only rebounded at a rate of 2.8 per cent – a low level given the severity of the 2009 decline. The muted growth in private sector activity was offset by public consumption, which grew by 2.3 per cent in 2010. This was because the expansionary fiscal policies implemented by the Labour government continued to make a positive contribution to growth for 2010, although the new government's fiscal consolidation policies threatened to diminish the contribution of public spending to GDP growth in the future. Given the significant nominal depreciation of sterling relative to its major trading partners since 2008, exports were expected to help offset weak domestic demand. However, while exports grew at 5.5 per cent, the fact that imports grew at a faster rate (8.6 per cent) caused net exports to make a negative contribution to GDP growth in 2010. This is consistent with the experiences of the other countries of the non-eurozone: rapid export growth requires incumbents to increase foreign market share and that new entrants enter export markets, both of which require time as well as improvements in cost competitiveness. In light of both the projected fiscal consolidation policies – primarily focused on expenditure reduction – and subdued private sector activity, export growth appeared to hold the key to whether the recovery in the United Kingdom economy would continue.

Conclusions

The recovery from the worst recession since World War II was, in general, anaemic and uneven. While the overall rate of growth in the non-eurozone was positive at 1.4 per cent for the unweighted average of the group as a whole, it was still lower than the overall rate of growth for the economies of the EU. This was especially worrying given that most economies of the non-eurozone had per capita income levels that were substantially lower than the EU average. As such, they would have expected to be growing at a faster rate than their richer neighbours. Instead, they were struggling to generate sufficient growth in domestic demand to help force a broad-based and persistent economic recovery. This looked unlikely to change soon, especially given the weakness of many of the private sector balance sheets of the countries covered here. In some countries, such as Hungary and the United Kingdom, the presence of both public and private sector balance sheet weaknesses meant that any recovery would be dogged by significant risks. Indeed, given the tendency for many economies to be reliant on external demand to generate growth, events in the wider economy looked to be of even more importance than usual. While some major developing economies, such as Brazil, China and India, continued to grow at healthy rates, doubts about the solvency of many European sovereigns, and the continued rise in commodity prices to near record levels, threatened to snuff out any nascent recovery.

This article examined the nature of the recovery across the non-eurozone in three sections. The first section traced developments on a number of important economic indicators, highlighting the heterogeneity of the recovery. After illustrating that variation in export growth and changes in domestic demand were of greatest importance in explaining the patchiness of the recovery, the second section attempted to identify those factors that help explain why some countries differed in the extent to which they were able to experience export growth and increased domestic demand. Here, it was argued that variation in export growth was related to one important factor: whether a country was open and trade-oriented prior to the onset of the Great Recession. If they were, they tended to benefit more from the growth in international trade. Other hypotheses, such as the importance of increased cost competitiveness, were not considered important. This was significant, considering the degree to which official discourse in 2010 had presented the issue of competitiveness as *the* most important challenge facing the EU (Tilford, 2011; Llewellyn and Westaway, 2011). Indeed, this point is perhaps even more important considering the findings from the analysis of the determinants of variation in the growth of domestic demand growth. Here, it was argued that changes in the REER and the level of unemployment were the two most important factors in explaining why domestic demand growth varied across the region. If the REER depreciated, and if unemployment rose, domestic demand growth tended to be much lower. Perhaps surprisingly, government efforts in undertaking fiscal tightening were not important;

neither was the extent of the pre-crisis credit boom. Thus, the evidence suggests that improvements in cost competitiveness over 2009 and 2010 not only failed to cause significant export growth, but they also contributed to the persistence of subdued domestic demand.

References

Commission of the European Communities (2010) *European Economic Forecast: Autumn 2010* (Brussels: Ecofin).

Connolly, R. (2010) 'The EU Economy: Member States Outside the Euro Area 2009'. *JCMS*, Vol. 48, s1, pp. 243–66.

Hausmann, R., Hwang, J. and Rodrik, D. (2006) 'What You Export Matters'. Harvard University Working Paper. Available at: «http://ksghome.harvard.edu/~drodrik/hhr.pdf».

Llewellyn, J. and Westaway, P. (2011) 'Europe's Pact is the First Step to Recovery'. *Financial Times*, 10 March. Available at: «http://www.ft.com/cms/s/0/91e9ac24-4b54-11e0-b2c2-00144feab49a.html#axzz1KT2ls09g».

Organisation for Economic Co-operation and Development (OECD) (2010) *World Economic Outlook* (Paris: OECD Press).

Reinhart, C. and Rogoff, K. (2009) *This Time is Different: Eight Centuries of Financial Folly* (Princeton, NJ: Princeton University Press).

Roubini, N. and Setser, B. (2004) *Bail-Outs or Bail-Ins? Responding to Financial Crises in Emerging Economies* (Washington, DC: Institute for International Economics).

Tilford, S. (2011) 'Europe's Damaging Obsession with "Competitiveness" '. Centre for European Reform blog. Available at: «http://centreforeuropeanreform.blogspot.com/2011/03/europes-damaging-obsession-with.html».

United Nations Comtrade (2010) *Commodity Trade Statistics Database* (New York: United Nations Statistics Division). Available at: «http://unstats.un.org/unsd/comtrade».

Wolf, M. (2009) *Fixing Global Finance: How to Curb Financial Crises in the 21st Century* (New Haven, CT: Yale University Press).

World Bank (2010) *World Financial Development Database*. Available at: «http://data.worldbank.org/».

JCMS 2011 Volume 49 Annual Review pp. 275–283

Chronology: The European Union in 2010

FABIAN GUY NEUNER
University of Oxford

At a Glance

Presidencies of the EU Council: Spain (1 January–30 June) and Belgium (1 July–31 December).

January

1	Spain takes over the EU Council Presidency.
1	Start of the European Year for Combating Poverty and Social Exclusion.
1	New rules for common fisheries policy come into force.
10	Ivo Josipović is elected president of Croatia.
11–19	European Parliament conducts hearings with nominees for College of Commissioners.
14	Greek government announces deficit reduction plan aiming at reducing the deficit to 2.8 per cent of GDP by 2012.
19	Commission outlines its long-term vision and targets for tackling declining biodiversity.
20	Nikiforos Diamandouros is re-elected European Ombudsman by the European Parliament.
21	Launch event for the 'European Year for Combating Poverty and Social Exclusion' in Madrid.

25	Council resolves to set up an EU mission to support the development of Somali security forces.
27–31	40th World Economic Forum in Davos.

February

3	Karolos Papoulias re-elected president of Greece in an indirect election.
3	Commission endorses Greece's deficit reduction measures and urges that the country takes steps to decrease its overall wage bill.
4	Conference on 'New Skills for New Jobs' in Brussels.
7	Viktor Yanukovych wins Ukrainian presidential election.
9	Barroso II Commission approved by the European Parliament.
9	New term of office for the Committee of the Regions begins with Mercedes Bresso becoming the institution's first female President.
9	Safer Internet Day. Commission launches campaign to encourage teenagers to use the Internet responsibly.
11	'112 Day' to raise awareness of the single European Emergency phone number.
20	Dutch government collapses after Labour Party withdraws from coalition.
24	The Commission and the European Investment Bank (EIB) welcome the Camdessus report on the EIB's external financing regime.

March

1–2	Brussels Tax Forum.
1–5	European e-Skills week aimed at highlighting growing demand for information and communication technology (ICT) skills for a competitive and innovative Europe.
2	Following a mid-term review of current programmes, the Commission increases funding for the European neighbourhood policy (ENP) for 2011–13.
3	Commission proposes 'Europe 2020' growth strategy for the coming decade.
4	The Secretariat of the Union for the Mediterranean is inaugurated with Ahmad Masa'deh as its first Secretary General.

5	Greek parliament passes Economy Protection Bill with further austerity measures.
5	Commission launches campaign to reduce gender pay gap across Member States.
6	Icelanders vote in a referendum to reject government proposals to provide loan guarantees to the Netherlands and the United Kingdom.
8	Social Affairs Ministers approve a plan for creating a European Microfinance Facility to support small entrepreneurs and the unemployed.
9	Commission proposes to establish an EU-wide European Heritage Label, which would act to recognize sites that symbolize European integration.
10–11	Commission organizes a conference aimed at discussing programmes to aid Europe's Roma community.
18–19	European Consumer Summit in Brussels.
20	Balkan Summit in Slovenia sees Western Balkan states lobby the EU over its commitment to enlargement and visa liberalization. Serbia boycotts the summit over the participation of Kosovo.
23–24	Conference celebrating the 25th Anniversary of the 'European Capital of Culture' initiative.
25–26	European Council. Adoption of the Europe 2020 targets and discussion on climate change and the internal security strategy. Eurozone countries approve plans to support Greece in handling its deficit.
31	Commission outlines proposed rules and procedures for European Citizens' Initiative.
31	Commission adopts the Commission Work Programme for 2010, which defines its priorities for the year.

April

8	The United States and Russia sign a new Strategic Arms Reduction Treaty (START) in Prague committing them to further nuclear disarmament.
8	Riots in Kyrgystan led to a coup and the ousting of President Kurmanbek Bakiyev.

10	Polish President Lech Kaczyński dies in a plane crash near the Russian city Smolensk along with 95 others, including many of the country's senior officials.
18	Derviş Eroğlu elected president of Northern Cyprus.
25	Viktor Orbán's conservative Fidesz wins an absolute majority in the Hungarian parliamentary elections and consequently commands a two-thirds majority with the Christian Democratic People's Party.
25	Heinz Fischer is re-elected president of Austria in a direct election that sees turnout fall to a historic low of 53.57 per cent.
27	Commission presents Green Paper aimed at supporting the cultural and creative industries.
28	Commission adopts 'European Strategy on Clean and Energy Efficient Vehicles' setting out a strategy for a cleaner and more energy-efficient trans-European transport system.

May

2	An EU–IMF (International Monetary Fund) rescue deal for emergency loans to Greece worth €110 billion is agreed at an emergency meeting of eurozone ministers.
6	United Kingdom general election. After some days of negotiation, a coalition government between the Conservative Party and the Liberal Democrats enters office with Conservative David Cameron as prime minister.
9	Euro area countries set up European Financial Stability Facility as a mechanism to support Member States in financial difficulty through issuing bonds.
12	Commission proposes strengthening the Stability and Growth Pact and closer economic monitoring.
12	Commission adopts progress reports for ENP countries.
18	Greek government receives its first loan instalment worth €14.5 billion.
25–26	Brussels Economic Forum.
28–29	Parliamentary elections in the Czech Republic see large drops in the support for both Social Democrats and Civic Democrats, although the latter subsequently form a three-party centre-right government with Petr Nečas as prime minister.
31	German President Horst Köhler resigns.

June

6 Slovenes vote in a referendum in favour of bringing a border dispute with Croatia before an international arbitration tribunal.

8 Meeting of EU finance ministers, where Estonia's bid to join the eurozone is accepted and agreement is reached to review Members' national budgets.

9 Dutch general election sees gains for the centre-right. Mark Rutte becomes prime minister.

12 Slovak parliamentary election sees Robert Fico's Direction-Social Democracy win the largest share of the votes, but it falls short of a majority. A four-party centre-right coalition is subsequently formed with Iveta Radičová as prime minister.

13 Belgian general election results in no party securing a majority in parliament triggering a long period of Cabinet formation negotiations.

17 European Council. The Europe 2020 strategy is adopted and plans for ensuring fiscal sustainability are discussed.

17 Iceland becomes an EU candidate country.

26–27 G20 Summit in Toronto. Key outcomes include agreement on cutting budget deficits and reducing debt-to-GDP ratios.

28 Seventh EU–OPEC (Organization of Oil Producing Countries) Energy Dialogue.

29 Pál Schmitt is elected president of Hungary in an indirect election.

30 Christian Wulff is elected president of Germany in an indirect election.

30 Commission adopts European tourism policy aimed at increasing the competitiveness of the European tourism sector.

July

1 Belgium takes over the EU Council Presidency.

1 New EU roaming rules enter into force, thus further cutting mobile phone roaming charges within the EU.

4 Bronisław Komorowski is elected president of Poland in the second round of elections.

7 Commission presents 'Green Paper on the Future of Pensions in Europe', which launches a public consultation on the issue.

8 The European Parliament votes in favour of establishing the European External Action Service.
14 Fourth EU–Brazil Summit.
16 Launch of European e-Justice Portal aimed at providing citizens with accessible legal information.
21 Slovenia becomes an OECD (Organisation for Economic Co-operation and Development) member.
22 ICJ (International Court of Justice) rules that Kosovo's 2008 declaration of independence was not in violation of international law.
23 The Committee of European Banking Supervisors (CEBS) conducts a stress test on 91 European banks, of which seven fail.
27 Start of EU accession negotiations with Iceland.

August
1 SWIFT agreement between the United States and the EU providing American authorities access to EU citizens' banking data enters into force.
11 EU provides financial aid worth €150 million for Pakistan after the country is struck by severe floods.

September
7 Commission President Barroso delivers inaugural State of the Union Address in Strasbourg.
12 Turks vote in a referendum on constitutional reform.
16 Special meeting of the European Council to discuss external policy and relations with strategic partners.
19 Swedish general election sees Fredrik Reinfeldt's centre-right coalition remain in power despite losing its absolute majority.
22 European Parliament backs plans for EU financial services reform.
27 President of Kosovo, Fatmir Sejdiu, resigns after a court ruling that he is breaching the constitution by leading a political party whilst holding office.
29 Commission follows up on prior speeches condemning the French treatment of the Roma and officially reiterates that free movement of citizens must apply.
30 The EU mission tasked with improving the security sector in Guinea-Bissau is completed.

October

2	Latvian parliamentary election sees an increase in the vote share of the incumbent coalition of Prime Minister Valdis Dombrovskis.
3	Presidential and parliamentary elections in Bosnia and Herzegovina.
6	EU–China summit in Brussels. Leaders sign an agreement on Oceanic Affairs and on the 2011 EU–China Year of Youth.
6	Commission launches 'Innovation Union' initiative, which is set to play a key role in increasing competiveness as part of the Europe 2020 strategy.
7	European Parliament supports proposals for visa liberalization with Albania and Bosnia and Herzegovina.
21	European Parliament awards Cuban dissident Guillermo Fariñas with the 2010 Sakharov Prize for Freedom of Thought.
25	Council passes on Serbia's EU accession application to the Commission.
27	Commission launches Single Market Act featuring new measures for generating jobs and growth.
28–29	European Council. The report of the task force on economic governance advocating more fiscal discipline and better co-operation and surveillance is endorsed. Members also discuss joint priorities for upcoming Seoul G20 summit and Cancún climate conference.

November

8	Visa liberalization for Albania and Bosnia and Herzegovina is adopted in the Council and due to enter into force soon after.
11–12	G20 summit in Seoul.
15	Commission adopts new strategy for promoting equal opportunities for people with disabilities.
19–20	Nato summit in Lisbon. The Alliance adopts a new Strategic Concept and discusses plans for a joint missile defence.
20	EU–US summit in Lisbon.
21	Ireland becomes the first country to officially request a bail-out package from the EU and the IMF.
22	After calls for a general election following the acceptance of the bail-out terms, Irish Prime Minister Brian Cowen announces that an election will take place in early 2011.

22	EU–Ukraine summit in Brussels.
22	10th Anniversary of EU–Russia Energy Dialogue marked by a meeting of the Permanent Partnership Council on Energy between the EU and Russia.
28	EU and IMF agree rescue plan for Irish economy consisting of support to the sum of €85 billion.
28	Moldovan parliamentary election. The Communist Party becomes the largest individual party, but is beaten overall by the Alliance for European Integration comprising the Liberal Democratic Party, the Democratic Party and the Liberal Party.
28	Swiss vote in a referendum in favour of the deportation of criminal foreigners.
29–30	EU–Africa summit in Libya. Leaders adopt the Joint Action Plan 2011–2013 and the Tripoli declaration calling for stronger co-operation in global economic affairs.

December

1	The European External Action Service is officially launched.
2	Commission launches communication campaign for the 'European Year of Volunteering 2011'.
8	Commission proposes EU strategy for the Danube region.
9	Estonia becomes an OECD member.
11	Conclusion of the Cancún climate conference sees new initiatives to reduce greenhouse emissions, including ways of aiding developing countries with the process.
15	European Parliament backs legislation allowing for the implementation of the European Citizens' Initiative.
16–17	European Council. Agreement is reached on a treaty amendment allowing for the establishment of a permanent mechanism to secure financial stability of the eurozone.
17	Montenegro granted EU candidate status.
19	Alexander Lukashenko is re-elected president of Belarus in an election that is criticized by parts of the international community for being flawed, and the ensuing violent crackdown is condemned.
20	A new media law enters into force in Hungary sparking controversy just days before the country is due to take over the EU Council Presidency.

21 Montenegrin prime minister, Milo Đukanović, one of the longest-serving leaders in the Balkans, resigns days after his country is granted EU candidate status.

22 Croatia makes progress towards EU membership by closing three further negotiation chapters, bringing the total number of closed chapters to 28 out of 35.

22 United States Senate backs the New START treaty with Russia.

JCMS 2011 Volume 49 Annual Review pp. 285–295

Index

Note: Italicized page references indicate information contained in tables.